PRAISE FOR Fire in the Ashes

A *Kirkus Reviews* Best Nonfiction Book of 2012

A *Booklist* 2012 Editor's Choice Selection

"Eschewing social science jargon and deploying extraordinary powers of observation and empathy, Kozol crafts dense, novelistic character studies that reveal the interplay between individual personality and the chaos of impoverished circumstances. Like a latter-day Dickens (but without the melodrama), he gives us another powerful indictment of America's treatment of the poor." —*Publishers Weekly* (starred)

"In this engaging, illuminating, often moving book, [Kozol] recounts the lives of poor black and Latino children–many now close friends–who once lived in Manhattan's Martinique Hotel. . . . Clear-eyed, compassionate, and hopeful." —*Kirkus Reviews* (starred)

"*Fire in the Ashes* isn't some saccharine account of how disadvantaged youth get a break and then triumph over adversity. Instead, Kozol shows us the very real costs of putting children in bad schools. . . . Throughout, Kozol connects with these kids and young adults on a human level, refusing to step onto some political soapbox." —*Boston Globe*

"Kozol's brilliant body of work shines a light not merely on the lives of the poor, but also into the dark night of the American soul." —*The Oregonian*

"An engaging look at the broader social implications of ignoring poverty as well as a very personal look at individuals struggling to overcome it." —*Booklist* (starred)

"Kozol's storytelling gifts shine through: with simple anecdotes that show the soulful humor, compassion, and wisdom that kindles progress among the survivors." —*Christian Science Monitor*

"*Fire in the Ashes* is a terrific book–powerful, insightful, and heartbreaking." —**David Berliner, author of *The Manufactured Crisis***

Also by Jonathan Kozol

DEATH AT AN EARLY AGE

FREE SCHOOLS

THE NIGHT IS DARK AND I AM FAR FROM HOME

CHILDREN OF THE REVOLUTION

ON BEING A TEACHER

ILLITERATE AMERICA

RACHEL AND HER CHILDREN

SAVAGE INEQUALITIES

AMAZING GRACE

ORDINARY RESURRECTIONS

THE SHAME OF THE NATION

LETTERS TO A YOUNG TEACHER

Fire in the Ashes

TWENTY-FIVE YEARS AMONG THE POOREST CHILDREN IN AMERICA

Jonathan Kozol

B\D\W\Y

BROADWAY BOOKS

NEW YORK

BROADWAY BOOKS and its logo, B\D\W\Y, are trademarks
of Random House, Inc.

Originally published in hardcover in the United States by
Crown Publishers, an imprint of the Crown Publishing Group,
a division of Random House, Inc., New York, in 2012.

Library of Congress Cataloging-in-Publication Data
Kozol, Jonathan.
    Fire in the ashes : twenty-five years among the poorest
children in America / Jonathan Kozol.
        p.   cm.
    1. Poor children—United States. 2. Poor families—
United States. 3. Education of children—United States.
4. Children—United States—Social conditions. I. Title.
HV741.K674   2012
362.77'56909747275—dc23   2012005183

ISBN 978-1-4000-5247-9
eISBN 978-0-7704-3595-0

Printed in the United States of America

Cover design by Darren Haggar
Cover photograph by Stephen Shames

10 9 8 7 6 5

First Paperback Edition

For Lisette and Angelo,
Pineapple and Jeremy,
Benjamin and Leonardo,
Lara and Mosquito,
Stephen and Miranda,
Antsy and Ariella.

And for Alice Washington.

They prevailed.

CONTENTS

TO THE READER

Over the course of many years I have been talking with a group of children in one of the poorest urban neighborhoods of the United States and have written several books about them and their families. Readers ask me frequently today if I've kept in contact with the children and if I know how many have prevailed against the obstacles they faced and, in those cases, how they managed to survive and how they kept their spirits strong amidst the tough conditions that surrounded them.

It has not been difficult to keep in contact with most of these children because so many of them, as they have grown older, have come to be among my closest friends. They call me on the phone. They send me texts and e-mails. We get together with each other when we can.

In telling the stories they've been sharing with me about the years since they were very young, I have begun by recapitulating moments in their childhood that set the scene for what their lives are like today. On some occasions, they have helped me to correct mistakes I've made or misimpressions I've conveyed in the writings that I did during those early years when we first met.

The names of the children, and grown-up children, and almost all the older adults I've described are disguised to protect their privacy, and many have been given different pseudonyms from those I've used before. Their exact ages, the locations of their homes, and other details of their lives have sometimes been disguised as well. Conversations on related topics are at times combined, and stories and events told to me out of order are resequenced. Further discussion of the way I wrote this book, and the ways that events and conversations have been edited, is provided in the text itself, as well as in the endnotes.

The stories in this book were brought to their conclusion in the weeks preceding January 2012. Many of the lives of children in these stories will, I expect, continue to take unforeseen and interesting directions. But this, for now, is where I must leave them. I hope the future will be kindly to them all.

PART ONE

The Shadow of the Past

CHAPTER 1

The Journey Begins

Christmas Eve of 1985 was not a good time for poor women and their children to depend on public kindness or prophetic reenactments of the Christian gospel at the hands of civic and commercial leaders in New York. It was a time when opulence among the city's newly minted rich and super-rich was flaunted with an unaccustomed boldness in the face of New York City's poor and homeless people, thousands of whom were packed into decrepit, drug-infested shelters, most of which were old hotels situated in the middle of Manhattan, some of which in decades past had been places of great elegance.

One of the largest shelters was the Martinique Hotel, across the street from Macy's and one block from Fifth Avenue. In this building, 1,400 children and about 400 of their parents struggled to prevail within a miserable warren of bleak and squalid rooms that offered some, at least, protection from the cold of winter, although many rooms in which

I visited with families in the last week of December were so poorly heated that the children huddled beneath blankets in the middle of the day and some wore mittens when they slept.

I remember placing calls on freezing nights from phone booths on Sixth Avenue or Broadway trying to reach Steven Banks, a Legal Aid attorney who performed innumerable rescue actions for the families in the Martinique that year. The wind that cut across the open space of Herald Square at night was fierce, the sidewalks felt like slabs of ice, and kids and parents from the Martinique who had to venture out for milk or bread or medicines would bundle up as best they could in layers of old clothes and coats, if they did have coats, or sweatshirts with the hoods drawn tight around their chins.

Dozens of kids I knew within the building suffered from chronic colds. Many were also racked by asthma and bronchitis. Infants suffered from diarrhea. Sleepless parents suffered from depression. Mothers wept in front of me.

I had never seen destitution like this in America before. Twenty years earlier, I had taught young children in the black community of Boston and had organized slum tenants there and lived within their neighborhood and had been in many homes where rats cohabited with children in their bedrooms. But sickness, squalor, and immiseration on the scale I was observing now were virtually unknown to me.

Almost every child that I came to know that winter in the Martinique was hungry. On repeated evenings when I went to interview a family I gave up asking questions when a boy or girl would eye the denim shoulder bag I used to carry, in which I often had an apple or some cookies or a box of raisins, and would give them what I had. Sometimes I would ask if I could look into the small refrigerators that the hotel had reluctantly provided to the families. Now and then I'd find a loaf of bread or several slices of bologna or a slice or two of pizza that had gone uneaten from the day before. Often there was nothing but a shriveled piece of fruit, a couple of jars of apple sauce, a tin of peanut butter, sometimes not even that.

I continued visiting the Martinique throughout the next two years. During that time, a play about impoverished children of the nineteenth century in Paris, called Les Misérables, opened to acclaim in the theater district of New York. Some of the more enterprising children in the Martinique would walk the twelve or fifteen blocks between the hotel and the theater district in late afternoons or evenings to panhandle in the streets around the theater or in front of restaurants nearby. Homeless women did this too, as well as many of the homeless men, some alcoholics and some mentally unwell, who slept in cardboard boxes on the sidewalks and in doorways of the buildings in the area.

The presence of these homeless people was not welcomed by the theater owners. People were paying a great deal of money to enjoy an entertainment fashioned from the misery of children of another era. The last thing that they wanted was to come out of the theater at the end and be obliged to see real children begging on the sidewalk right in front of them.

The problem was resolved to some degree when police and private guards employed by local businesses developed strategies for cleaning out the homeless—sanitation terms like "cleaning out" were used without embarrassment— from the streets around the theaters. Meanwhile, on the East Side of Manhattan, another group of business leaders went a little further by employing people in the homeless population to drive out other homeless people from Grand Central Station, where they had been taking refuge from the cold for several years by sleeping in the station's waiting rooms.

The ultimate solution, which required the removal of these homeless families from the midtown sections of Manhattan altogether, took a few more years to carry out successfully. In the interim, despite the efforts of the theater owners, many of the older children from the Martinique would manage to slip past the hired guards or the police and walk up to theater-goers, who would sometimes hand them a few dollars.

The younger children from the Martinique, however, did their begging for the most part close to home within the blocks surrounding the hotel, where they would run into the streets when drivers slowed their cars as the lights were changing and where a driver whose compassion overcame his irritation might roll down his window far enough to give the kids some money. Those who were inclined to castigate the parents of these children for letting them go out into the streets at night might have relented somewhat if they understood how rapidly the competence of many of these parents had come to be eroded by the harshness of conditions in that building.

Scenarios of broken will and loss of good decision-making skills were apparent everywhere. Some of the parents were emotionally ill when they arrived here; but those who weren't would frequently succumb to the pervasive atmosphere of insecurity and high anxiety that suffused the filthy corridors and crowded living spaces of the Martinique. Many who had not used drugs before this time became drug users in a setting in which heroin and crack cocaine were readily available. (The sixteenth floor of the Martinique Hotel—there were seventeen floors in all, but the top two were unoccupied—was operated, with the knowledge and, apparently, cooperation of some of the guards, as an open market for drug users.) A number of people became HIV-infected under these conditions, although in 1985 the term was not yet widely recognized among some of the residents and many did not understand exactly why it was that they were growing ill.

The conditions under which these people had to live were not unknown to New York City's social service system or to its political administration. Anybody who was able to get past the guards, as I did repeatedly with the cooperation of two sympathetic social workers who enabled me to get into the upper floors and visit families pretty much at will, could not avoid, unless he closed his eyes, the sight of overflowing garbage piled in the landings and of children who, for lack of other options, played amidst that garbage.

But physical unhealthiness, the prevalence of drug addiction, and the documented presence of widely known carcinogens (open containers of asbestos, for example, and asbestos-coated pipes in the lobby of the building) were not the worst of the destructive forces children and their families had to undergo. The Martinique, as I was forced to recognize when the social workers started talking candidly to me during the months to come, was not merely a despairing place, diseased and dangerous for those who had no choice but to remain there; it also was a place of flagrant and straightforward criminality on the part of management and ownership. A young man with a raw, salacious smile, to whom the social workers made it a special point to introduce me and who, they told me, was a relative of one of the two owners of the building, used the power he was thus afforded to induce young women to provide him with erotic favors in exchange for items that they needed, such as cribs and linens for their children.

"He boasts about it," one of the two social workers told me. "He describes it to us openly, and gleefully. He goes into considerable detail. . . ." Some of the guards, the social worker said, took advantage of the younger mothers too, as one of those mothers, a smart and savvy woman who told me she had had to fight off their advances, reported to me at the time and has repeated since.

There was no need for secrecy, it seemed, because there was a sense that this was "a closed system," where rules of normal law and normal governance did not apply. Complaint or protest would have no effect except to prompt the guards or manager to punish the complaining woman by denying her essential services or else, if the manager so wished, by calling the police and charging her with one of many forms of misbehavior that were common in a building in which almost every person had to break some rule or operate some petty scam in order to survive.

Cooking, for example, was officially prohibited because of fire dangers, but the city's meager allocation of subsistence funds to purchase food made it unthinkable to buy it from a restaurant and forced the mothers in the Martinique to cook their children's meals in secret, then conceal their hot plates when inspectors from the city came around. The management cooperated with the tenants by providing them with garbage bags to cover up the hot plates on inspection days while, at the same time, it pretended not to know that this was going on. When mothers were reluctant to provide the guards who were hired to protect them with the favors they expected, the guards could use the cooking scam or other scams much like it as a way to break down their resistance.

Children, of course, observed the humiliation of their mothers. The little ones, too young to go to school, might perhaps be sent out to the corridors; but most of the mothers would not dare to let them wander too far from the bedroom door. Even the kids who never witnessed these activities first-hand could not fail to be aware of them. I used to wonder what enduring influence all of this would have upon the capability of children in the building to believe in any kind of elemental decency in people who have power over their existence. Would they later find it hard to trust the teachers in their public schools? Would they develop an endemic wariness about investing faith in any older person of authority? Would they love their mothers all the more for having done the best they could to protect them from this nightmare, or would they harbor a resentment that their mothers were not able to avoid this situation in the first place?

One of the social workers who befriended me that year, a sensitive man who had studied early childhood development as an undergraduate at Yale, spoke of the Martinique in unsparing language as "New York City's midtown death camp for the spirits of poor children." He knew that I was Jewish and he asked me later if this choice of language had offended me. I told him it did not. I thought it was justified.

Two years later, I published a book about the Martinique Hotel. It appeared first in two successive issues of The New Yorker magazine, and this, in turn, attracted interest from the other media. The Nightline television program, moderated at the time by the journalist Ted Koppel, asked me to go back into the Martinique with a camera crew and do a documentary on the families I had known. The social workers and some of the mothers helped to get the camera crew and the producer past the guards and up into the building. The camera itself was hidden in a baby carriage by one of the mothers, who rolled it through the lobby without attracting scrutiny and brought it with her on an elevator to the floor where she was living. She then accompanied us into other bedrooms whose occupants had told me they were not afraid to answer questions.

By the time we had finished with the final interview, however, a guard on an upper floor had become suspicious, banged at the door, which we did not open, then notified the management. The manager, an unpleasant character by the

name of Sal Tuccelli who carried a pistol in an ankle holster, confronted us with several other guards and insisted
that the cameramen hand over the material they had just
recorded. When they refused, the manager and guards
reacted in the same way they routinely did with residents
who defied or disobeyed them. I was slammed against a
metal wall. One of the cameramen was seriously injured.
The TV producer, an unintimidated woman, removed
one of her high-heel shoes and used it to defend us. By this
point, the police had been alerted. The cameramen got out
of the building with the video.

I knew, of course, that journalists were not welcome
in the building and that the social workers who had made
my visits possible were taking risks in doing so. But until
this time I had never witnessed so directly the extremes to
which the management would go in the interest of conceal-
ment. It reminded me more vividly than ever that the city
and the owners of the Martinique, with whom the city had
contracted to sequester homeless people at a price tag of
$8 million yearly for those 400 families, were determined
to discourage any troublesome exposure of the social crime
in which they were colluding.

It also left me with a visceral reminder of the terror
mothers and their children would experience when the
guards or, more frequently, the manager would hammer at
their doors early in the morning if, for example, the rental
check paid by the city, through no fault of their own, had
not arrived on time. "Six a.m.," one of the mothers told me.
"He bangs on the door. You open up. There he is in the
hallway with his gun. 'Where's your rent?'"

This is the way that one of the richest cities in the world
treated the most vulnerable children in its midst a quarter
century ago. When these hotels were finally closed in 1988
and 1989, not for reasons of compassion but because of the
enormous damage the visibility of so much desperation was

doing to the image of the city and its elected leaders, most of the several dozen families I had come to know, all but two of whom were black or Latino, were shipped en masse into several of the most impoverished and profoundly segregated sections of the Bronx, far from the sight of tourists and the media. These were communities that already had the city's highest rates of HIV infection, the greatest concentration of drug-addicted people, of people who had serious psychiatric illnesses, women with diabetes, women with undiagnosed malignancies, and among the highest rates of pediatric asthma in the nation.

The misérables, although they were no longer homeless, would continue nonetheless to live under conditions of physical and psychological adversity that were only incrementally less harmful than the ones they had endured in the preceding years. In one of the neighborhoods in which the largest numbers of the homeless were resettled, the only medical facility was a city-run institution known as Lincoln Hospital, which underwent the loss of its accreditation more than once because of errors by the staff that led to the deaths of at least a dozen patients, two of whom were infants. For the mentally unwell, psychiatric care of the thoroughgoing kind lavishly available six subway stops away in the costly and exclusive Upper East Side of Manhattan was all but impossible to find. Children, meanwhile, many of whom had had their education interrupted or repeatedly disrupted during their homeless years, found themselves consigned to public schools that, in the absoluteness of their racial isolation, resembled those of Mississippi fifty or one hundred years before.

So this is where they sent them. And this is where I followed them, invited by their parents to visit them on weekend afternoons or in the evenings during a school holiday, to keep alive the friendships we had formed when they were in the shelters. I went to their schools. I got to know their teachers. I went to their churches. I got to know their pastors. I went to their hospitals, sometimes at their own request when they were ill because they thought that it might win them more attention. So I became acquainted with a number of their doctors, many of whom were selfless and devoted individuals who did everything they could to compensate for scarcities in the basic services that doctors elsewhere know they can depend upon.

I did this, off and on, for more than fifteen years. Then, beginning in 2005, I lost track of some families for a time when my father, who'd been ill for several years, entered an acute phase of his illness, and, within the same two years, both he and my mother passed away. It took another year before I could regain my sense of equilibrium. At that point I began returning to those neighborhoods again and meeting once more with the families I had known. Some of the children were still in their teenage years. Those whom I had met when they were in the Martinique were already in their twenties. We had long talks. We took long walks. Sometimes we would spend an evening having dinner in the neighborhood. When I was home we kept in touch by phone and mail, and by e-mail in the case of those who had computers. In these ways we rebuilt our friendships.

What happened to these children? What happened to their families? Some prevailed, a few triumphantly. Most survived, even at a rather modest level of survival. Others did not. This will be their story.

CHAPTER 2

Eric and His Sister

One of the nicest but most fragile people that I knew who was in the shelter system at the time when I was visiting the Martinique was a shy and gentle woman whose name was Victoria.

Vicky had been shunted through a number of the shelters from 1984 until the end of 1989. Her longest stay was in a place known as the Prince George Hotel on West 28th Street, four blocks from the Martinique.

When she came into the shelters, Vicky had been suffering from clinical depression and periodic seizures, for which she had been treated at a hospital on Roosevelt Island, which is in the midst of the East River. Her husband, who was caring for their children at the time, had not been well for many years, the consequence of a degenerative illness that, as best I understood, he had contracted as a young man growing up in Georgia. He passed away a short time after Vicky came out of the hospital.

At this juncture in her life, with no money in her pocket, and no prospects of a job, and with two young children who had no one else to care for them, she began to make her way into the less-than-friendly channels of the shelter apparatus, moving at first, as was the case with all home-less families, from one so-called "short-term shelter" to the next. The psychological and physical exhaustion families underwent when they were moving constantly tended to have a predictable effect. It undermined whatever capabil-ity for good clear-headed thinking might still exist within the spirits of the stronger women while, in the case of those like Vicky who were not strong at all, it simply added to their pre-existent instability.

Vicky, as she told me later, fell into a "zombie-like" condition—she felt, she said, "like I was walkin' in my sleep"—a condition that continued when she was living on a "permanent placement," as the city termed it, in a room at the Prince George.

The building, which was owned at the time that Vicky moved there by one of the two owners of the Martinique—it was later taken over by another owner with a record of illegal operations who subsequently served a lengthy term in prison for defrauding creditors of $100 million—was less depressing physically, at least on the lobby floor, than was the Martinique, but it made its claim to notoriety for other reasons of its own. Although the manager of the Martinique had some degree of governance over the Prince George as well, the day-to-day administrator was a man who'd been convicted of abusing his own daughter, beating her and leaving her locked up at home, "alone and without food," according to the New York Daily News. His daughter had been taken from him by the city to protect her from addi-tional endangerment.

The city, wrote the columnist Bob Herbert, who was then a writer for the Daily News, "takes one child out of

[his] care and then hands him over 1,000 more." There were at least 1,200 children in the Prince George at the time.

Children were endangered in other ways as well. Fires kept on breaking out—at one point, four or five times in a week. A three-year-old was burned to death while Vicky's family lived there. The fires were alleged to have been caused by arson, but tenants told me some of them resulted from the carelessness of drug abusers who were cooking crack cocaine right there in their bedrooms—a not-uncommon practice in those days when crack was just emerging as a drug of choice among the very poor.

This, then, is the setting in which Vicky and her children found themselves at a time when Vicky was already ill and loaded with anxiety. Her daughter, who was named Lisette and was only seven when all of this began, suffered less than did her brother, Eric, who was four years older. As in the case of many of the other children in the building who were nearing adolescence, he was very much aware of the sordidness of his surroundings, the unscrupulous behavior of the governing officials, the open market for narcotics, as well as the various semi-legal or illegal strategies other children of his age had inventively developed in order to pick up a little money that they sometimes, but not always, used to help their families. It would be another four years from the time that Vicky's family came into this building until the day when they got out.

When I met Vicky and her children in the Bronx in 1993, they were living in Mott Haven, which was then, and remains today, the single poorest neighborhood in the poorest borough of New York.

Vicky's home, although it was on a street that was a well-known center for the sale of drugs—heroin, specifically—was two blocks from a church on St. Ann's Avenue,

an Episcopal church called St. Ann's, that was a place of
safety for children in the neighborhood. The church, a
beautiful old stone building with a tall white spire at the
top of its bell tower, had a large expanse of lawn on a pleasant hillside where there were swings and slides and a sprin-
kler for the younger children, and a court where older kids
played basketball.

I spent a good part of the 1990s visiting St. Ann's
because it ran an excellent and innovative afterschool, in
which I was able to talk at length with children and was
sometimes asked to help with their tutorials. Naturally, it
wasn't long before I also grew acquainted with some of their
parents and with other adults who gravitated to the church
for the sense of solace that they found in the inviting and
informal atmosphere the pastor had created.

The priest of the church, an extraordinary woman
whose name is Martha Overall, came to St. Ann's with a
deep commitment to the children of the neighborhood. She
was also well equipped to help the parents of the children
deal with the legal problems and bureaucratic obstacles
that people who depended upon welfare inevitably faced. A
graduate of Radcliffe College, where she had studied eco-
nomics, she also drew upon the adversarial and strategic
skills she had acquired as a lawyer who had been a protégé
of a famous litigator by the name of Louis Nizer.

Even while she practiced law, Martha had been working as a volunteer and advocate for families in Mott Haven,
so when she turned her back upon the law and chose a
life of service in the ministry, she already had a thorough
understanding of the sense of helplessness that people in
the area frequently experienced in dealing with their land-
lords or with government officials. She was masterful, and
she could be very tough, in her confrontations with people
in positions of authority. But she was warm and gentle with
people in the parish who came to her in need.

Vicky quickly grew attached to Martha, and she and the children soon began to come to church almost every Sunday. On the weekdays, Eric sometimes came there on his own, mostly to play basketball. Now and then, he brought his sister with him.

Eric struck me as a complicated boy. In spite of all he had been through, he had an element of likability and even of good humor. But he found it difficult to be transparent in his conversations and relationships with older people at the church who took an interest in him. As I watched him in the next few years, I could not help noticing the frequently evasive—maybe self-protective—way that he would speak to grown-ups when they questioned him. It was a hint, but only that, that he was concealing things that might stir up worries for his mother if she knew of them.

But she worried anyway. She told me she had seen this tendency—"not always bein' straight with me" is the way she put it—starting in the period when they were still at the Prince George. But she said she'd noticed this more frequently since they'd been resettled in the Bronx. She said she never knew what he was holding back, but she was watching him uneasily. . . .

One day in the fall of 1995, Vicky came into the church while I was helping at the afterschool. She came right up behind me and leaned down and whispered "Hi!" before I knew that she was there. She seemed in such a pleasant mood that it surprised me when, a moment later, she asked with a slight tremble in her voice if I had the time to go outside and talk with her.

As soon as we had left the church, she began to cry. She didn't tell me what was wrong, and I didn't ask. She was wearing sneakers, baggy slacks, a loose-fitting sweater, and a floppy-looking hat. Her clothes were clean but her appearance was disheveled.

We went out for a walk.

Sometimes when a person that I know appears to be distraught, I have a tendency to think there has to be an explanation that I can discover if I ask exactly the right questions. I feel embarrassed later when I realize that there isn't any simple answer to my questions. Usually I know this in advance but, because of something in my personality or education, I often fall into this trap of thinking that the answer lies in talkative solutions. Walking around without a destination sometimes leaves an open space that isn't filled already with my own predictive suppositions.

Vicky never told me exactly what it was that made her cry that afternoon. I knew, of course, she was concerned about her children. Eric, who was sixteen now, was not doing well in school. The high school he attended was one of those places, misleadingly referred to as "academies," familiar in the Bronx and other inner-city neighborhoods, where the course of study had been stripped of programs that might stimulate a student academically and instead was geared to practical and terminal instruction. Having lost so many years of education while he had been homeless—most of the children in the shelters, as I've noted, had seen their schooling interrupted frequently—his basic skills were already very low. His attendance was, in any case, haphazard.

Vicky couldn't help him much because she'd had so little education of her own. Her mother had died when she was five and, for some reason she did not explain, she was taken from her father and given to a guardian who, however, seemed to have abandoned the customary obligations of a guardian. She had had to leave school during junior high, which she said was not unusual in the rural part of Georgia where she had been born, and went to work "cleanin' houses, doin' laundry for white people" for most of the next four years. By the time her son was born and she was married and her husband brought her to New York, schooling was no longer in her mind. Although her writing skills were good (she had learned a kind of slanted printing in her grade-school years), she had little understanding of the work that Eric was supposed to do at his alleged "academy."

Lisette was in the seventh grade and was a better student but had also been assigned to a bottom-rated school, which was called a "school for medical careers" but did not offer courses that would likely lead to any kind of medical career beyond, perhaps, a low-paid job within a nursing home, and pretty much precluded any opportunity to move on to the kind of high school that would open up the possibilities for college.

The apartment where the city had resettled them consisted of three tiny rooms on the fourth floor of a six-story building where there was no elevator, no bell, and no intercom. To visit with Vicky you had to yell up from the street and she or Eric or Lisette would lean out of their window and throw down the key to the front door.

Vicky and her children were living on a welfare stipend which, including food stamps and some other benefits, amounted to approximately $7,000 yearly. (According to Martha, this was even less than the average income for a family in the area, which she pegged at $8,000 for a year's subsistence.) She supplemented this by getting up at 5:00 a.m. two days a week to go to a food pantry at one of the housing projects, where she had to be assigned a ticket with a number to establish her priority but then was forced to wait for an hour and a half, or else go home and then return, before she actually received a bag of groceries.

The only job she'd had since moving to the Bronx was cleaning houses or apartments in Manhattan, which, she said, was something she was glad to do, but was also forced to do as part of her welfare obligation in New York. "One lady, Mrs. Jacobs, lived on Second Avenue. The other one lived—let me see, on 14th Street, somewhere around Green-wich Village." Both were elderly; one was home-bound. "They were nice to me," she said but for some reason she could not explain, this heavily promoted "work experience program" lasted only six months and did not lead to per-manent employment.

She was candid with me, and herself, in her recogni-tion that at least some of the suffering she had undergone had been of her own making. While she had been home-less, she had grown attached to a kindly-seeming man who was good to her at first but who was subject to depressive swings of mood and soon began abusing her. Once she had her own apartment, she took out an order of protection, but her boyfriend kept on coming back, she said, when he was depressed or hungry. Sometimes when he showed up at the door, she told me that she lacked the will to keep him out. On more than one occasion, he had beaten her severely.

I asked her if she prayed.

"I do pray—but not out loud." She said, "I pray inside."

Amidst the sadness of the conversation, she kept reaching out for gaiety. A nervous laugh would precede the revelation of a longing or a memory that brought an evanes-cent sense of satisfaction to her mind. "I pray," she said, "for something that I haven't done for thirteen years."

I asked her what it was.

"To pick up my knitting needles," she replied.

A soft smile lighted up her eyes. "I used to make a sweater in three weeks if I had nothin' to upset me. I'd start when it was summertime and I'd have six sweaters made for Christmas. . . . If you ever see me get my needles out again, you'll know I'm feelin' happy."

At the corner of Brook Avenue, she stopped next to the stairs that led down to the subway station, looking in a vague, distracted way at a woman in a long skirt who was selling bunches of chrysanthemums and roses. She reached out her hand in the direction of the roses but it seemed she didn't dare to touch them.

"Would you like them?"

"One rose," she replied.

Tiny drops of water sparkled on the petals. She held the flower in her hand against her chest as we were walking back in the direction of St. Ann's. At the corner, she looked left and right. Then, with relief, she told me, "There you go!" and waved across the street.

Lisette was coming up the avenue with a couple of her friends. When she saw her mother she ran into her arms. Taking a bunch of papers from her backpack, she showed her a book report she'd done that day at school. It had been marked A-plus by her teacher. Her mother studied the book report, kissed her on the cheek, then handed her the keys to the apartment and two dollars to buy something at the store.

"An A-plus on a book report doesn't mean a whole lot at this school she goes to," Vicky said once Lisette was gone. "Her teachers like her. They do the best they can. But I don't think that they can give her what a girl with her potential ought to have. . . .

"You see, this is the best that I can get for her right now. I don't accept it—yet I do, because I don't know any choice I have." But a moment after that her gaiety returned. "See?" she said. "I know she's home. She's safe upstairs and we have food to eat. And so, for now, I'm happy. There you go!"

Her moods were like that. Sometimes sadness. Sometimes gaiety. Sometimes a bright burst of jubilation. Then she would crash down—so fast—into the pit of a depressive darkness. Then she would be fighting back again and searching for her jubilation like a person looking for an object that she'd put away into a drawer somewhere and temporarily could not be found. She laughed that nervous laugh, it seemed, when she was near the tipping point between exhilaration and surrender.

In November 1996, a doctor called me from his office in a small town in Montana. He said his name was Dr. William Edwards. He told me that a group of people at his church had read my book Amazing Grace, about the children in the Bronx, and had called a meeting of their congregation. The members of the church, he said, decided that it was "appropriate" for them "to find a place in our community" for any family that believed they'd have a better chance in life in a setting very different from New York.

I did not know how I should react to this idea at first. I'd never received a call like that from a total stranger and, although I knew almost nothing of Montana, I found it hard to picture any family that I knew beginning life all over in a place so far away, and so unlike New York.

But the doctor's explanations were so plain and simple—it was a nice town, he said, the schools were good, the congregation was prepared to find a house and fix it up and pay the rent at first and help out with the food expenses for a while, and he was a family doctor and had children and grandchildren of his own—that I told him I'd pass all this information on to Reverend Overall and that she would likely call him back if there was ever any interest from a family at St. Ann's.

I pass on a number of more modest offers and suggestions every year to ministers and teachers and other people working in poor neighborhoods and never know for sure if they'll materialize. Some of them do. Churches and synagogues routinely ask me for the names of schools or churches in the Bronx and frequently they follow through with shipments of computers, books, and other educational materials. Religious congregations from as far away as Maine and Pennsylvania have invited groups of children from St. Ann's to visit them for extended periods of time. But moving an entire family some 2,000 miles to a small town in Montana that I'd never heard of was in a different ballpark altogether.

There's another reason why I hesitated to respond to Dr. Edwards's invitation. There is an intimidating rhetoric of cultural defensiveness in many inner-city neighborhoods like those of the South Bronx, which sometimes has the power to inhibit any actions that might tend to break down racial borders and to stigmatize the people who propose them as "invasive" or "paternalistic." There is a kind of mantra that one often hears from local power brokers in neighborhoods like these that the way to "fix" a ghettoized community is, first of all, never to describe it in such terms and, second, to *remain* there and do everything you can to improve it and promote its reputation. Those who choose to leave are seen as vaguely traitorous, and those who help them leave are often seen as traitorous as well.

Sometimes ideology and rhetoric like this can introduce an element of complicated and neurotic inhibition into issues that should be decided by the people they will actually affect. I wasted a few days debating whether to dismiss the whole idea and, at one point, I nearly threw away the name and number of the doctor. Then, to end my indecision, I sent the information he had given me to Martha and more or less forgot about it for a while. . . .

A month later, in the middle of December, Vicky came into St. Ann's in a state of desolation: beaten again, eyes purple, worried sick about her son, who was not attending school, worried about welfare, worried about clinic visits, worried about rent and food.

The telephone in the office rang while she was sitting there talking to the pastor. "It was the doctor from Montana," Martha told me later. I didn't know if she had called him earlier that day or if the timing of his phone call was a sheer coincidence.

"We had another meeting," Dr. Edwards said. "The invitation is still there."

Martha told him, "Wait a minute," and, looking at Victoria, she told her there was someone on the phone that she might like to talk with.

"I had to leave the office then and go downstairs into the afterschool," she said. "When I came back, Vicky and the doctor were still talking. When she put the phone down, I asked her what she thought. She reached out for my hands. It must have seemed unreal to her. I told her that she ought to give herself a lot of time to think about it and discuss it with the children. I gave her Dr. Edwards's number and told her she could call him anytime she wanted, and I suggested that she ought to question him some more.

"That was only about two weeks ago. Lisette came in today and said, 'Guess what? We're moving to Montana!'"

About a week later, I went to Vicky's home. I didn't want to spoil her excitement, or that of the children, but I thought I ought to tell her some of the reservations I had had ever since the first call I'd received. My concerns, I quickly realized, were not hers. When I told her, for example, that there wasn't likely to be more than a small number of black people in the town where she was going, she said that she already realized that.

"You're not concerned at leaving all your friends here, leaving everything you're used to?"

"I *want* to leave," she said.

The living room in which she slept was already filled with shipping boxes she had gotten from the church.

"You're sure that you can handle it?"

"I won't know unless I try," she answered.

Another week went by. . . .

"In about two hours," Martha told me on the phone, "Vicky and Eric and Lisette will reach their new home in Montana. Dr. Edwards had tears in his voice on the phone today when he called to check on the arrangements. The whole community seems to have gotten together to rent a house for them, and put in some furniture, and work out all the other details so that they'll feel welcome when they get there. I think that everybody knows it isn't going to be easy. . . .

"Vicky was up all last night. I brought her a scale so she could weigh the packages for UPS. She told me she wanted to get her hair done but there wasn't time because the kids were so excited that they were no help to her at all.

"I think that she was happy with a kind of totally 'free' happiness I have never seen in her before. She spoke of taking up her knitting once again, and letter-writing, and she said she'd like to have a garden. She'll be forty-eight in March.

"A neighbor of Dr. Edwards used his frequent-flier miles to pay for the tickets, but there was some kind of glitch and we only got two tickets so I bought the third one—for Lisette. The woman at the desk gave her an upgrade to first class!

"We had lunch at the airport. They were off at two p.m. I think they had to change planes in Chicago."

– II –

One month later, on my answering machine: "Jonathan, this is me, Vicky. Oh yes! I'm tellin' you! I'm really here! I'm in Montana."

She left her number. I called her back as soon as I got home.

"Jonathan!" It was the first time I had ever talked with her when she didn't need to struggle to sound cheerful.

"Have you ever eaten elk?"

"No," I said. "Are you eating elk?"

"Yes!" she said.

"Where do you get it?"

"At the store."

"What's it like?"

"It tastes like steak. You broil it. Delicious!"

"How are the kids?"

"They're in school."

"Any problems?"

"No," she said. "Not yet."

"Any black kids in the school?"

"No," she said, "except for them."

"Does that bother them?"

"I don't think so," she replied, "because they know it doesn't bother me."

The only thing that bothered her, she said, was walking to the store. "People here? They drive real fast. And there isn't any stoplights on this street at all. None on the next street either, come to think of it. None on the next street after that. In fact, there isn't any stoplights anywhere in town.

"And, oh! The girl next door—Diane?—she drives me from the IGA if I got too much to carry in my arms.

"I'm tellin' you! There's a lot of friendly people here!

"One lady came to bring me milk and asked me, 'I don't mean no harm, but are you prejudiced?' I told her no, because I'm not. She looked at me and then the two of us began to laugh! Because—you know?—you'd think the question would have been the other way around. . . .

"It's like everybody wants to know: How did I ever get here? Well, I want to know that too! The only thing Dr. Edwards told me is that they was goin' to choose *someone.* It was something they made up their minds about."

"What's the church like?"

"Made of logs."

"What's it called?"

"Trinity Church."

"What denomination is it?"

"Christian."

"What can you see looking out your windows?"

"Mountains!" she replied. "They're on almost every side."

"Is it snowing?"

"Only in the mountains."

"What's it look like?"

"Beautiful!"

"The day you got there, when you were coming off the plane—what was it like? Was Dr. Edwards waiting?"

"Yes, he was there. Not only him. It seemed like everyone in town was there. They had their cars pulled up: twenty people, maybe more. Then Dr. Edwards took us to this house. He said, 'This will be your home.' Then he took us to the church. He said, 'This will be your church.' Then the stores began to send us food. Four stores. Each one gave us groceries: a hundred dollars from each store.

"Oh, Jonathan! It's cold here in the winter, but the hearts of people in this town are warm."

In the first days after she arrived, she said, she had to

struggle to convince herself that she was really there. "The first night, after Dr. Edwards and his wife were gone? I told the children, 'Leave me be. I need to sit here in this chair.' I told them not to turn on no TV. It's just as well, because they only got three stations here and one of them goes off at six o'clock."

"What's the house like?"

"Oh yeah! Well, I'm in the livin' room right now. It would make up two of them that I used to have. I got two sofas. One of them's a sofa-bed. Over at the other end, there's a dining room and kitchen, which is kind of small, but they're both connected, and I got a washer and a dryer, and I got a microwave which is up above the stove. Three bedrooms. One of them is mine. Other two is down the hall. Seems like it's got everything I need."

"Where do kids there go for fun?"

"To school. McDonald's. Burger King. The IGA. To ranches. To the church. . . ."

"They go to ranches?"

"Me and Lisette, we went three days ago."

"How did you get there?"

"Chrissy picked us up."

"Who's Chrissy?"

"One of my friends."

"Have you made many friends?"

"Oh yes!"

I heard shouting in the background.

"Wait a minute. . . ."

Then Lisette picked up the phone.

I asked her whether everything was going good at school.

"My school is fine!"

"How big is it?

"Fifteen students."

"In the school?"

"No! In my class."

"Are the students nice to you?"

"Yes," she said.

"You feel okay? You're happy there?"

"I don't want to live in any other place."

In April, Vicky sent me a big envelope of pictures of the mountains, and the ranch-like house in which they were living, and the one-story wooden church, which looked like a log cabin. In one of the photographs there were six or seven wooden houses, very tiny, at the bottom of the photo. Above the houses, filling nine-tenths of the picture, there was a spectacular blue sky, with white and gray clouds rolling in from the distant mountains. A single tree, its slender branches reaching high. A small white pick-up truck beneath it. "Looking down the street," she'd written on the back, "the sky goes on forever."

When I phoned her the next night, she told me she was spending more time at the church.

"Sunday," she said, "I put my name down on the list for Hospitality Committee."

"What does that mean?"

"You see, after the service here, we all go in and eat our meal together. Members of the church, we take turns cookin' for each other. I wanted to make lemon cakes, because I'm good at bakin'. So I put my name down for next Sunday."

"How's Lisette?"

"Doin' okay. Gettin' B's—but could get A's, her teacher says. Needs to get her papers done. Do her homework every night. They give them a lot to do. This is something new to her."

When I asked the same thing about Eric, though, she sounded more uncertain.

"He's havin' a harder time. Missed too much back in

New York. No one here can figure out what they was doin' with him at his school. Principal says they're tryin' hard to catch him up. Dr. Edwards's talkin' with him now."

"You sound good."

"I'm feelin' good," she said, "but I still have times when I get scared that something's goin' to go wrong. . . ."

A few months later, at the start of June:

"I got a job."

"What are you doing?"

"Bakin' cookies, fryin' donuts—at the IGA."

"What does it pay?"

"Six dollars twenty-five." She'd started with a part-time job at Burger King, she said, "but IGA pays better."

She said that Dr. Edwards gave the kids some spending money for a while after they arrived, "so they could do things with their friends." But they didn't need it now. Eric was working at the IGA—"couple of hours, after school." Lisette, meanwhile, was baby-sitting for their neighbors. "She put up these little cards at the IGA. People call her. Mostly weekends. Mothers say she's really good. Feeds the children. Washes them. Tells them stories. Gets them into bed. Sings them songs. If it's late they drive her home."

In July, we talked again. She said she still was working at the IGA. "Doin' thirty hours now. Rent here is four-fifty. Church covers two-fifty and I pay the rest. Next month I'll be payin' fifty more. Long as I get thirty hours I think I can handle it."

She told me she had joined a group of women who were having problems like the ones that she'd been through, some of them with alcohol, but most of them related to abusive treatment at the hands of men. "I go to meetings at the church. Tuesday nights. Fifteen women. Some are single mothers, same as me. I was scared to talk at first. I'm talkin' now. It's hard for them to make me stop."

When we spoke the next time she told me that Lisette had done "something she shouldn't do" and "got herself in trouble"—not bad trouble, it turned out, but enough to worry Vicky for a time. One of the girls she knew from school had been teaching her to drive. "Kids out here," Vicky said, "they start to drive when they can reach the pedals!"

"What's the legal age?" I asked.

"I think you have to be sixteen. But this is . . . something different here! They do it anyway."

The girl who had been driving, Vicky said, banged into another person's car. Both the girls had to go to court. "The judge gave them a scolding and he made them pay a fine. They also have to pay the owner of the car for what they did. She's been payin' from her baby-sitting money. I think she owes him fifteen dollars more."

I asked if Dr. Edwards was still visiting a lot.

"Oh yes! He's here a couple times a week. Last week all of us had the flu. He came and gave us medicine and shots."

She said that he'd been taking them on long rides out into the wilderness to see the cattle ranges and the wild animal preserves. "He's forever doing that. He loves his car. We went out with the kids this week to look at one of the abandoned mines."

"What kind of mines?"

"Gold mines!"

"How old is Dr. Edwards?"

"Seventy? Sixty? I'd say maybe sixty-five. . . . He's got grandchildren who are Lisette's age. Two of them are girls."

"What does he look like?"

"He's a tall man, healthy-looking. Loves to do things with the kids outdoors. He's got gray hair."

"Is he a religious man?"

"Oh yes. I'd say he must be a religious man. He don't *talk* religion but I know that he's religious."

"How do you know?"

"You know it by the way somebody acts."

At the start of August, Martha sent me a reminder that I'd said I'd transfer money to Vicky, which we promised we would do to help her out with buying school clothes for the fall. I had a small private fund that I'd established for this purpose and for other relatively minor needs that families faced. Sometimes only a couple hundred dollars, at the moment it was needed, could help a family catch up with their rent before they got an order of eviction. For most of the families I knew in the Bronx, few of whom had bank accounts, I had grown accustomed to making wire transfers. I asked Vicky whether she would like the money sent by Western Union or if she'd prefer I send a check to Dr. Edwards, who would cash it for her.

She said I didn't need to send her money but, when I said it was a promise we had made, she said I could send the check directly to her home.

"How will you cash it?"

"I don't need to cash it yet. I'll put it in the bank."

"You opened up a bank account?"

"Checking," she replied.

"How long is it since you had a bank account?"

"I never had a bank account in my entire life before. Jonathan, I'm *tellin'* you! This is the first time. . . ."

End of summer: Vicky called to tell me that Lisette had had an accident.

"She was with her girlfriend out at someone's ranch that Dr. Edwards knows. They was runnin' with the horses and she wasn't lookin' and she ran into a hole or something that was full of water. Hurt her ankle. She's on crutches. Hoppin' around from room to room. I'll be relieved when she goes back to school.

"Oh, did I tell you? Eric's got a girlfriend. Actually, he's had a lot of different girlfriends since we got here to this town. He doesn't stick with them too long. He goes through them awful fast. We came here eight months ago? I think he's had a different girl for every month since we arrived. . . .

"Oh yes! Dr. Edwards had us to his house for dinner Sunday night. He invited a friend of his, a high school principal from another town. A *black* school principal. There you go! He says he wants to talk with Eric more. He says that Eric needs to do a lot of work if he wants to keep up with his class."

Her voice was strong and energized. She said that she was working hard—"doin' forty hours now." Between her job, her meetings at the church, getting the children set for school, and keeping on top of them to clean their rooms ("Eric's room is an embarrassment," she said. "He throws his things all over the floor"), it sounded as if she didn't have a lot of time to dwell upon the past.

"Do you ever miss New York?"

"No," she said. "I do not. But I miss some *people* there.

"I was thinkin'—once I feel more settled here, I might go back to St. Ann's. Maybe I won't tell them. Just walk in the door one day and say, 'Well, here I am!' If I do, I'd like to go by bus this time, and not by plane, because I'd like to see what's down there on the ground.

"Oh yeah! I forgot to tell you that I found my knitting needles. My friend Diane? She took me to the mall in Bozeman and I got some beautiful blue yarn. I'm using a pattern that my other girlfriend gave me."

"What are you making?"

"Makin' a sweater—for Lisette. Finished with one sleeve. Workin' on the other now. This pattern's not too hard. If I have the time, I'm goin' to make a couple more of them by Christmas."

Shy voice: "Jonathan?"

"Yes," I said.

"If I made one for you, would you wear it?"

"Are you kidding?"

"There you go!"

— III —

Christmas Eve.

Vicky called to tell me that she had another job. "It's in a home for the elderly. I'm a dietary aide. It's my third job, and I hope the last one.

"I started Monday. I had to learn about the job. Then, on Tuesday, I did a double shift. Started at six-thirty, went to two o'clock. Then went back at four and worked until ten-thirty. I *like* old people! Some are disabled. Some have lost their memories. When I have a break, I like to sit and talk with them. . . .

"Lisette?" she said. "She's at the skating rink. They call it 'The Skating Palace' here. My friend Diane? She *likes* Lisette. She gave her ice skates as a present.

"The church gave us a Christmas tree. Members of the church came over and they helped me decorate it. Oh yeah! It's for Lisette. Not for me. I'm forty-nine years old!"

She said they still were taking rides with Dr. Edwards. "There's a town here in Montana which is called Big Timber. Smoky skies. It's by an Indian reserve. . . . I love to go on rides with him. Lisette too. I told him that he takes the place of my father for me. I never seen my Daddy since I was in junior high.

"I think he's up in Billings now to see one of his patients. He has patients all over Montana. . . .

"Did I tell you that we have a woodstove in the living room? Oh yes! When it's cold, we heat with wood, because the gas bill gets so high. Now my friend Yolanda, who lives down the street, has been bringin' wood to us, because her mother's got a truck. It's piled out there in the porch so we can keep it dry."

Lisette was fourteen by now and continued to do well in school. Dr. Edwards's granddaughters were her closest friends. In the spring, however, Dr. Edwards told me that the three of them had gotten into trouble. "They were apprehended at the mall in Bozeman. Shoplifting," he reported. "In fairness, I do not condemn Lisette as harshly as the others." It had been his granddaughter, the oldest of the two, who had been "the instigator," he believed. "They were given public service to perform. Lisette will do her service at an animal reserve.

"I'm confident that she'll come out of this okay. She's a loving girl, so boisterous and warm! And she accepts affection easily. My wife and I take her out to dinner when we can. We took her out a week ago after the court hearing. My wife is very fond of her. She hugs us both a lot."

Eric, on the other hand, was a source of more and more concern to him. "When I told him what had happened to Lisette, his response was awful cold. To quote him: 'I don't see why I should care.' I've spent more time with him than with Lisette. His grades at school are really bad. I'm taking him to Bozeman with me once a week for a tutorial in reading that a friend of mine arranged. So we have a chance to talk, to the degree that he will open up to me at all.

"I told him that I have to make a trip out to Seattle in the summer and I said that I'd enjoy it very much if he'd like to come with me. We could camp out on the way, on the Columbia River. I told him we could do some rafting. But he was not responsive."

During the summer, Lisette managed to get into minor troubles once again, "nothing bad," Dr. Edwards said, "but I talked about this with her principal and we struck on an idea."

There was, he said, "an excellent program" for students of her age—"takes place in Yellowstone. . . . Three months long. Counseling and leadership, and learning to mark trails. Learning about conservation right there in the wild. They don't indulge them. There's a firmness that is always ready to exert itself if a student pushes things too far."

His hope, he said, was to "catch" Lisette before the minor troubles she'd been getting into grew into much bigger ones. He said he believed, as did her principal and teachers, that she was a gifted child and could do honors work in high school and go on to college, but only if she gained a stronger sense of self-control—and, he added, "of self-understanding." He said that she did not object to his suggestion. "In fact," he added, "she became excited at the thought of going out there in the wilderness."

It proved to be a good idea, as I gathered from a letter Lisette wrote to me from Yellowstone, maybe six weeks later.

"Dear Jonathan,

"Hi! Hello! It's Lisette here. I am in the woods right now. I'm here for three months. Clearing trails. . . . Cool, huh?"

It was a short note. She didn't give me many details. "I hope that everything is going good for you," she ended in her neat and curly schoolgirl printing. "Please write back. Love, Lisette."

Two weeks later, I got another optimistic note from Dr. Edwards. "The big news: Lisette has been doing extremely well at Yellowstone." He and Vicky and his wife, he said, had had "the great experience" of going out to see her when the students' parents were allowed to visit after they had been there in the wilderness two months. "I'd have given a hundred bucks for you to be there with us."

At the end of the day, he said, "we all sat in a circle. Lisette and the other kids talked about the parts of the experience that mattered most to them. Lots of tears and hugs among the kids and counselors. She comes home in one more month. Here's some pictures of her that I know you'll like."

In one of the pictures, Lisette was running with a bunch of other kids across a grove of trees. The branches, covered with thick foliage, were hanging almost to the ground. In another, a close-up, she was wearing something like an army jacket and a woolen hat that was pulled down to her forehead and was smiling brightly, with a look of mischief, right into the camera. On the back of the picture Dr. Edwards wrote, "When they came back from the woods, Lisette told us, 'I feel like one dirty bird.' They wash themselves *and* their clothes in cold lakes and streams—no soap! But she's a happy camper."

The news continued to be good after she returned to school. "She's really blossoming," Dr. Edwards told me. "Doing honors, getting A's, and the school by reputation is one of the best ones in the area. She's popular among the other students, does cheerleading, sings in the choir. But she's careful about boys. . . ."

The news about her brother was less cheerful. "I'm sad to tell you he dropped out of school last week because the school will not allow a student to continue to play sports if he has failing grades, and that was just about the only thing he really seemed to care about. The school was willing to work with him and give him extra help. His teachers didn't want him to drop out. The truth is that he never gave it a real try.

"He's repeated once already. Now he's over eighteen and has no degree and no longer has a job. He doesn't stay at home a lot. He seems to stay with different girls, until they've had enough of him. Then he crashes with Victoria. Then he's gone again.

"When I try to talk with him, he turns away his eyes. He tells me that he'd like to join the military. But they won't accept him. They insist on a diploma. My friend, who is a principal in another district"—this was the black principal that Vicky had described—"has talked with Eric several times. He tells me that he 'closes down' and gives him almost no replies.

"So Vicky has her hands full. When Eric's home, the house becomes a hangout for a whole group of his friends and, to be quite blunt about it, not the kinds of friends I'd like to see him with. Vicky works 'til late at night, so she can't control this. And, when she's there, the boys are pretty rude to her."

The news continued to be worrisome through the fall and winter of the year. By the beginning of their third year in Montana, Vicky started falling into the depressive moods from which she used to suffer in New York. "She's deeply troubled about Eric," Dr. Edwards said. "I've put her on some mild medication and it seems to make a difference. She's been successful in her job. She tells me that she loves it. I hope that she'll keep on. . . ."

He wrote me six months later, in June of 1999, with another mixed report: "Lisette remains a spot of brightness in a zone of growing darkness. Eric's a loose cannon. His most recent girlfriend, with whom he's been living now for nearly half a year—the very attractive daughter of a very white truck-driver who happens to be a Christian fundamentalist—is now very pregnant." Her father, he said, "is in a frantic state and is known here as a man that you don't want to mess with. So Eric's in some danger, which I've cautioned him about. I've also spoken with the father."

Two months later: "The police have put a warrant out for Eric. It seems he's been involved in robberies with one of his problematic friends. I gather they've been doing this repeatedly. Amazingly, his girlfriend sticks it out with him, although it's been real stormy. 'Hurricane force' is how I would describe it. I'm surprised her father hasn't popped him."

The racial factor, he surmised, was always in the background and, with Eric out of school, out of work, living off a girl he had made pregnant, Dr. Edwards speculated that her father "may well look at Eric as a prime example of the racial nightmare—'irresponsible and dangerous young black man'—appearing in real life." Still, no father, he observed, even one without the slightest bit of bigotry, could be expected to be empathetic and forgiving toward a boy who put his daughter in this situation. All the father knew was that his daughter, who was Eric's age but was a student at the university by now, was living with a man who had given ample evidence that he was unprepared to be a husband that his daughter could rely upon. When he heard that Eric was arrested, he had yet another reason for concern.

Throughout this time, Vicky and I remained in contact with each other, but her letters and her phone calls had become less candid and informative than they'd been before. On a few occasions she confirmed what Dr. Edwards had been telling me, but not in full and, most often, long after the fact.

"Eric?" she said. "He's with his girlfriend quite a lot, but he keeps on comin' back. I *cannot* put him out." She said that she could not forget how hard it was for Eric when they had been homeless and before they even got into the shelters. "We were sleeping in a friend's house. If we got there and the door was locked, we slept out in the hallway. Lisette was just a baby then. He was the one that went and asked for food at the White Castle. So I sometimes ask myself: Am I the one to blame for all the troubles that he's had? But he makes it very hard. . . ."

She didn't tell me yet that he'd dropped out of school. She didn't speak about his girlfriend's pregnancy. She didn't say he'd been arrested. She didn't speak about the medication Dr. Edwards gave her. She did say, "I been prayin' for my son. I'm askin' God to help me."

When we spoke the next time, she said that she had finally made a trip back to New York but had somehow lost the will to go back to St. Ann's and had come back quickly. While she was gone, Lisette had been staying with Dr. Edwards and his wife. Eric, meanwhile, had been fighting with his girlfriend so, in Vicky's absence, he went back into her house and, because he had no key—"I told him that I didn't want him goin' there while I was in New York"—he'd broken in with several of his friends, "messed up the place, rang up a huge bill on my phone, and robbed me of some money I had left there."

"Where is he now?"

"He's back with his girlfriend, but he comes here when he wants. If I'm at work he pries the window open."

She said that Eric's girlfriend had come to the house alone after Eric robbed her. "Yeah! She knew. She found out that he done it. So she came and told me she was sorry, and she stayed and talked with me while he was gone off somewhere with his friends. She's a sweet girl and I know she likes me and I found out quite a lot. She told me Eric isn't treatin' her the way he should. He yells at her. She says he's raised his hand to her."

This information, Vicky said, had saddened her tremendously. The thought that he had been abusive to this girl, who trusted him and was in love with him, "made me disappointed in my son."

It was a while after that before I heard from her again. Her telephone was disconnected for a time because she never caught up with the bills that Eric left her. She wrote me a few letters, and in one of them she opened up more fully than before about the troubles Eric had been going through. "Got three weeks for stealing gas. It was for his girlfriend's car. He uses it whenever he likes. He goes out riding with his friends." His girlfriend was afraid of saying no to him, she said.

She also told me that the break-ins Eric made into her house and the wildness of the friends he brought with him were causing problems with her neighbors, and she said her landlord spoke with her about this. I was glad she was confiding in me once again, but I was worried by the growing time-lag between the news that I received from Dr. Edwards and the news that Vicky felt prepared to share with me.

The letter ended on a slightly upbeat note. "Lisette still goes to church with me. Church members taking turns to pick us up on Sundays. I'm trying to think positive.

"I'm ending this letter now.

"God bless you.

"Victoria."

— IV —

Vicky had said that she was trying to "think positive." But positive thinking, as highly recommended as it is, can be overrated as a salutary and sufficient answer to calamitous conditions that are far beyond the power of an individual to alter or control in more than small degrees. For all the efforts she had made, for all the help her neighbors gave her, for all the love and loyalty Dr. Edwards never ceased to demonstrate to her and to her children, Vicky found herself unable to escape the shadow of her history.

It was Eric's uncontrollable behavior that finally brought her down. In April of 2000, after Eric once again had broken into Vicky's house with a number of his friends while she was at her job and Lisette was working late at school, the police were called by people in the neighborhood—"music blasting and loud voices," Dr. Edwards said—and Vicky was at last evicted from her home.

Although the members of the church helped her get resettled, she fell into a state of bad depression once again and, having earlier been careful about overuse of alcohol—a couple of beers late at night when she came home from work, maybe something stronger on the weekends when she was relaxing with a friend—she now began to drink much sooner in the day in order to subdue the feelings of foreboding that had overtaken her.

"After doing a good job at the nursing home," Dr. Edwards wrote to me, "and having recently been given a nice raise in pay, she abruptly quit. She simply was unable to get up and out into the world and face the pressures of the day. Alcohol and antidepressant medications, as you know, can be a deadly brew. I'm going to start all over, if she'll let me, with another intervention."

In a follow-up note in May, he was more hopeful, but cautiously so. "Vicky has joined a twelve-step program. It was begun by a young physician here in Bozeman, an excellent man who, unhappily, developed an addiction—to Demerol, I think—while he was in training, and is very good and sensitive with people in her situation. He's been successful with a number of my patients but in Vicky's case I have to say I've got my fingers crossed. She's fallen deep into her drinking. I don't know if she can stop." When I asked what she was living on, he said she was on welfare and, he thought, she might be doing part-time work when she was well enough to handle it.

It was more than seven months after that before I heard from Vicky. Her phone had been cut off again after her eviction, but she said, "I got a new phone now." To my surprise, and a bit to my confusion, she sounded upbeat and excited when she called.

"Oh yes! You know what I did? I took the bus to Georgia and I saw my Daddy! He's seventy-four. I hadn't seen him since I was fourteen. His birthday was on Christmas Day. I made him a sweater. Same as yours, except in green.

"Did I tell you that my father's a musician? Yes! He's in a gospel choir. They were having a rehearsal on the day before I left. I said, 'Daddy, you're going to rehearsal. Would you let me come with you?' My father was so happy!"

She didn't say a word about the latest difficulties Dr. Edwards had described. Not a mention of the job she'd given up, the twelve-step program she'd begun, the struggle she'd been going through to fight off her depression. And she said nothing this time in reference to her son. The same sense of disconnect I'd noted in our conversations from the year before left me with a great deal of uneasiness again.

In his letters, Dr. Edwards's references to Eric had become increasingly disheartening. "I've tried again and again to sit him down and talk with him, but he isn't interested, doesn't want to listen, doesn't want to tell me anything at all." He said that Eric's girlfriend had ended their relationship. He also said he had some reason to believe that Eric and his friends were "gravitating into drugs or stolen pharmaceuticals." He noted, too, that Eric was now living in his own apartment and, by all appearances, paying his own rent. So he said he had to wonder where the money came from.

In the summer of that year—it was now 2001—he told me Vicky was no longer showing up for meetings at her twelve-step program. He also said she'd moved again, and more than once, as I discovered later. "I stopped by to visit with her just a week ago. She'd been drinking heavily. It was hard to get straight answers from her. It's as if she's sitting there just waiting for the bad news she's expecting."

Six weeks went by.

"Jonathan," Vicky said in a message on my phone. "I have something terrible to tell you. I lost my son two days ago. Eric was shot—shot with a shotgun to his head. He would have been twenty-two this Sunday." She left me her phone number. When I called her back, her voice was blurred and breaking. "I don't know how to say this," she began. "My son has taken his own life. . . .

"Day he died, I'd called him in the mornin'. He said that he was with his friends, playin' cards and havin' fun." Then, all of a sudden, she reported, Eric sounded very scared. "'Mummy, I don't feel no good. I need your help.' I said, 'Okay. Come over here right now.'

"A few minutes later, he was at the door. He came in by his self, and then his friends came in. I didn't know why he let them come with him, but I was thinkin' they'll be gone and then he'll be alone with me. They went into another room and it was quiet for a while. Then I heard it, right behind the wall, and I went in and saw the shotgun layin' there across the floor. There was blood all over him. It was comin' from his head. . . .

"Next thing, the police was there. Police was comin' up the stairs. Then they was tryin' to revive him. Then they put him on a stretcher and they carried him downstairs and took him to the hospital, but they said I shouldn't come. But fifteen minutes after that another man from the police, he took me with him in his car and said that he would stay with me. Then a doctor came out from the door and he got up and spoke to him, and then he sat down next to me and held my hands and told me that my son was dead.

"He asked me was there anyone I would want to contact and I told him Dr. Edwards. But Dr. Edwards, he'd already heard. And he came in and he was there and he took me to my house. And then his wife. And other people from the church. They wouldn't let me be alone. And, after that, Lisette was there. And Dr. Edwards's wife went outside to talk with her."

I asked her whether anybody close to him, anyone who cared for him, had told her that he was depressed before she spoke with him that day.

"No one. No one knew. He just kept it in. I told Lisette I pray from this she'll always tell me what she's feelin' when she's feelin' bad. 'Never hold it in,' I said, 'because I been there and I love you and I couldn't bear it if I lost you too. . . .'"

Dr. Edwards mourned for Eric like the father he had tried to be for him. He condemned himself for never having found a way to penetrate those walls of isolation in which Eric had enclosed himself. "Starting months ago," he said, "I had my struggles about being the prime mover, asking whether everything that he was going through was somehow of my doing. I've tried to come to peace with this, but I haven't given up my questioning. It's going to be a long time, I'm afraid, before I do.

"There are some who are convinced it was a homicide. Several of his friends, as I believe you know, had followed him into that room, and no one has explained what they were doing when that shot rang out. But the police have interviewed the boys and studied the case carefully, and all the evidence seems to confirm it was a suicide."

Again and again, he came back to the question of

his own responsibility. "I realized there were going to be problems from the first time Vicky opened up to me. And after she had been here for a while she confided in me more and she told me quite a lot of what the kids had undergone when they were in New York. But I overestimated the potential of a different place and different opportunities to overcome what I had hoped they'd left behind."

Weeks after Eric's death, I found that I kept coming back to what Vicky said he'd told her on the phone. "Mummy, I don't feel no good. I need your help"—and her reply, "Come over here right now." For all of the defensive toughness and aloofness others saw in him, he had spoken to his mother in that moment in the way that frightened children do. If he had only come alone and told her what he feared, might she have held him in her arms and given him the sense of safety he was asking for? Could she have been for him, in the hour when he needed it, the mother she herself had never had?

From that time on, Dr. Edwards and those members of the church who were Vicky's closest friends did everything they could to help her and Lisette to reconstruct at least some semblance of stability. Lisette regained her footing rather quickly. She was now a senior and continued getting honors grades and was making plans to go to college. She was, Dr. Edwards said, "a mature and capable young woman" and "happily in love" with an only slightly older man, a student at the university—"a serious and decent guy by the name of Thomas who is very much in love with her as well." He said that she'd been living with him for a time, but it seemed important to him to explain that they were "married under common law" which, he wanted me to know, "is binding in Montana."

A short time later, he told me she was pregnant but he was confident that this would not prevent her graduating high school and proceeding with her plans for higher education. "We had dinner with them, and Lisette made clear that she has no intention of returning to New York. She's looking at some colleges around Atlanta now. She and Thomas seem to have a good perspective on the choices they'll be making. As a couple, they seem very solid, very strong."

Vicky, on the other hand, continued to be almost inconsolable. "I went over there to visit her the other night. She told me she was drinking. But she didn't need to tell me. I could see that she was pickled when she came to the front door. I'd been told she was starting a new job, but there's no way she could have gone to work in the condition that I saw."

I spoke with Vicky very seldom after that. Usually her voice was faint and her words were often slurred and the little information that she chose to share with me was never very clear. Before long, there were no more messages from Vicky on my phone. I didn't know if she had moved again. The most recent number she had given me appeared to be cut off.

In one of the final letters that he sent me, Dr. Edwards said, "I don't see Vicky anymore, which saddens me, but she no longer seeks my company. I've tried my best to keep in touch. My wife and I drive over there from time to time, but we never find her home and the messages I leave for her are not returned."

Eight months after Eric died, I received a very grown-up and reflective letter from Lisette. "Since my brother was laid down to rest, my mother has been struggling. Dr. Edwards says he told you she's been drinking. She was broken by my brother's death. I love her, but I have to use my strength to save myself.

"Thomas and I are doing our best to pay our bills and

taking good care of our daughter. We were married in a church on May 15. I graduate next week. Then we're going to move south so I can enter college in September."

She said that they had changed their plans and were looking at a town near Myrtle Beach because her husband's relatives were living in that area. Her husband had applied for transfer to a college there, which she would be attending too.

They must have moved soon after that. I wasn't sure if she received the letter I had sent her in reply. Dr. Edwards, who was well into his seventies by now, was no longer able to maintain the pace he used to keep, and he soon retired. Within another year or so, he told me he had lost all contact with Lisette and Vicky. Many years went by before I got word of them again.

It came in a phone call from South Carolina in 2009. Lisette still had a little of that buoyant schoolgirl voice that had endeared her to so many people in her teenage years, but she was twenty-six by now, the mother of four children. With time taken off to raise the children, she was heading toward completion of her studies to become a paralegal. Her husband was completing a degree in dentistry.

Her mother, she said, had suffered greatly in her final years from pancreatic cancer. "Her social worker called me from Montana and told me she would probably not live for very long. We brought her here to stay with us. She started chemotherapy. We took her to a hospital in Charleston to receive her treatments and we thought that she was doing well, until she just stopped eating. She had lived eleven months. She died at home with our kids around her. She's buried at the cemetery with my husband's family."

In her final words she said, "I'm going to give a good life to my children. I have to do it. I'm the one who made it through. I'm a stronger person now. I guess that I was always stronger than I knew.

"Please give my love to Martha when you speak to her. And if you're ever here near Myrtle Beach we would love to have you come and visit us. We have room for you to stay. If you like, I'll take you out to see my mother's grave. I know how much she meant to you.

"Okay? I have to go! Say a prayer for me!"

CHAPTER 3

Pietro and His Children

No two parents I encountered in the late years of the 1980s and the early 1990s could have seemed more different from each other than Pietro Locatello and Victoria. Distinct from one another in their family histories and in the make-up of their families, in their quirks of personality and qualities of character, not to speak of the most obvious distinctions, which were race and gender, the only common bond that I could see at the time when we became acquainted was the fact that both had fallen into homelessness at the same unhappy time in New York City's history and that both were very fragile people when they went into the shelters.

Pietro had been a doorman and a maintenance worker at a building in Manhattan when his wife was strangled on the beach at Coney Island by one of several men with whom she'd been involved during her years of marriage to Pietro. The man, apparently, was a narcotics user and had killed her in a fit of jealousy when she told him she had other lovers. Pietro was emotionally dependent on his wife and for this reason, as I gather, had forced himself to tolerate her infidelities. After her death, his world fell apart. For a long time after that he could barely function.

His wife had left him with three children. Pietro's mother, a widowed woman in her sixties, moved in to help him with the children, and this had made it possible to keep the kids together. But Pietro was too shaken to continue with his full-time job and, even with the part-time jobs he somehow pieced together, he fell behind on rental payments and the family was, at last, evicted. It was this that led him to take recourse to the city's homeless system, and this in turn had brought him to the bleak and narrow room in which I would get to know him in the Martinique Hotel.

On the day before Christmas 1985, one of the social workers I have mentioned who enabled me to get into the building introduced me to Pietro when I was in his office. The social worker told him, as he felt obliged to do, that I was a writer and that I would like to do some interviews with families in the building. Pietro seemed to hesitate at first, then asked if I would like to come upstairs and see where he was living. He gave me his room number and I told him I'd be back there in the evening.

The children—Christopher, ten years old, Ellie, who was five, and Miranda, four—were in their beds by the time that I had gotten past the guards and climbed the stairway to their room. The girls were asleep. Christopher was still awake and fully dressed, sitting on the top bunk of the three-bunk bed with a blanket wrapped around his shoulders. A tall boy for his age, vigilant and tense in his expression, and unnaturally pale, he had an emaciated look. So, too, did his father. Pietro, who was over six feet tall and whose weight had dropped from 165 to 120 in the two years he'd been living here, had a skeletal appearance.

His mother—"Grandma," as he and the children called her—was not there when I arrived. She had fallen in the stairwell on the night before and was at the hospital, Pietro said, for a check-up to make certain that she had no major injuries.

The room appeared at first to be unheated. Then Pietro pointed out to me that in the window opposite the beds there was a broken pane of glass that he had covered over with a sheet of garbage plastic but which still admitted cold air from outside.

That night, and on later nights when I returned, Christopher said very little. As with other children I would meet that winter, it was obvious to me that he was often hungry and perhaps was wondering if I had some food with me. Seeing that look, I'd sometimes give Pietro ten or twenty dollars so he could go across the street and stock up on food supplies. Or else, if I was sure that I could get in past the guards again, I'd go out and buy some milk and cereal and other items on my own. Christopher would climb down from the bed and eat the cereal in silence. He made it clear that he had no special wish to talk with me. I had the sense that he regarded me distrustfully.

Like other boys about his age, he would go out in the afternoons and evenings to panhandle in the traffic on Sixth Avenue or Broadway or else, on the opposite side of Herald Square, on the sidewalk out in front of Macy's. His father did not want to let him do this but, he told me, "At his age, I simply cannot keep him in a cage within this room. It feels like a prison to him. All his friends are out there in the streets. He wants to be there with them."

Christopher had apparently become adept at extracting money from the tourists and commuters, and now and then he brought some of the money home or used it to buy presents for his sisters. Mostly, however, he was using it to pay for meals while he was out, his father said, or else to pay for cheap and gaudy-looking trinkets (phony gold chains and the like) that were popular among his friends, many of whom were older than he was.

Pietro worried that a boy as young as Christopher might attract the notice of police, although there were so many boys doing the same thing that this may have been unlikely. But he had another reason for concern. Christopher was a handsome boy. His white-blond hair, unkempt as it was, pale blue eyes, and sharp-featured jaw made him a target, as his father feared, for older men he might encounter in the streets.

The following year, a man who came into the Martinique with one of the groups that organized activities for children in the shelter began to buy him presents—"Frisbee things that lighted up," his father said, "inexpensive things at first"—but then he bought him an expensive coat and took him off one weekend to a country house somewhere on Long Island without Pietro knowing where he was.

When Christopher returned on Sunday night, he acted rather secretive to Grandma and his father and, in his conversations with Pietro in the months to come, I noticed that he spoke to him in tones of thinly veiled contempt, as if he felt that, by Pietro's inability to give him things that other people could afford to buy him, he had lost the right to exercise authority and no longer held the status of a father in his eyes.

His sisters, meanwhile, being the young children that they were, had not lost the sweetness and the trusting qualities of childhood. The girls were thin and had pale complexions, like their brother, but they were playful and affectionate to me when I was there and would chatter gaily with each other and with me and Grandma. And, to their father, they never showed a hint of the hostility that Christopher displayed when he was in the room—although, increasingly (he was nearly eleven now) he was seldom in the room on the evenings I was there. There were times when I would stay as late as midnight talking with Pietro and, when I left, the boy had not returned.

I had no reason, at this stage of things, to recognize a pattern in the way that Christopher behaved, in distinction from the way the little girls behaved and the trust that they invested in their father and grandmother. I did not know Vicky yet, or Eric, or Lisette. It was a long time after that before I met them at St. Ann's. And, even then, although I could not fail to notice parallels between the boys' behavior, I was not inclined to put things into patterns. I thought about the kids and families I was meeting exactly as I saw them: different families, different kids, with the sole exception that all of them had undergone a time of destitution and all had lived for periods of years in places as unwholesome as the Martinique Hotel. Whether or not the consequence of that experience, in each and every case, would be enduring, or injuriously so—or what form that injury might take in kids of different ages and different dispositions—still remained unclear to me, as it does to some degree even today.

– II –

Three years after I had met him in the Martinique, Pietro and his family were resettled by the city in a section of the Bronx, known as the East Tremont area, that was only slightly less impoverished and drug-ridden than the area around St. Ann's.

The first time I went to see them was a warm and sunny August afternoon in 1990. Pietro was at the local grocery, where he was packing bags. He did this in the afternoons to make a little money which, like many people in the poorest sections of the Bronx, he did not report for fear of being cut from food stamps and the other welfare benefits that he depended on. Christopher was not at home. Ellie was out visiting a friend. Grandma and Miranda were sitting in the living room with a little boy, a five-year-old, whose mother lived nearby.

The boy, whose name was Bruno, had white scars around his eyes. He'd been burned in a household fire, one of many that had leveled buildings in the area. Headlines about fires in the South Bronx were familiar in those days: "FIERY TOMB FOR TWO BRONX KIDS," "TRAPPED TOT KILLED IN APARTMENT BLAZE," "APARTMENT FIRE KILLS BRONX BOY." Bruno had been fortunate to get away with nothing worse than two white scars.

Miranda was sitting on the sofa, holding a black kitten on her lap, one of three stray kittens they had found on the landing just outside the door. Bruno, meanwhile, was sitting on the floor playing with a big white duck—not a toy duck, but a real one—that began to quack at me when I came in the door. The kittens didn't chase the duck, Miranda said, because his quacking frightened them. The duck, she told me, had been given to her by a man who lived downstairs. She had named him Oscar.

Pietro wouldn't be returning from his job for at least another hour. So, when Miranda asked me, I agreed to go out for a walk with her and Bruno to a nearby park. Once we got out on the street I took them by their hands, but Bruno fairly flew along East Tremont Avenue, tugging us both after him. We passed a block where heaps of trash— refrigerators with their doors torn off, tattered sofas, pieces of linoleum, and green plastic bags of garbage—had been piled high. But, at the park, the flowers were in bloom: tulips, hyacinths, and daffodils, and white and yellow daisies. The children knelt down on the grass and Miranda spelled the flowers' names except for one, "hyacinth," which she said she couldn't spell because she'd never heard the word before.

At a food stand in the park we bought a box of popcorn, which we ate on the way home. Walking back along a street we didn't take before, we passed another vacant lot, surrounded by a wire fence, in which another patch of flowers was in bloom. The children tried in vain to reach them through the spaces in the fence. Bruno settled for a dandelion, which he said he'd bring home to his mother.

Pietro had come back from work by the time that we returned. He scooped up the smallest of the kittens and held it on his lap while we sat down to talk. Miranda and the little boy took the duck into the bedroom with them while her father talked to me about a problem he was having with his welfare worker, who had told him that she thought it was extravagant for them to keep so many cats.

"'You haven't got enough to feed yourself,' she said. 'That's why we give you food stamps. Do you think your food stamps are supposed to feed your cats?'"

He said that they had put the duck into a closet in the bedroom when the welfare worker came. "What would she have said if Oscar had got out and walked into the living room?

"I know," he said, "it seems a little crazy for us to keep a duck in the apartment. But the children love him, and the neighborhood is so depressing and they have so little. I just want them to remember that they're children. . . .

"We feed the cats a little milk. I bought some cornmeal for the duck. It only cost three dollars and it lasts about two months. We don't have a TV. So it's something to distract them."

A month later, he told me on the phone: "The welfare worker came by without notice. She saw the duck. He went right up and quacked at her."

"What did she say?"

"She says we ought to put him in a pot and cook him."

"Were the kids there?"

"Yes," he said. "She said it right in front of them. She says she won't report me if we want to keep the cats. But she says that Oscar has to be evicted."

The girls, he said, were crying when she left.

"From a certain point of view, I guess it's understand-able. She figures that we have so little money and we're asking them for something—for the food stamps, for the rent. So I guess she's thinking, 'This is something they can do without.' And that's correct. But my children have to do without so much. Having animals to play with is a lit-tle thing, I guess. It's a little 'extra.' I guess they figure it's too much. It's hard to know the answer: What's too much? What's enough? Kids need clothing. They need food. They need a roof above their heads. Do they also need to have a pet?"

I asked him what he planned to do with Oscar.

"He's still here. No eviction papers yet!"

Pietro was arrested once while he was in the Mar-tinique. He stole an Easter basket for the children from a Woolworth's store. He had to make a court appearance but the judge, it seems, was understanding of the situation. He let him off with a token punishment, something like a couple months' probation, or maybe just a warning. His sins, such as I knew of them, struck me as pretty trivial. He loved his kids. He did the very best he could to make up for the poverty in which they had to live and whatever they remembered from the time within the Martinique, which was not, after all, a matter of an Easter basket or three kit-tens and a duck but was a *real* offense, and one for which nobody had to pay a punishment except for those who were its victims. This brings us back to Christopher.

* * *

In the background of the children's lives, beyond the quacking of the duck and the battle that Pietro waged (and which I thought that he enjoyed to some degree) against the wishes of a somewhat uptight social worker who was doing only what she had been trained to do, there was a cloud forming. Christopher was absent from his home every time I went there. He was close to fifteen now and Pietro told me that he had no power to control him. Grandma, he said, was the one that Christopher confided in. But Grandma's bond to Christopher did not strike me as a wholly healthy one. She made up lies in his defense when I asked her where he was at night or if she knew what he was doing. There was something worrisome and puzzling, I thought, about the blindness of her loyalty to Christopher.

Miranda later told me he had pretty much dropped out of school, if he'd ever shown up at his school at all since the time they'd been resettled in the neighborhood. It appeared the public school, whichever one it was to which he'd been assigned, made only the most cursory attempts to find him.

He was already several years below the level of an average student of his age, because he'd lost so many years of education when the family had been homeless. Although the children in the Martinique, officially at least, had been assigned to public schools, many never got there, or, because of bureaucratic chaos or the failure of the schools to communicate with parents, there would be a long delay before they were enrolled. It often took four months or more before the city noticed that some of these kids were sitting in their rooms at the hotel all day without a school to go to.

By the time the family got out of the Martinique, in any case, Christopher's rebellious attitude and defiance of adult authority would have posed a challenge for attendance officers at almost any middle school, even if they gave it a real try. It would have required an inordinate degree of compassionate attention, not only in the schools but in a broad array of public institutions, to have had the slightest chance of turning back this very angry adolescent from the way that he was heading.

By his fifteenth birthday, he had been in juvenile detention twice for stealing cars and stripping them. From that point on, he was in and out of court and, within another three years, he would serve the first of several sentences at New York City's sprawling prison out at Rikers Island.

Miranda was nearly twelve years old at the time when Christopher first went to Rikers Island. She and her sister were going to a Catholic school, which they had attended since they moved into the Bronx. The small foundation I'd established, which was supported by readers of my books, was indirectly paying for tuition. My assistant sent the money to Pietro, rather than the school, because I thought that it was better for the children to enable him to make these payments on his own.

The children went to school in clean clothes every day. When Pietro didn't have the money for the laundromat, he or Grandma washed their clothes at home. He couldn't afford to buy the kind of clothing for the girls I know he would have liked, but what he did buy was in proper taste—no short skirts or tight revealing blouses, which many of the adolescent girls they knew were wearing.

"The other teenage girls we knew were hanging out with boys," Miranda said when we talked about her childhood ten or twelve years later. "A lot of them got pregnant and had children by the time they were fifteen. But Ellie and I did not turn out that way. I was playing with dolls still when I was in junior high. Daddy and Grandma wouldn't let us out at night. If they did, they'd call us in by eight.

People in the neighborhood treated us as if they knew we were protected, that we were a close family."

Those who knew the family well enough to be aware of what was going on with Christopher, or had observed his rough behavior for themselves, did their best not to give Pietro the impression that they thought he was responsible. They knew he had a sense of guilt, which also came across in letters that he wrote to me. They tried not to compound it.

Pietro hoped that Christopher's experience at Rikers Island might have left him scared enough to stay away from dangerous activities. He hoped that it had chastened him. But Christopher's trajectory over the next years continued on its downward slide, and, far from being sobered by the time he spent in jail, he seemed to have become more hardened, more emboldened.

The culmination came in 1995 before he was twenty, when he and three other young men grabbed a boy they did not know in the subway in the Bronx and threw him on the train tracks. The boy would very likely have been crushed beneath the train that was approaching if bystanders had not climbed into the pit beside the tracks to rescue him. Christopher was convicted of attempted homicide, and served the next seven years in prison—"upstate," as most families that I knew euphemistically described the penitentiaries where inmates served long sentences.

The prison where he served the longest portion of his sentence was seven hours from New York City. The girls went once a month to visit him with Grandma and Pietro—fourteen hours on the bus, leaving the Bronx at 2:00 a.m. on Saturday nights, returning home at 10:00 p.m. on Sundays. "There was something that I couldn't figure out about his attitude," Miranda said. "He didn't act the way you'd think someone would act in prison. It was like 'no big deal.'

Like he didn't want to think that he was up there in that prison for a reason."

After I had had no contact with him for so many years, he now began to write me letters that were postmarked in the town of Alden, which, I found by looking at a map, was roughly equidistant between Buffalo and Attica, the latter of which was the site of yet another penitentiary, historically notorious because of a prisoner revolt and resultant massacre of prisoners that had taken place there thirty years before. Both prisons, like most of the large state prisons in New York, were sited in white areas—and highly valued by the local residents and politicians for the jobs that they supplied—while the vast majority of inmates in these institutions were black or Hispanic. Thousands of incarcerated men of color from the streets of the South Bronx and other poor and segregated sections of New York underpinned the economic life of these upstate communities. Christopher, with his clear blue eyes and pale white skin and white-blond hair, inevitably attracted the attention of his fellow inmates.

His letters began in a polite and friendly tone, telling me for instance that he hoped that I was in "The Very Best of Health" and sending his best wishes to my research aide who, however, did not know him other than from having forwarded a message now and then that his father, for some reason, asked her to convey to him. I wanted to believe that the good-natured feelings in these letters were sincere; but since I hadn't seen him or spoken even briefly with him since the years in which he used to glare distrustfully at me while he was in the Martinique, the familiarity with which he addressed me now had an unconvincing sound. He spoke of his father with no softening of feelings and said that it was Grandma who had always taken care of him.

Sooner or later, he would come around to asking me

to send him money, or, in two instances—attributing to me more power than I had—asking me to intervene in efforts he was making to obtain a hearing to reduce his sentence. I agreed to do this once, at his father's pleading, and wrote a letter that alluded to the damage Christopher had undergone from his association with the older adolescent boys who had been his mentors in deception and some minor forms of criminality while he was in the Martinique. I cited Mario Cuomo, the former New York governor, who came away with horror from a visit to the Martinique and likened it to "a scene out of Dickens."

But, as hard as I tried, I knew that there was something unpersuasive in my letter. The truth is that I'd written it reluctantly because there was nothing in his correspondence with me, or in the things his father and Miranda had passed on to me after having visited the prison, that even hinted at a feeling of repentance for the crime that he'd committed.

A year later, he thanked me for that letter but asked me for another. Again, there was no indication that he felt remorseful or responsible for what he'd done. And he remained belittling in reference to his father, although Pietro was the only person who consistently attempted to assist him while he was in prison, sending money orders, for example, so Christopher could purchase clothes for winter.

"This Jail thing is Real Rough," he said in that second letter. "A lot of cutting's, a lot of stabbing's. I want to get out." He enclosed a photo of himself. His hair was gone. His head was shaven to the skull. He looked very muscular.

He told me he was known as "White Boy" to the men with whom he was imprisoned, and gave me the impression that he felt he was at greater risk of danger for this reason. But I worried more about the harm that he might do if he were released with no apparent alteration in his values or his temperament. This time, despite the pressure that his letter placed on me, I did not reply to him.

Meanwhile, on East Tremont Avenue, the efforts that Pietro had been making for so long to provide the children with as much stability as possible were thwarted unexpectedly when they were evicted from their home. The federal housing subsidy, known as Section 8, which he, like other homeless people, had been given when he moved out of the Martinique, had been withheld for no apparent reason other than the bureaucratic workings of a system that was famous for its arbitrary and erratic operation and its seeming lack of rationality. As a result, his landlord was not getting rental payments other than the small subsidiary funds that tenants had to pay and which Pietro scraped together on his own.

Miranda was seventeen, her sister eighteen, when they were evicted. All at once, the household in which they'd been living in the decade since they left the Martinique, and where they had known at least a fair degree of continuity and safety, was ripped apart by forces that Pietro never really understood and could not control.

"Daddy and Grandma moved into a single room in somebody's apartment near where we'd been living," said Miranda. She and her sister moved in for a while with a friend who lived in the same neighborhood. Ellie, who was married a year later when she was nineteen—she had a baby by that time—would be taken in and treated kindly by her husband's family before they saved enough to rent their own apartment.

Young as she was, and shy and understated as she'd always been, Miranda had to cope with the reality that, at least in economic terms, she was suddenly, as she put it, "out there on my own." She had to find a job, and find a place she could afford to live, and this, in turn, compelled her to drop out of school before she could complete her senior year.

After a number of fits and starts, she pulled herself together and was able to obtain a job, then a series of different jobs, none of which paid very well but gave her nonetheless her first experience of even partial self-reliance. One of the earliest jobs she got, which had been assigned to her under New York's workfare regulations, was, she said, "a short-term thing, clean-up work, raking leaves and stuff like that" in the public parks, "but only for six months," after which she found her way into longer-lasting jobs.

"One of them was over there at Yankee Stadium," she said, "doing counter work." Another job was "at a bakery on 82nd Street near Madison," where she was on a part-time basis, what she termed "on-call," but she said, "they called a lot." When she wasn't working at the bakery, she braided hair for women on the sidewalk of East Tremont Avenue. "I'd set up a chair outside. I might make a hundred dollars in an afternoon if I had three customers."

At one point, she also said, "I took a course in home care," and soon was getting long-term jobs taking care of people who were ill and needed a companion to look after them. She told me she enjoyed this work. "It was mostly older women. They reminded me of Grandma."

At this time, while Christopher was still away in prison and Grandma and Pietro were living in their rented room, Miranda, who was almost twenty and had led a very careful life in terms of her relationships with men, became, she said, a bit less careful "with a guy I'd always known and thought of as a friend, not in the romantic way. Then one night, you can guess. First time in my life. And, presto! I was pregnant. . . ."

While she was pregnant, she continued working for one of the women, who, she told me, "lived up there in

Riverdale"—a mostly white and affluent community. But, as her pregnancy advanced and she began to have some spells of dizziness and weakness, she said that she passed out one night in the lady's living room. She was permitted to come back to work. "But, only two weeks after that, I passed out again." At the hospital, she was diagnosed with dehydration and anxiety and was told it was not wise for her to work for the remainder of her pregnancy.

This time, it seems, the welfare system worked the way it ought to work for women in her situation. As an expectant mother, she was placed on rent assistance and provided with the welfare benefits, including food stamps, she would need to take care of her baby. By the time her son was born, she had found a small apartment in the St. Ann's neighborhood. After another year had passed, she took on a part-time job. Her little boy was cared for by a neighbor in the afternoons while she was at work.

This, then, was her situation at the time when Christopher, after having served nearly the full length of his sentence, with the reduction of a single year that had been commuted to parole, returned to the South Bronx.

– III –

"When Christopher came out of prison," said Miranda, "I was the only one who had a home that he could come to. He was my brother. I had my hands full with my baby and my job, so I didn't know what I should do, but he had no other place. I was his 'security,' he told me. You can see how little space I have"—she gestured to her bedroom and a smaller room that held the baby's bed, and the very tiny living room in which she had no furniture other than the sofa we were sitting on—"but I took him in. . . ."

"I gave him my bed and I slept on the couch, because you know how tall he is. I washed his clothes. I cooked his meals. He used to tell me he was 'getting things together,' but he was out late almost every night. Sometimes he'd be out until the morning."

I was not surprised when she said he broke the terms of his parole within a year after he got out of prison. "He went back twice, each time for about six months. The second time was in 2004, I think—or maybe in 2005." When he was out, he was back in her apartment. "He managed to get little jobs. He was a good talker. But he couldn't hold them. He was late too many times and people got fed up with him." Even when he had a job, "there was always something else going on that he wouldn't talk about. . . .

"Finally," she said, "he got a really good job in Manhattan at an exercise salon called Equinox. He told me how much money he was making and the people he was meeting. He had been bulked-up in prison," where, he told her, he'd been lifting weights and doing other body-building exercises. "He was in terrific shape. . . . But even then, when he was making money, he wouldn't help me with the food. He spent his money on himself. Stupid things. He bought himself expensive clothes. He bought a car, an old red Honda, from a friend, but he would get angry with me when I asked if he would drive me to my job or help me with the rent, the part of it that I was s'posed to pay.

"I was overworking myself, rushing off to do my job, doing everything I could to take care of my baby, filling out the forms I had to do to keep my rent assistance. Lots of forms for different things. Plus, also checking up on Daddy, going there to make sure he and Grandma were okay. Christopher, when he came back from work, just layin' there. . . . I was only twenty-four. Christopher was thirty. But he wouldn't help me."

Christopher finally quit his job at Equinox, she said.

"By this time, I knew that he was doing stuff he shouldn't do because he had a lot of cash. It seemed like he was making more than he had made at Equinox.

"At last I told him he would have to leave." She spoke about this with a sense of sorrow at her inability to keep him there and, as I suspect she may have wistfully believed, to function as a counterforce, by her availability and physical proximity, against his seemingly compulsive inclination to do almost anything that would get him into trouble once again. But, she said, "I had no choice. I was afraid of breaking down. The tension was too much for me."

During this time, Pietro kept in contact with me, mostly in long letters written from the room that he was sharing with his mother. His letters began, typically, on a long and crowded page, would continue on another page if he had another piece of paper, and then on smaller scraps of paper or the backs of envelopes or whatever other bits of paper he might have around.

What came across consistently was the comfort he received from knowing that Miranda never let too many days go by without checking up on him and that her sister's situation with her husband and his family seemed secure and, of course, the happiness he took in seeing his new grandson when Miranda brought him there to visit him.

His greatest worry had to do with Grandma, who was over eighty-five years old by now and had started to display the symptoms of Alzheimer's. He came back to their room one night and found she wasn't there and had to go into the streets and look around for several blocks until he found her sitting on a corner, looking lost and scared. He recognized that he might need to put her in a nursing home before too long and, because he'd never lived without her since his wife had died, I think he felt a sense of dread, perhaps the kind of panic that a child might have felt—as if his mother's presence in his life gave him his only sense of continuity and safety.

A few months later: "The time I feared the most has come. God knows how hard it is to be apart from her. The days are not the same." But, he wrote, "it's safe to say it was the right decision. I know she's getting the right diet, healthy meals. People there making sure she gets her medicines on time."

He reminisced about an afternoon when he was in the Martinique and Grandma had invited me to join them for Thanksgiving. "My mother was so proud that she could make a real Thanksgiving dinner for us on a hot plate, which was all we had. I know you will remember this, because you wrote about it in your book." He made a reference to one of the guards at the hotel who refused to let me go upstairs at first and made me wait there in the lobby for an hour without telling them that I was there. "But we did it! Grandma kept the dinner warm. And she was so happy. Thank God for those memories!"

A year later: "As you can see, I got some paper I can write on." After telling me he'd seen his mother "at the home," he reverted to his thoughts about the time we'd met and he told me something that he'd never said before. "In all honesty," he wrote, "I didn't trust you at the start. So many people coming there at Christmas—feeling good about themselves. Looking at the horror show. Land of the Living Dead. . . ." He said he didn't start to trust me until I kept coming back. "I'm glad you did, because you got to know us good. And you got to know the girls." That, he said, "is something that I'm thankful for."

He also reminisced about a pleasant kind of teasing, a good-natured to-and-fro, that had evolved between us, after we had gotten to be friends, because of the baseball rivalry between New York and Boston. He was, of course, a Yankees fan. When I told him I had lived most of my life in Boston, he could not resist the opportunity to convey his sympathies to me every time Boston came to play there in the Bronx. In his letters, he continued teasing me. It was something trivial, but light-hearted and familiar, that he was holding on to even when the other items in a letter were not light at all.

In three of his letters he went into detail about Christopher. In the first letter, which had followed shortly after Christopher came home from prison but before he started breaking his parole, Pietro sounded somewhat optimistic. "My son just got a job about a week ago. He's doing well, Jonathan, and with the job I think that he feels good about himself. . . . Good news there. He's acting more responsibly."

Another letter: "I seen my son today. Miranda brought him here to visit me. He says he's going to apply to college." I didn't want to second-guess Pietro, but I wondered whether Christopher might have had in mind one of those job-related institutes that many people in the poorest neighborhoods who have only meager education, and little understanding of distinctions between different kinds of higher education, speak of interchangeably as "colleges." It didn't seem believable to me that, after all the years of schooling he had missed, he would have the rudimentary skills that would be prerequisites for college.

But there were two lines in the letter that I wanted very much to find believable. "Christopher," Pietro said, "told me, 'You look good, Pop.' He hugged me, Jonathan! He said he wanted to see more of me."

The comfort he derived from this one moment of affection did not, however, last for long. In a subsequent letter he appeared crestfallen because of a painful confrontation that his son provoked by what amounted to an act of thievery from Grandma.

Grandma, as I've mentioned, had a blind spot when it came to Christopher, and her inability to gauge his sense of judgment, as well as his ethical reliability, had worsened with the onset of dementia. At some date I've been unable to pin down, she had given Christopher the legal right to oversee financial matters for her, such as a small widow's pension she received and which she'd been using through the years to help Pietro and the children—all three children, and not solely Christopher.

It turned out there was an accumulation of a fair amount of money in her pension fund of which, apparently, she'd been unaware. Christopher, according to Miranda, "decided that he had the right to take this money for himself" and not share it with his sisters. "Daddy was opposed to this. He knew that Grandma still might have expenses that we'd need to pay for while she was still living." Whatever was left upon her death, Pietro said, should be divided equally.

In his letter, Pietro did not go into these details. He simply said, "My son has disappointed me. He's trying to get hold of money that does not belong to him. When I told him I would not permit this, he was very rude to me. I told him, 'I'm your father. You're my son. I want you to obey me.'" But Christopher, he said, had suddenly grown cold again. "My son has turned away from me."

Miranda said that it was worse than that. "When Daddy said it wasn't right for him to take the money, my brother really slammed him—'I'm the one in charge of things.' He could be a monster."

Starting in the winter of 2005, about a year after Grandma went into the nursing home, there were references in Pietro's letters to difficulties he was having with a growing weakness in his arms and legs, which, according to the doctors he had seen, was the consequence of a debilitation of bone structure.

The factors that had led to this debilitation were something of a mystery to me, and they would remain so. It may be that he was leaving something out. It may be that he did not entirely understand whatever explanation or whatever diagnostic possibilities a doctor had conveyed to him. He did say it was growing hard for him to keep on with the work he had been doing. Apart from packing bags and bringing them to the homes of older people who did not have strength enough to carry them, he also had a part-time job for a man who owned a furniture and dry-goods store. He would pay Pietro as much as forty dollars in a day for moving heavy pieces out onto the sidewalk for display and moving them inside again when the store was closing.

"Jonathan," he said, "I'm only fifty-five years old, but my legs are giving up on me."

Within another year he had to give up both these jobs as his body had progressively grown weaker. In one of the last letters that he sent me, he indicated that his health had gone into a steep decline. In the same letter he also said that he had moved into another rented room, which he thought might be the reason why the letters I was writing were not reaching him or, if he got them, only after long delays.

"Jonathan, my friend," he wrote, "I got two letters from you in one day and I have so much to say. My health is broken but my hands aren't broken, so I still can write to you. . . .

"These are trying times for me. Some days there is nothing left except my will. I know that God in His ways has some reason for what has befallen me, but I can't surrender for my children's sake. I need a lot of doctor care and I'm keeping my appointments but I feel I'm fighting without weapons."

He spoke of "God's intentions" for him in this time of weakness, and later in the letter he made a reference to God's "plan," which he said he did not know but that he knew he had no other choice but to accept.

Pietro rarely spoke to me about religion in the years I'd known him, but Miranda said he'd been religious as a child and had gone to church each Sunday with his mother until he was twelve years old. It seemed that in his sickness he was reaching back for this. He also spoke again about how much he'd counted on his mother and how much he missed her. God and Grandma seemed to come together at this moment in his memory.

In the only other letter he had strength to write, he said that he was "counting up my blessings. . . . Both my daughters grew up into healthy women. In the days in the hotel I never thought we'd get this far. I didn't dare to think ahead. So that's one thing I'm thankful for. Ellie has her children and Miranda has her little boy. And she's been so good to me and kind to me and patient with me, Jonathan! I guess you know she's always been my angel and I know she's strong of heart and she's out there kicking. God knows she took a licking. Won't say more about that now. . . .

"Hope my writing's not too bad. Please excuse. Out of paper.

"Goodbye Friend. Until next time, Pietro."

It was not long after that before Miranda had to move him to a place that she first referred to as "a rehabilitation center" but which, as she clarified this later, was actually a hospice for chronically ill people. He was in a wheelchair now, she told me. On occasion, if a friend who had a car would help her, she would bring him to her home to visit and have dinner, and her sister and her children would come over. I noticed that she didn't say whether Christopher was there, and I didn't ask her.

Pietro had a stroke that winter and, although he

partially recovered, the damage to his heart and pulmo-
nary function, according to the doctor that Miranda spoke
to, left him with a very poor prognosis. It was, the doctor
said, unlikely that he would survive for long.

At the end, Miranda said, "he was going back and
forth into the hospital. He went in a final time a couple
weeks before he died. He had the nerve to ask me for a
cigarette! He cursed me out when I said they wouldn't let
him smoke there. And, besides, I told him that I didn't have
one anyway. So then I said, 'Okay, Daddy, I'll go out and
buy you some.' He cursed me out some more, but it was all
in fun. . . . Two days later, he was dead. I'd signed the DNR
six months ahead."

Pietro's death preceded that of Grandma by only a few
months. He never did achieve the reconciliation with his
son that he had prayed for. Of all the disappointments he
had undergone, it was this, Miranda said, that she believed
had been most painful for him.

Pietro's long-enduring anguish over Christopher was,
of course, a very different matter from the kind of long,
lamenting sorrow Vicky underwent as Eric slipped away
from her. And Miranda's often torturous relationship with
Christopher, for as long as she could keep him in her home,
was obviously very different from the bond between Lisette
and Eric, who had not subjected her to the financial exploitation that Miranda underwent. Still, there are similarities.
The survival and the stamina of the younger sister and the
growing hardness and the loss of stable bearings in the
older brother are what I had in mind in saying, as I did, that
I did not look for "patterns" but could not escape the sense
that there were parallels.

Christopher and Eric were not the only boys I knew
who received their first induction into cynical behavior,
distancing, dishonesty, and patterns of evasiveness in the

homeless shelters and in the years that followed when they were resettled in impoverished neighborhoods that had the fewest services of social intervention on the part of public institutions. Christopher's story stands apart for me, however, because I was present, physically, repeatedly, at the point of incubation. I saw that look of hunger in his eyes. I saw him wolfing down that cereal and milk. I saw him running out into the traffic when the cars slowed down on Broadway, hoping for a couple dollars to be handed through a window. I also knew he'd seen the needle-users buying what they needed in the hallways and the stairways of the Martinique Hotel. He probably saw them shooting up as well. I could not forget this.

One afternoon three years ago, Christopher called Miranda while I was with her and her son, and when she told him I was there, he asked to say hello to me. He sounded elated on the phone and said he'd like to get together with me sometime soon. For Miranda's sake, I said I'd like that too. I gave him my phone number. He said he had no number of his own but would send a message to me through Miranda.

I asked what he was doing and he told me things were "going great" but, when I pressed him just a little, he replied that he was "late" and had to rush and offered me no further information.

The spirited tone within his voice struck me, after I hung up, as just a bit *too* spirited. Miranda had already told me he was dealing drugs again after having quit his job at Equinox. She had also made it clear that he had long since gone beyond the relatively lowly stage of selling at street level. He was "into something big"—that's the way Miranda put it. Whatever "something big" implied, it reawakened the concern I'd had more than ten years before, when he wrote to me from prison asking for my help with the parole board in reduction of his sentence. As I've said, I complied with his request, but not enthusiastically, because I did not know what he might do upon release. He'd attempted once to take a person's life. Might he succeed the next time?

Even now, as he was moving back into the zone of danger, there were people who did not give up on Christopher. A charitable agency that worked with former inmates not only kept on reaching out to him but gave him a part-time job, which Miranda said that he held on to for a while. An outreach worker from the agency, who lived in the neighborhood—"close to Cypress Ave," she said, "right next to the Bruckner"—gave Christopher a place to stay. "He had his own bedroom there."

Miranda said she wasn't sure the outreach worker recognized that Christopher was selling drugs. But, because the agency in question tended to employ men and women who had been in prison and had been through major troubles of their own and had had direct acquaintance with the life within the streets, it seems likely that the outreach worker must have known that Christopher had by no means turned his back upon that life, and had given him a room in his apartment precisely for that reason—to protect him from himself, if that still was possible.

"This particular morning," said Miranda, "I came back from an appointment that I had to go to at the hospital, and my phone was ringing, and it was the guy that he was staying with. I had had a talk with Christopher two nights before. He owed me forty dollars and I knew he had the money but, you know—same old thing—he didn't want to pay me.

"I got so mad! I told him I was short of money. I only had about two dollars in my wallet. I told him I was going to kill him if he kept me waiting.

"Next day? He doesn't call. Doesn't come. No Christopher. I have to borrow from my friend to get some milk and sandwich meat and a can of macaroni. . . .

"Now it's Thursday and this guy, his counselor, is calling me, and I'm still so pissed at him. He says, 'I need to talk with you.' So I say, 'What happened? Did he get himself locked up again?' He says, 'No, he didn't get locked up.' So I'm thinking: What else did he do this time? It's like—you know, I've been through this for so many years with Christopher. Whatever stupid thing he's done is *not* going to surprise me.

"So he says, 'I'm coming there to talk with you.'

"He comes in. By this time I'm getting scared. He sits down. I'm standin' up. He seems like he's afraid to look at me.

"So he says, 'Someone called for him this morning. He was in his bedroom, so I went to wake him up. I told him there was someone on the phone for him. But he didn't answer me. So I touched him on the arm. . . .'"

Miranda said, "My brother's dead."

"Yes," he said. "He was cold. There was no sign of breathing."

"Take me there. I want to see my brother."

So he brought her to the house. "He was layin' there. He had on his shorts and T-shirt. That was all he wore at night. Those were his pajamas." She didn't tell me if she saw the hypodermic he had used. "But that was it. That was how my brother died. He overdosed on heroin. Possibly," she said, "it was some bad shit somebody had given him. . . ." She wanted to believe his death was not intentional.

Christopher was the white boy. He did this in New York. Eric was the black guy. He did it in Montana. One with a needle. One with a shotgun. The differences are there.

– IV –

Miranda speaks of Christopher with torn emotions nowadays.

"You see?" she said to me one night. "He got the bad part of the deal when we were young. For me and Ellie, even back when we were in the Martinique, we never felt we had to be so hard and cold because we had our Grandma and our Daddy to take care of us. We would never have to go into the streets. Besides, we thought, 'Our brother does it *for* us.' Like he'd bring us presents now and then—little things, nothing real expensive, but he didn't need to do it, so that *did* mean something to us. He was our big brother. It was like, 'He'll be looking out for us. . . .' "

She told me that he'd found "his little group of friends" at the hotel—"Shaun and Kwan, who were his age, and another boy, Segundo, and some others who were older. They were the ones who went out to the street with him. Sometimes I'd wake up when he came in. I'd hear my father scolding him."

She also recollected that she and her sister became curious about the man who took him off for visits on the weekends. I asked if she was jealous of the presents he was giving him. "No," she said. "I was too young to know jealous. I was only at that age when I was beginning to ask questions to myself. Who was this guy who took my brother off alone and what was he after?"

Later, she said, living in the Bronx, "Christopher began to do his disappearing acts." But she said she didn't worry too much at the start. "I guess I thought whatever scheme was going on, 'well, that's what he has to do.' I didn't even want to guess what he was up to."

It was only when he was arrested and sent to Rikers Island that Miranda said she understood there was "something going wrong" in Christopher—"I mean that there was something really messed-up in my brother's head." But even then, and even after he had been to prison and came back to stay with her and she could see how hardened he'd become—"I knew that he was not no angel, and I won't pretend"—she never ceased to feel a bond of loyalty and love for him. "No matter what he did, I loved him still, because he was my brother." This, she said, was "why it was so hard for me to put him out. . . ."

Miranda leads a somewhat lonely life today but, living close to St. Ann's Church, she has friends to boost her up at moments when she's overwhelmed by memories. Since Christopher died, I've seen her much more often, maybe twelve or fifteen times, than in the previous ten years. Her son is doing well in school. She reads him books. She helps him with his math. She goes to school for meetings with his teacher. He has a fish tank and two cages of small animals. She goes to work while he's at school. She's working extra hours at the bakery this winter, in the weeks preceding Christmas, so that she can earn enough to buy him a computer.

"I'm twenty-nine," she told me when I spent an evening with her in November. "I don't think I want another boyfriend. The only men I tend to see are boys I went to school with. So, you know, it wouldn't be romantic. . . ."

I've seen her eyes fill up with tears when she's speaking of her father and her brother. But she has a dignified demeanor, a quiet sense of self-respect, and now and then, when she's in an upbeat mood and tells me something funny that happened, for example, while she was at work, I see a flash of the comedic side that helped her father to get through his times of tribulation. She's still quite thin, as when I met her in the Martinique when she was a four-year-old. Her hair is long. Her skin is pale. The pallor lends her an ethereal look. One of the older women at St. Ann's tells her she's a beautiful girl. But she does not believe this.

CHAPTER 4

Silvio:
Invincible

Vicky and Pietro were highly vulnerable people when they went into the shelters, and both of them came out of that experience with badly shaken confidence. But there were other people who went through the shelter years yet struck me at the time we met as nearly indestructible.

One of them was Ariella Patterson, a self-possessed and level-headed woman, the mother of two boys, one almost six years old and the other nine, who had become homeless when the house where they were living had gone up in fire after an explosion in the boiler room. She had two sisters, but both of them had families of their own and could not take her into their apartments. Her mother was an alcoholic and could be of no assistance to her.

Like others in her situation, Ariella was obliged to look to the city's welfare system and its homeless agency for shelter and to navigate a series of perplexing rules and regulations that had been established as deterrence strategies to discourage homeless people like herself from requesting shelter in the first place.

The keystone of the system of deterrence was an institution—there were two of them in those days, called Emergency Assistance Units—in which a homeless family was allowed to stay initially, sleeping on the floor, or else on chairs or tables, in an undivided space with other homeless families until it was determined if they qualified for placement in one of the hotels.

The EAUs, as they were known, were horrendous places. Homeless people, including women in their final months of pregnancy, would sometimes have to stay for weeks. Some went into labor while they waited there. Visitors were generally not allowed to enter—an even more restrictive policy than the one that was in place at most of the hotels. I got into both of them with the help of Steven Banks, the Legal Aid attorney, who, in one instance, brought me through the entryway and walked me past the guards himself. Once I was admitted, I was pretty much ignored and was able to remain within those buildings very late at night, watching mothers placing coats or other clothing on the tables or the floor for their kids to sleep on, and talking with those mothers who were too upset or scared to go to sleep at all.

One of the city's motives in requiring these periods of temporary insecurity for newly homeless people was, according to the Legal Aid attorney, to "test" these families in order to discern whether they were genuinely desperate in their need for shelter. If they left an EAU before the city came to a decision, this would indicate that they were not "truly homeless" and were not deserving of additional assistance.

After this experience, people were unlikely to reject an opportunity to move into any place the city chose to put them where they would have a room of their own and beds their kids could sleep on. Thus it was that Ariella now began a long progression from one of the city's shelters to another. "Some of them," she said, "were not as bad as others. One of them was a Travelodge where the city put some homeless people, which was reasonably decent, but we only got to stay there for three weeks." Another one, not so decent, was a place where rooms were rented out to prostitutes, but in which a number of rooms or sometimes an entire floor, were set aside for homeless people and their children.

Her longest stay was at the Martinique Hotel. To this day, she still recalls a child at the Martinique, "a little girl nine years old," whose mother hadn't been there long and wasn't yet familiar with the dangers that the building held. She sent her down the hallway to throw away the garbage in one of those barrels that were placed at every landing. "She was raped next to the garbage bins," Ariella told me.

"Another mother, a lady with two babies who lived a couple doors from me—people called her 'Cookie,' very young and very shy and very frightened of the building. . . . She started sleeping with the guards because they promised her protection."

It was, she said, "a cesspool, the worst place in the world that you could be with children." People today, she added, ask her "whether it was 'traumatizing' to be living there. I tell them, No. 'Traumatizing' is too nice and too genteel. It was a nightmare. It was hell on earth.'"

She had a vivid memory of details of the building that I remembered too: the row of pay phones in the back part of the lobby, the sheets of plywood that had been set up around the check-in area, maybe for protective reasons, and the elevators, some of which would work, and some would not, where mothers and their children waited in a line for the next one to arrive—which is why it was often easier and quicker to go up the stairs.

Getting out of the shelter system, finding a real home,

going through the protocols for obtaining rent assistance, could, she said, be something of a nightmare too.

"'You came on the wrong day. Come back again next Tuesday.' 'The form you filled out wasn't right. It's not the one we needed. You need to get the other form,' even though this was the only one they'd given you. 'Go to this address'—it would be some other office maybe forty blocks away. Long lines. Wait your turn. Go back to the first place once you've got the form. 'You didn't fill it out correctly. You were supposed to get it signed by your welfare worker. . . .'"

But she did it, more effectively than most, and kept her cool and maintained her composure. And maybe, as a consequence, she was treated more respectfully by the people that she had to deal with than were many of the other homeless families that she knew.

"I always dressed so carefully! I spoke to them politely. I think they may have thought that I was 'more refined' because of my appearance and because I'd had more education"—she had finished high school and had some credits in post-secondary classes—"than most of the people they were dealing with." Then, too, even while she had been homeless, Ariella had been volunteering with a charitable group that provided lunches to the parents and the children in the building, and this may have worked to her advantage in the eyes of those who handled placements of the homeless population.

In any event, when they found her an apartment, it was in the same Mott Haven neighborhood as the one where Vicky and her children would be living before long. The building itself was relatively new, dating from the early 1970s, but it was surrounded by a twenty-square-block area of indescribably depressing and decrepit buildings, known as the Diego-Beekman Houses, in which the use and sale of heroin and crack cocaine were almost as widespread and unhidden as had been the case within the Martinique.

Subsidized by federal funds but owned and run by a private corporation, the Diego-Beekman complex encompassed nearly forty buildings in which Ariella estimated that as many as 4,000 children and their parents were residing. The buildings were routinely cited for serious infractions of the law, "immediate health and safety risks" that were termed by federal examiners "major" and "life-threatening," gross sanitation dangers such as sewage back-up that had been accumulating on the basement floors, rats coming out of cupboards and falling through ceiling holes from one apartment to the one below.

One of the most serious problems, Ariella said, was the failure of the company to provide the buildings at all times with secure and solid outside doors with working locks to keep intruders out—and to make appropriate repairs to doors that had been vandalized or locks that had been broken—which, she said, was perhaps the major reason why people who were selling drugs found Diego-Beekman a perfect place to operate.

"Slip into a building anytime they liked. Sell in the hallway. Sell from a stairwell. Sell from the corridor of one of the upper floors. Sell from the apartment of somebody they terrified, who didn't dare to throw them out. . . ."

The company that owned the Diego-Beekman buildings was an out-of-state corporation that was based in Boston. Its primary investor (I remember my embarrassment when I discovered this) happened to reside in the same suburban area in which my mother and father lived for more than thirty years. The man, whose name was Gerald Schuster, was notorious in Massachusetts for a long-established record as a negligent and predatory owner of slum housing in the black community of Boston, as well as for anti-labor practices in a chain of nursing homes he operated. But nothing he had done in Massachusetts was even in the ballpark with the sheer dimensions of his operation in New York.

I would later spend considerable time in a number of his buildings because so many of the children I was meeting in the Bronx were Mr. Schuster's tenants. There was one building in that complex that I got to know particularly well because I went there several times to interview the family of a child named Bernardo after he'd been killed by falling from an upper floor through an empty elevator shaft. The elevator door wasn't working properly and would open unpredictably even when there was no elevator there. The tenants had complained about the danger many times; but the company refused to make repairs. Bernardo's body landed on the steel roof of the elevator unit, which had stopped four floors beneath his own. He was not found until his blood began to drip on passengers.

Mr. Schuster managed to clean up his image at a later time by making contributions to important Democratic politicians, some of them strong advocates for the very people he had treated with contempt and whose lives he had imperilled—Richard Gephardt, Christopher Dodd, John Kerry, and Barack Obama, among others—or by giving parties to raise funds on their behalf. The Boston press now calls the former slumlord a "philanthropist."

Ariella was fortunate that her own apartment building was not a part of Mr. Schuster's complex. But virtually all her neighbors did live in those buildings and no one in the area could totally escape the atmosphere of danger that was ever present in that vast expanse of housing. "Some people did lead reasonably stable lives in the Diego-Beekmans," Ariella said. "Some kept their spirits up, decorated their apartments nicely, gave their kids a good sense of security, and protected them from getting into risky situations. I think it was much harder for the families that had come out of the shelters. You just can't put that many people who are shaky and unstable, and children who are loaded with a lot of pent-up anger, into a single neighborhood without it having some effect on almost everyone."

This, in any case, is her own portrayal of the world in which she now set out to make a new home for her family.

— II —

Once Ariella moved into the neighborhood, she had quickly taken steps to find a job that could support her family. When she was younger, she had worked in entry-level jobs in office buildings and in sales and marketing. With this background, she was able to obtain a sales position at a chain of children's stores and subsequently worked for two large chains of clothing stores in which she began in merchandising but in time moved on to supervisory positions. One of the jobs she liked the most was for a chain of army-navy stores in which she began in sales but later was promoted to an office job and worked directly with the owner of the company.

When we met in 1993, she was earning $16,000 yearly. As low as this may sound to anyone who knows the cost of living in New York, it was twice the average family income in Mott Haven, which, as I have noted, was about $8,000 at the time. She joked with me that, by the standards of the neighborhood, $16,000 made her feel like she was "almost middle class."

As soon as she'd begun to work, she used whatever money she had left, after she had paid for food and clothes and for her share of rent, to compensate her children in every way she could for the years of homelessness they had been through. One of her boys, Silvio, was twelve years old when they moved into the neighborhood. Armando, the younger boy, was nearly nine.

"On the weekends, I would dress them up and take them to Manhattan. I took them to museums. I took them to concert halls. I took them out to restaurants. There was a nice one, The Sign of the Dove, somewhere on Third Avenue, that wasn't too expensive. . . .

"I wanted them to see everything I'd never had when I was a child and I wanted them to know that they could have this someday if they did their studies and did not drop out of school and, as I hoped, someday went on to college. I wanted them to understand that life as they were seeing it around them in the neighborhood did not necessarily have to define them."

She was hopeful at the start that this was having some effect upon their way of thinking of the future, but she realized before long that the efforts she was making to expand their cultural exposure—precisely what so many educators recommend to parents of an inner-city child—were too episodic, and too far detached from the world in which they led their ordinary lives, to counteract the tide of violence and drug-related wildness that was sweeping through the area.

In the case of Silvio, who was old enough to have experienced more keenly than his brother the sordidness and stigma of a setting like the Martinique, who had looked into that "cesspool," as she'd called it, and seen the patterns of behavior and defensive strategies that festered there, Ariella found it very difficult to eradicate the imprint this had left upon his image of himself and the way he looked upon his options in the years ahead of him.

"Even when my situation had become more stable, he could not regain his own stability," she said.

"I was working full-time now. My boss had moved his office to New Jersey. He'd been robbed too many times here in the Bronx. So I had a long ride to get to work each day. I had to take the Number 6 train to get to Grand Central.

Then I took the shuttle to Times Square. Then I took a bus on New Jersey Transit at the Port Authority and, after that, I had to get another bus to get to our office. It could take an hour and a half from the time I left my home until the time I got there.

"Coming back could take even longer because, at night after a certain hour, one of the buses wasn't running. So I was getting home too late to keep an eye on Silvio after he got out of school. I wasn't there to watch him. . . .

"He started gathering a group of friends around him. He was in the fifth grade, still in elementary school, because he'd missed so much of school when we were in the shelters. His teachers were complaining about his bad behavior. He was causing havoc at the school. He was breaking exit signs, smashing doors, smoking weed when he was in the bathroom.

"By the time he got to middle school he was having sex. He was a handsome boy and looked older than he was. And the girls were drawn to him. He started stealing. Little things at first. Then bigger, more expensive things. He'd give presents to the girls. Then he'd steal things from their homes. He got away with it. It seemed as if he thought he could do anything he liked. He thought he was invincible."

She asked if I remembered an old movie, Scarface, that starred Al Pacino as a refugee from Cuba who became a powerful drug dealer in Miami. "Silvio loved that. Fancy cars. Swanky clothes. Money! And the jewelry! The glamour and excitement of the life within the streets, and the power that went with it."

Not long after that, she said, "he started stealing stuff from *me* as well, right out of my bedroom. Money I had hidden in my bureau—which I would have given to him if I knew he needed it." And, although she said she hated to see other parents striking their own children, "I was scared I might do it too, and would really hurt him because, no matter what I said to him, or how many times I said it, I realized that I couldn't hold him back.

"One day, when I had just been paid, he took my entire salary and cashed it on his own. There were people who would do that for you if you knew the place to go. . . . I lost all my self-control. I gave him a real beating."

At last, she did what other parents in the neighborhood were sometimes forced to do when they saw a child falling out of their control. She filed a legal document known as a PINS petition—the acronym means "person in need of supervision"—so that she could send him to a group home where he'd be protected, or so she believed, from the trouble he was courting by the recklessness of his behavior.

"When I went to visit him on family day, he'd be screaming at the staff. 'Fuck you! Fuck you too!' They'd have to restrain him. They told me once, 'He's lucky this is family day.' Otherwise, they would have treated him more harshly."

Within two months, he was begging her to bring him home. "'Mom,' he'd say, 'take me out of here. I'm going to kill myself if I have to stay.'" She waited another month, but after it became apparent that they had no power to control him there—"he was growing more defiant than before"—she threw up her hands at last and brought him home with her.

"It was August by that time, just two weeks before his fourteenth birthday. When school began, I went up and had a long talk with the counselor. And I talked with Silvio at night. *Every* night. And I wasn't pulling punches with him. I was being strict with him." For a while, she believed that he was calming down.

"Okay. October. He wasn't showing up at school. He began to steal again. One night he stole my pager. This was long before I had a cell phone, so the pager was important to me for my job. And I also needed it in case his brother had to reach me while I was at work. . . .

"That night, he was riding in a car with a group of

older boys. One of them grabbed the pager from him. He told him, 'Give it back.' He said it wasn't his—it was his mother's. But the boy refused. Silvio reached out and tried to grab it from him," which, she said, in that situation, "was not a good idea." The boy that he was fighting with was holding a box cutter in his hand. "When Silvio reached out again, he slashed away at Silvio. He sliced his face apart."

Ariella wasn't certain how he got out of the car. "But," she said, "it couldn't have been far from here. When I saw him at the door, he had his hands across his face. When he took his hands down I could see the blood all over him. They had to give him sixty-seven stitches at the hospital to put his face together."

I told her that I would have thought this would frighten almost any kid enough to stop him cold or at least make him far more cautious. But, she said, it didn't work that way with Silvio. "The scar, to him, was like a badge of honor. On Halloween, we were at my sister's house. He told my sister, 'Look at me. I'm Scarface.'"

After that, she said, "I had to put him back into the home. But they still could not control him. He would run away from there any time he had a chance. It wasn't like a lockup. There weren't any gates or bars. The only thing the guards could do was put you in restraint if you acted violent or threatened someone else. They'd wrestle you down to the ground and twist your arms behind your back. But it was easy to get out at night. And he always knew there were people he could stay with.

"One night when he ran away he came to the apartment. I sat him down and talked with him. I told him he was going with me in the morning to enroll in a new school. He didn't put up any disagreement. He was in a quiet mood and he seemed to open up to me a little more than usual. He promised he would try to change. I cooked him a good dinner, one of the things he loved the most, steak and rice and pigeon peas. We talked some more. He seemed happy to be home. So, that night, I was hopeful."

But, as Ariella told me later, "I must have known even then that I was grasping at a straw." The reassuring conversation they had had turned out to be the calm before a storm. "Two nights later, at around ten-thirty, he told me he was going out, because he said he needed something at the corner store. I told him, 'No. I don't want you out there at this hour.' Only a moment after that, while I was in my bedroom, he was out the door."

According to one of the boys who hung out with Silvio, he did, in fact, go up to the corner store to buy himself some cigarettes. Then, however, instead of coming back to the apartment, he and his friend walked up to the station at Brook Avenue, where they met some other friends, and they took the Number 6 train down into Manhattan. Then they caught another Number 6 train, this one coming back in the direction they'd just come from.

"This time, however, when they got back to the Bronx they did not get off at Brook, but continued riding—past Brook, past Cypress, past St. Mary's, and they kept on going. . . .

"These were the old trains," Ariella said when she was explaining to me what had happened next. "The connectors in between the cars were something like a metal lattice that the kids could climb on. A lot of kids were doing this, climbing up between the cars to get onto the roof, then lying flat and riding through the tunnels, which was known as 'surfing' and was a crazy thing to do, and very, very dangerous.

"But Silvio was fearless. Two of them were lying down but two of them were sitting up, and one of them was Silvio. It was like a game of chicken. Who would take the biggest risk? Which one was the bravest?

"One of them was sitting on the front edge of the car,

so he was facing forward. The other one, Silvio, was on the back edge of the car ahead, so he was facing backwards.

"There are two bridges over the tracks in between two stations. One of them is Whitlock. The other one is Elder. The first bridge is higher than the second one. He lowered his head and got past it safely. The second bridge came up fast, but he didn't know this. He lifted his head and waved to his friends. The steel girder struck his skull. His body fell headfirst between the cars.

"One of his friends pulled him in and held his arms around him. He said his body was convulsing. One of Silvio's hands shook twice. Then, his friend said, he stopped moving.

"He was fourteen and three months. I later learned that he had died at 5:58 a.m. . . .

"A detective was at my house at eight. When I heard him knocking, I thought it was Silvio. I'd been worried all night long. I said, 'I'm going to give him the beating of his life!'

"When I opened the door the officer was standing there with two frightened-looking boys. They were staring at me with this look of horror in their eyes. One of them had drops of blood all over him. He was the one who'd been holding Silvio. But he was too scared to talk. The officer let the boys go home. Then he asked me, 'Are you Mrs. Patterson? Do you have a son named Silvio?'"

When she answered that she did, the officer asked if she had someone she was close to, because, she said, "he didn't want to tell me this while I was all alone.

"I told him I had no one there except my son Armando. He was getting dressed for school. So I asked the officer to come into my bedroom. That was when he told me."

After the officer had done his best to comfort her, and given her instructions about going to the morgue, because the body had to be identified, she told me, "I was on 'automatic' for a while. I sent Armando off to school. I couldn't cry. I was numb. I sat there on the sofa and was staring out the window. 'What have I done? What do I do?' I called a friend. She wasn't home. I called my older sister, Ana. I went there to her house. But I couldn't talk to her. I ran outside to her backyard. It was raining. Finally, she came out and made me come inside."

Her sister, she said, "was good to me. She held her arms around me. She made me drink a cup of tea. Then she brought me back to my apartment."

Soon after that, she said, her younger sister came. Then co-workers from her job arrived. "I was fortunate that the man I worked for was compassionate and kind. He came directly to my house and handed me the money I would need to bury him.

"Then my sisters took me to the morgue. Then they took me to pick out a casket. Then I had to find a church that would do the burial. The Catholic church that I attended said they couldn't do it. They told me that I lived in the wrong zip code. I'd been there a week before to pray to God to help me. But they wouldn't bury him." She had to find another Catholic church so she could have a funeral for Silvio.

Her mother, she said, offered her no comfort. "The first thing she told me when I said that he had died? 'It's your fault—for having him.' She'd never been a mother to me. But from that time on I hated her."

For a long while after that, she said, "I hid from myself. I turned my feelings outward—into anger. I was angry at God, angry at the Catholic church, angry at my mother." In the end, however, she turned her anger inward and was forced to ask herself if she *was*, in fact, to blame for never having found a way to save him from himself. All the early efforts she had made, the visits to museums and concert halls and restaurants and other nice and interesting places in Manhattan, all those efforts to expose him to some of the normal things that children in the safer and less troubled sections of New York might ordinarily enjoy—was there ever any chance at all that this would make the slightest difference for a boy who'd seen what he'd already seen and whose chosen avatar of the triumphant and exciting life had been a movie character, who came to his own demise, as it happened, in a hail of bullets, by the name of "Scarface"?

"That movie was a curse to him," Ariella said. But it was not the only curse, as she knew well, which is why she kept on questioning herself.

– III –

Ariella's capability for level-headed thinking was badly shattered by her guilt and sorrow about Silvio. But even as she struggled to dig out of the depression she was in, she had to make the best decisions that she could for her surviving son.

"I kept my job but cut my hours so that I could be here with Armando from the time that he got out of school. My biggest worry now was how his brother's death was going to affect him."

Armando, she reminded me, had still been very young when they were in the shelters. "He hadn't seen the things that Silvio had seen or, if he did, he was still too innocent and young to have 'connected' with them." So the time when they'd been in the Martinique and similar hotels, she felt, had not affected him directly. "The influence was indirect. He learned things from his brother. . . .

"He was always hand-in-glove with Silvio. He looked up to him. And more and more, once Silvio began to win his stripes among the kids he knew here in the Bronx, he saw him as a leader, as a kind of hero to the boys who hung around with him."

Silvio, as she had said, thought he was invincible. "Armando had believed this too. And even after Silvio was gone, he still held on to this idea somehow. His brother, in his mind, was *still* indestructible."

Ariella wanted him to give up this idea. "I needed him to understand that Silvio was not the hero he believed. His brother had destroyed himself. But I was not my normal self. My guilt was eating me alive. So, even though I was there with him more than I'd been with Silvio, I wasn't there in the way Armando needed me to be.

"Meanwhile, we were still in the same neighborhood. Drug use, which was bad already, was increasing at the time. The biggest drug lord was a very scary guy whose sister was a friend of mine when I was in school, before he started selling drugs—or, anyway, before I knew that he was selling them. He was named George Calderon. His sister's name was Lourdes, but people called her Sugar. Later on, she got a good job as a clerk at Lincoln Hospital. She seemed like a nice person." It was not until her brother took over the area, Ariella said, that she realized that her friend was in the business with him, "although I guess it isn't so surprising when you realize how much money he was taking in."

At the height of his power, from 1987 to 1992, Calderon was renting sections of the sidewalks to lower-level dealers. "Once the city started moving homeless families here," she said, "his business was exploding" because so many of those people had already been addicted.

I'd heard stories about Calderon before, some of them from a former dealer who had rented space from Calderon and who told me that the drug lord ran his operation from a building on a corner of St. Ann's—which, Ariella said, was only one block from the church.

"It's important that you understand that all this was

wide-open. People were terrified of Calderon, because he was ruthless if someone didn't pay him. But in the eyes of teenage boys hanging out there in the streets who saw him in his fancy chains and flamboyant clothing, he was a celebrity. And because the stuff he sold was good, people who were desperate for drugs knew they could depend on him." When he died—he was shot in 1992, a year before I came there—"he was given something like a presidential funeral right here at St. Ann's. . . .

"Anyway," she went on, "up until the day he died, Calderon controlled one side of St. Ann's Avenue. On the other side—I mean, on *this* side of St. Ann's in the Diego-Beekmans—there was another group of dealers called the Wild Cowboys. So this is what I mean in saying it was all around us. This is what Armando saw every time I let him out to play and every day when he came back from school. You couldn't get away from it."

Armando was eleven in 1989 when his brother died. "By the time he was twelve, dealers in the neighborhood began to give him small amounts of money." This was not, she said, an act of generosity or because some of the dealers had been friends with Silvio, although Armando might have seen it in that way. It was a prelude, she explained, to the next stage of entanglement, one in which young people of his age were used to carry drugs for older dealers.

The reasoning behind the use of children in this role, Ariella said, had to do with the degree of punishment that would be meted out to children, as opposed to grown-ups, who were caught in the possession of narcotics. A dealer who was sixteen years of age or more would, if he were caught, be tried before an adult court. If he was convicted, depending on the circumstances and amount of drugs that he was carrying, he stood the risk of being sent away for a good stretch in prison. A boy of twelve or thirteen, on the other hand, would be brought before a family court, where a hearing would take place and the evidence would be considered. In extreme cases, he might be consigned to juvenile detention. That would be the worst. Far more frequently, he would simply be remanded to his parent or his guardian with a lecture and a warning.

As a consequence of this, a child of Armando's age could be very useful to drug dealers at a relatively small risk to himself. Thus it was that, even as his mother was clamping down on him more strictly and severely than she'd done with Silvio, and succeeded for a time in keeping him at home with her at night in the apartment, and making sure he did his homework and that he went off to school each day, Armando nonetheless was growing more familiar with that other world, "the life," with all the dangers and attractions that it held, which had seemed so glamorous and so exciting to his brother. Before another year had passed, Ariella would discover she was every bit as powerless to keep Armando from the streets as she had been with Silvio.

At the same time, although his school attendance was much better than his brother's, the schools in which he was enrolled were among the most deficient in the New York system. At his elementary school, P.S. 65, Armando had been diagnosed with "learning disabilities," but the school did not provide him with the specialized instruction required under state and federal legislation for a student who had been identified as having special needs.

"They gave the kids with special needs teachers with no expertise and expected parents to accept this. You know, 'minority parents don't make waves.' And even if you did complain, it didn't make a difference. . . . So even though he failed his courses they would pass him on from grade to grade. He wasn't learning, but they kept promoting him and sent him on to middle school."

The middle school he attended—one of two failing schools to which most children in the neighborhood were regularly steered—was no more attentive to his needs than his elementary school had been. But, once again, he was promoted automatically and subsequently sent on to a high school, known as Monroe High, one of the city's bottom-rated schools, where four of every five kids who came into the ninth grade had been ejected or dropped out before their twelfth-grade year. But even a much better high school would, I'm fairly sure, have found it difficult to make a difference in the way that he was heading by this time.

"He dropped out a month before the end of the ninth grade," Ariella said. "I wasn't thinking clearly. I didn't know as much as I do now about some of the special schools to which he might have been admitted. So I let him stay at home for the last weeks of the year. At least I thought that I could keep him out of trouble here."

But, as she said she should have learned from her experience with Silvio, she realized quickly that her hopes that she could keep him safe at home were, "to say the least, naïve."

He never did go back to school. "What I mean," she said, "is that he wouldn't *stay* in school on any routine basis after that." And, by the time he was sixteen, he was no longer merely an apprentice to the older dealers, serving as their courier. "He was selling" and, she said, "other dealers were recruiting him," because he was apparently so good at it. "And no matter what I did, he was slipping out at night, sometimes after I had gone to sleep, or if I went out to the store or was at a tenants' meeting right here in the building."

I asked her if she'd thought, prior to this time, of taking out a PINS petition on him, as she'd done with Silvio, but she said, "It didn't work for Silvio. They couldn't keep him in the home. If I couldn't get Armando under my control, I did not believe a group home like the one where Silvio had been was going to change anything."

At seventeen, Armando was arrested by police with a

weapon on him. "A friend, he said, had slipped a loaded gun into his pocket"—although, because I've heard this explanation many times from others who were caught with weapons on them in the street, I had to wonder whether he was telling her the truth. In any case, she said, "When I went to court with him, the judge released him to my custody"—perhaps because it was his first arrest. But this may not have been the favor to him that it seemed, because "within a matter of days he was back there in the streets again."

He continued selling drugs but, for now, not using them, at least so far as Ariella could perceive. "He was smoking weed," she said, but this was so common among adolescents in the area, as it is today with kids of the same age in white suburban neighborhoods, that it didn't cause her the alarm she would have felt if she thought that he was getting into hard narcotics.

She had much greater reason for alarm when he was arrested one year later for possession of cocaine and heroin on the Lower East Side of Manhattan. He was given five years on probation. "But, a few months later, he was tried again, this time on 'conspiracy to sell,' and was given four to nine. They let him out in four and a half. When he came out he was a different person."

As was the case with Christopher, Armando had acquired a lot more of the skills of criminality while he served his sentence. He'd also gotten deeper into using drugs— "this was *while* he was in prison," Ariella emphasized—and not simply selling them. "When he went in, he was smoking weed. By the time that he came home, he was using heroin. He'd become addicted. . . ."

"It took about a year," she said, "before I could get him to go into rehab, which he stuck to for a while." But after a time, instead of shooting heroin, he was drinking heavily, and when he was drinking he'd become combative. "'No one's going to mess with me or I'm going to kill them.'"

He was tough but, like his brother, not as tough as he believed. "When he was very drunk one night and offended someone at a party, the guy that he insulted stabbed him in the arm, cracked his skull, and cut off two of his right fingers."

Soon after that, he went back to heroin—"using it and dealing it," she said. He'd been twenty-two when he got out of prison but, because of violations of parole, he was back in prison, or at Rikers Island, seven times during the next four years.

Ariella told me only recently that Armando had been married while he was in prison, or between his prison stays, and had had two children. Looking back, she wondered if this might have been his ultimate salvation. His wife had never given up on him. "She was constant in her loyalty. She had known him since she was thirteen. When he came back from his final sentence, she was there to make a home for him."

While he'd been in prison in the years when he kept breaking his parole, she had brought the children with her when she'd gone to visit him. The older child was a boy, whom I never got to know. The other was a little girl, whose name is Inocencia and whom I've met several times, a three-year-old when he was serving his last sentence. "When they came to bring him back to jail that final time, it happened to be on the baby's birthday. They took him away in front of her before she had her party. . . .

"He swore to me he'd never be away again for another of his children's birthdays. I don't know what it was. The look on her face, a child's face? A sense of shame that he had let her down again? I think that something changed in him from that day on."

It would not be accurate to say that, since Armando came home to the South Bronx after his last stay in prison, he has made an easy and untroubled readjustment to life on the outside. As a former convict and with the limitations of his education, he has found it difficult to obtain the kinds of jobs that can support his family. He and his wife have been evicted twice. One of those times, the family landed in a homeless shelter. The second time, Ariella moved them into her apartment for a year until they could afford a new apartment.

During that year, Ariella said, she had some lengthy conversations with Armando's wife, who had been on welfare since the children had been born. "I told her, 'Get off welfare. You don't need it. You can get a decent job. Let Armando be the one who takes care of the children. Let him be the household parent for a while. Let him learn to be a father.'" She said that she was hoping this would be a way for him to learn responsibility and that his wife, meanwhile, could break out of the welfare trap and find out what it's like to have some economic independence of her own.

"She went out and got a job at Staples. Then she went to Whole Foods. She's been working there five years. . . .

"I'd like to see Armando get into a good job of his own. For now, he does some part-time work, but his real job is his family. He's always home before the kids come back from school. He doesn't drink. He doesn't put himself into positions that are going to cause problems. Inocencia is nine years old. She has a little laptop and she's teaching him the way to use computers. She teases him because, you know, she's very smart and little kids don't find it hard to pick up on computers. It's not quite as easy for her father. . . .

"Armando," she said, "survived somehow. He lives for his wife and children now. He tells me that he feels a sense of peace at last. That's something I don't think he's ever felt since he was a young boy."

— IV —

There's one further chapter to this story.

Ariella has two younger boys. I've known them both for many years—one of them, the older of the two, whose name is Stephen, more closely than the other. He was in the second grade when I met him at the afterschool at St. Ann's Church, where I used to tutor him whenever I was there for an extended time, and often saw him also at his public school. Ariella had learned a great deal more by now about the local schools. So, instead of sending Stephen to P.S. 65, the elementary school to which the older boys had gone, she was able to enroll him in a better elementary school a couple blocks away, known as P.S. 30.

One of his teachers told me that, at first, he was "a lot to handle," because his moods tended to be highly change-able. He was easily distracted, and distracting to the other children, at some moments in the day. At other times, he'd withdraw into himself and would have a look of sadness in his eyes.

One afternoon, when I was with him at St. Ann's, we went into the sanctuary with a slightly younger boy who was also at the afterschool. Stephen looked up at the stained-glass windows that portrayed the Stations of the Cross and his eyes filled up with tears.

"I know someone up there," he said softly.

The other boy asked him, "Who?"

"My brother Silvio," Stephen replied.

The younger child patted Stephen on the arm until he had stopped crying.

This was at a time when Stephen was going on the weekends with his mother to the prison where Armando was incarcerated. "He did go through some times of deep depression," Ariella told me. "There was a good psychiatric center for young children at Mount Sinai Hospital. So I made him an appointment there"—which was an act of more aggressive intervention on her part than she had taken with the older boys, because Mount Sinai was not in the Bronx and it was believed by people in her neighborhood to be a place that served primarily the white and middle class, which may perhaps have been an accurate impression. But Stephen received good treatment there, and his depression dissipated greatly over the next years.

When he finished elementary school, Ariella took no chances on the middle school Armando had attended. Instead, she got him into a less violent and more successful school at some distance from their home where he wouldn't be subjected to the same peer pressures as his older brothers were. He went on to high school, where he became more social and outgoing than before. He didn't study as much as he should but managed to get reasonable grades, although she added that she thought the teachers there were "fudging grades to make the school look better than it was." In any event, he buckled down enough to graduate on time and went to a two-year college, but broke off his studies for a while and worked as a tutor at St. Ann's. He's planning now to return to college because he has a more specific sense of motivation than before. He's developed a compelling interest in the field of criminology with a focus upon counseling and mentoring young people before they get in trouble with the law.

Ariella's youngest son, a serious boy, is in his final year at high school now. Ariella brought him up to Cambridge to visit me last winter. He's very bright and studies hard. His grades are good. He wanted to see Harvard University. He doesn't open up to me as easily as Stephen does. He keeps his feelings to himself, but I know that he has high ambitions.

After Ariella's bad experience with the church that wouldn't bury Silvio, she's become an active and committed member of St. Ann's. Reverend Overall provides her with an office there from which she does outreach work to other parents in the Bronx. Three years ago she was given grant-support by an Episcopal foundation in New York to organize an anti-gun and anti-violence campaign. Working with a number of existing groups of activists and parents in the area, she helped produce a stirring piece of video in which mothers speak about the losses of the children whom they could not save.

Projects of this nature, and efforts to reach out to influential and supportive sectors in the mainstream of society, have come to be her dedication. She speaks from time to time at universities and colleges. "I spoke at New York University," she told me recently. "The students wanted to find out how anybody could survive on $16,000 in New York, even twenty years ago!"—which she said "was not the subject I had planned to speak about."

She holds her own effectively with people in the world of academia. "I don't need a Ph.D. to talk about the things I know. I'm not intimidated by professors when they question me. I can handle their linguistics and gymnastics." When they ask her "how to stop the violence" but, she says, "don't want to hear about the way they put our kids in neighborhoods that are most violent already—you know, 'put them in the fire, then tell them to stop burning'—I don't let them throw that at me. I know what an oxymoron is. I'm not afraid to answer."

Still, for all her reestablished confidence, Ariella lives with memories that no mother who has lost a son, and nearly lost another, can ever put out of her mind. She was not as nearly indestructible as I had initially imagined. She was broken by the death of Silvio. It took her many years to regain her equilibrium and, even then, she could not save

Armando from the troubles that he underwent. But she's done a good job with the younger children and she tries to be of service to her neighbors.

I find I like to talk with her as often as I can. It feels to me as if I'm standing with her on a very solid piece of ground after a tornado's passed. Strength, it seems, in somebody who had a lot of courage to begin with, can at last renew itself.

CHAPTER 5

Alice Washington:
The Details of Life

This will be a different kind of story.

Alice Washington was forty-two years old when I got to know her in the Martinique Hotel. Like most others who were in the Martinique, she had been projected into home-lessness, not by a single crisis (as, in Ariella's case, a fire in her home), but by a combination of intertwined events that she had to cope with almost simultaneously.

First, she learned that she had cancer in her large intestine and needed to have surgery. She had, in all, three operations, and they were successful. But in the months before she had regained her strength, her husband, who, she said, had always been a drinker, began to drink more heavily. He soon became abusive to her, verbally at first, then physically.

Unlike many women in these situations, Alice was not willing to tolerate this treatment in the hope that things might change. One night after he had raised his hand to her

and struck her—only once, but that was enough for her—
she made up her mind to leave him to his drinking and get
out of the house in which they had been living since their
children had been born.

She had three children, two of whom were teenage
girls. The other was a boy of twelve. Unable to continue
working while she was recovering from surgery—she had
been a secretary for most of the twenty years since she completed high school and a two-year business course—she
had no option but to turn to welfare and to look for shelter
via the same chaotic agencies that others in her situation
needed to depend upon.

She and her children ended up at one of the EAUs that
Ariella had described and which I later visited. For several
nights the city was unable to assign her to a shelter. When
a place was finally found, it was in a small hotel, but she
never got beyond the door. When she arrived at 1:00 a.m.,
she was told the hotel had no space for her. At 2:00 a.m.,
back at the EAU, she was forced to sign a paper formally
refusing placement at the hotel that had just refused her.

They spent another seven nights at the EAU, after
which they were sent to one of the more notorious shelters
in the city, a hotel called the Holland, which was on 42nd
Street, a few blocks from Times Square.

At the time when they were sent there, only certain
floors of the hotel, those in greatest disrepair, were used to
house the homeless. The floor where Alice and her children stayed had no running water. "Even the toilet had
no water," Alice said. "We had to carry buckets to a bar
across the street," where someone from the bar came out
on the sidewalk with a hose and filled the buckets for them,
because homeless people weren't allowed inside.

"I couldn't let my children live like that," she said.

Two days later, returning to the EAU, she had to sign
another document in which she rejected the shelter they

had found for her and was given a "referral slip" that she was told she must deliver to a welfare center in another part of town. She spent the next day waiting at the welfare center before they shut the doors on her and told her that they couldn't help her. It was a long while after that before the people at the EAU figured out what they would do with her.

Finally, after forty-five days of homelessness, Alice and her children were provided with a small room—four beds, two chairs, and a tabletop refrigerator—in the Martinique Hotel. They would live there for the next four years.

It was in the Martinique, in the second week of January, 1986, that she and I first met. She was standing near the elevator on the seventh floor, talking with a man, another resident of the hotel, whom I had met a couple nights before. We chatted only briefly and she made a few sardonic cracks about the garbage piled up and spilling out of barrels all around us on the landing. When I happened to remark that I had seen the manager, Mr. Tuccelli, downstairs in the lobby, she told me to be careful when he was around but, before she could continue, the elevator opened. Two unfriendly-looking guards came out. She cut the conversation off abruptly and went down the stairs.

The following day, however, when she saw me near the social workers' office in a hallway on the second floor, she walked right up to me and picked up on our interrupted conversation and invited me to come and visit in her room. In the next few months we came to be good friends.

What attracted me to Alice from the very start was her irreverent sense of humor and her absolute refusal to succumb to the passivity that was induced in many of the others who were living in the Martinique. A natural leader among women in the building, she had an acerbic wit and a sophisticated sense of well-directed anger that enlivened her perceptions and opinions. When I ventured an opinion of my own that she believed to be naïve, she didn't hesitate to tell me so directly. I sensed that she enjoyed these opportunities to take me down a peg or two because it soon enabled us to move beyond the usual banalities that dominate an "interview relationship" and to get to know each other on a far more equal basis than is common in these situations.

She was a politically sophisticated woman. When she came upon a story in one of the papers that offended her intelligence, she would cut it out and write her often pungent comments in the margins. Understatements and omissions in the daily press in stories on the homeless and places like the Martinique stirred up her indignation. The organized abuse of women in the building, she believed, would have made front-page headlines in the press if those who were the victims were not overwhelmingly black and Latino. When I was initially reluctant to agree with her, she grew impatient and she said, "Come on! You know they wouldn't tolerate disgusting things like this for women like your mother or your sister!"

Alice was a good "decoder" of the words and subtle biases and innuendoes in news stories. It was she who pointed out to me, for instance, that the papers were referring to the presence of so many homeless people in this section of Manhattan as essentially a sanitation problem. Plumbing imagery was being used in speaking of "a back-up" in the homeless population, which had caused "the overflow" to spill into the old hotels around Times Square.

"They already know the place to put their sewage," Alice noted cuttingly. "They haven't yet decided where to put their homeless people. But I promise you it won't be anyplace where they will have to see us every morning."

She was right, of course; and when the city, as I've noted, started shutting down these big midtown hotels in the final years of the 1980s, and massive relocations of the homeless population went into effect, she was not surprised to learn that almost all the people she had known within the Martinique were going to be moved to the South Bronx. Even those who put up some resistance against moving into neighborhoods where they knew their children would be isolated from good public schools and decent health facilities were made to understand that this decision was not in their hands. They would be shown apartments that the city had prepared for them. If they did not like what they were shown, they could of course refuse it and look elsewhere; but from that point on, as they were made to understand, they would be on their own.

Alice tried a little harder than some of the others did to fight the city's relocation plans. She studied lists of housing units in Manhattan and she walked the streets and spent entire days in tracking down the leads she'd found. After several weeks, she told me of a building she had seen on Second Avenue, not far from Bellevue Hospital, which, she was told, accepted federal housing subsidies like those that she and other mothers in the Martinique had finally received.

There was, admittedly, more than a little wistful innocence in this attempt, and I suspect that at some level Alice knew she wasn't going to win. And still, as spunky and determined as she was, there were a couple weeks in which I thought that she might pull it off. When she told me she had gone into the rental office of the building she had looked at and had learned that there would soon be vacancies, I started to believe that she might actually succeed.

Her hopes, however, would be swiftly dashed.

"I told my social worker where the building was, and asked her to put in my application," she reported a week later. "She went in back to talk to someone else, and she was in there for a good long while. When she came out she said that she was very sorry but it wasn't going to work.

"'You know, Mrs. Washington? They don't seem to have no openings in that building for you now. But I think

we've found a *real* nice place for you to live in the South
Bronx.'"

"What did you say?" I asked.

"What *could* I say?" she said. "I knew she didn't want
to hurt my feelings. This was a black lady and we both
knew what was in the other's mind. So pretty soon, she
says, they're going to be takin' some of us to see this building in the Bronx.

"I guess I knew this thing was really settled in advance,"
she said at last. "I gave it my best shot. It didn't work. So, in
another month or two, I'll have to pack my stuff and tell the
kids to pack their things. I think that we'll be gone before
December."

Alice's prediction was only slightly premature. Soon
after New Year's—it was 1988 by now—she and her children were moved into a rat-infested building on a street
called Boston Road, which intersected with East Tremont
Avenue, not far from the block where Pietro and his children would be living before long.

It was in that building, in the years that followed, that
the friendship that had formed between us in the Martinique grew into a deeper bond that made it possible to
talk with one another about our private lives and personal
affairs without the sense of circumspection that we might
have felt at first. We came to trust each other and to share
our fears and worries with each other. (I had worries of
my own—about my father, who was in the early stages of
Alzheimer's, and my mother, who was frail and elderly.)
For the most part, however, we simply had relaxed and
pleasant times together during which we'd talk for hours
about things that were entirely unrelated to the policies
and politics and difficult conditions that surrounded her
existence.

Even when she needed to discuss with me something
that was painful or laden with anxiety, she never lost the

capability to look into the face of danger with a sense of dignity and, even at the hardest times, with a gift for finding ironies and pointing to comedic aspects of a situation that would likely not have held the slightest possibilities of humor for most other people that I knew. Anger at the big things, but laughter at the oddest details of the very small things—"an eye for incongruities" is the way I thought of it—enabled her repeatedly to rise above calamitous realities.

– II –

One winter evening, two years after she had left the Martinique, I walked up the hill from the station at East Tremont to the building where she lived, pressed the button by her name, listened for the lock to click, which always came too fast, waited for it to click again, and went inside and down two lengthy corridors to her apartment door.

Alice was in an upbeat mood and, as often was the case when she was in good spirits, she took the greatest pleasure in talking about food.

I asked her what she'd had to eat that day.

"You know—what I always eat when I can afford to. My lamb chops and my baked potato, and my garlic bread. Did I tell you I enjoy a baked potato? All you have to do is put it under the cold water tap and pat it with a paper towel. Pat it light so, as it bakes, it don't get dry. Then you rub some margarine or butter on the skin and wrap it up in foil. Wrap it up with butter, it comes out real nice. It looks like something you would get in a good restaurant."

"Do you use margarine or butter?"

"Parkay is cheaper but I love the taste of butter," she replied. "Try to get *whipped* butter. Breakstone's is the best. I'm pretty sure that you can get it at your store. . . ."

Instructive details about cooking different kinds of food became a routine part of almost every conversation we would have in the next year. "I cook my broccoli in a steamer," she told me on another night, "so the broccoli stays green. Otherwise you boil away the minerals and vitamins. I do the same with butter beans and green peas. My mother taught me that."

She reported to me on a box of grapefruit I had ordered for her—one of those gift packages that are shipped directly to a person's home from a company in Florida. "There was twelve big grapefruits in there. Ruby red. I had a half of one of them this morning with my raisin toast.

"Jonathan, they're good! There's so much juice in there! You take it from the carton and you feel it with your hands. Even without sugar they're so sweet!"

Her conversations about food were intermingled frequently with her affection for her mother and her memories of families she grew up with in a neighborhood where many Jewish people still were living at the time.

"Do you like smoked salmon?" she inquired.

"I love it," I replied.

"Me too," she said. "My children say that I could live on bagels and smoked salmon."

"How did you get a taste for that?" I asked.

"From my mother," she replied.

She told me that they lived above a Jewish store when she was young—"a delicatessen and a restaurant combined"—and she said she also had known Jewish girls at school.

"What do you call the soup that Jewish people make from beets?"

"Borscht," I said.

"That's it. My mother made me taste it once. I didn't like it."

"I don't like it either," I admitted.

"They say it's not too bad with sour cream," she said, as if she was trying to persuade herself to reconsider it.

Her mother's liking for Jewish foods seemed to be associated for her in a reassuring way with the friendships she had had not only with her Jewish classmates but with older Jewish people—"elderly people," Alice said, whom she liked to talk to when she was a child.

She told me that her mother had an office job with an interracial group in the 1960s in a building on the Upper West Side of Manhattan that was then, and is today, a beehive of religious activism. Between her mother's friends at work and her own friends at school, she had had a lot more contact with white people in that era than she and her children did today. I knew she was nostalgic for those days.

One night, maybe six or eight weeks later when I was there for dinner, Alice became irritated with herself because she had forgotten to put glasses on the table.

She asked me what I'd like to drink: "Tonic or iced tea?" She still called soda "tonic," as my mother did.

I asked what kind she had and she replied, "Cream soda."

I told her that I hadn't seen a bottle of cream soda since I was a child fifty years before.

"Where do you get it?"

"At the store," she said. "I'm sure they have it up there where you live." She poured it into a glass with ice, poured herself a glass as well, and came back to the table.

We had a nice dinner, with baked apples for dessert. After we had eaten, she held her hands around a cup of coffee and a smile slowly came across her face.

"How's that little friend of yours who had a little baby?"

I was surprised that she remembered her: a young

woman who was helping me in the preceding winter and who called her three or four times when I was away from home.

"She's fine," I said.

"What does she look like?"

"She's got freckles," I replied, "and long red hair."

"How old is she?"

"Twenty-eight or twenty-nine."

"She sounded very young," she said. "Her baby never would stop crying!"

"She was teething then, I think."

"I told her what to do."

After an authoritative pause, she made this observation: "She was very formal on the phone with me at first. She wouldn't call me anything but 'Mrs. Washington.' I told her, 'How come I can call you by your first name but you won't use mine?'"

"I think that she was shy."

"I thought so, too. I told her I was no one to be scared of. 'I'm a mother just like you,' I said. 'From this point on, you call me by your first name or you don't call me at all. We either talk like friends or we don't talk.'"

She got to know a number of my friends over the years and frequently made observations to me later in regard to a peculiar awkwardness in one, a sense of insecurity or sadness in another—or, in one case I remember from the year before, an overeagerness to please. I often thought she could have been a therapist because she was so gifted at unpeeling superficial explanations, which she did sometimes by teasing people slightly, but her teasing almost always had a playfulness about it.

She was, however, not reluctant to give strong advice when she thought that someone needed it. She reproached me many times when I grew impatient with my mother, who often drove me to distraction by complaining to me of the problems that my father caused her, because of his increasing loss of memory. "You're going to lose her some-day. When you do, it will torment you to remember any-thing unkind you ever said to her. You've been blessed that she's still here. My mother died when she was forty-six. I would have given anything to have my mother with me still. Remember what I'm saying."

Friends can give advice like this, intending well but doing harm. Sometimes they don't realize that the kinds of words they use, and the tone that they assume, can be crippling to you; sometimes perhaps they do. Alice was dif-ferent in this sense. She understood a lot about fragility in people that she cared for. Even when she grew impatient with mistakes she thought her friends were making, she never showed the slightest wish to demonstrate her com-petence at the cost of someone else's self-respect. This was one of the qualities in Alice for which, in time, I came to be most grateful.

Dinner with Alice: 1992.

She had not been feeling well. She said that she'd had very little appetite the week before and couldn't get herself to eat and didn't have much energy. She said she'd seen her doctor, who told her she was running a low fever—a prob-lem that, she mentioned passingly, she'd had several times that year. But tonight she felt much better and she said she wasn't tired, so I stayed there late.

After coffee and dessert she lit a menthol cigarette. She had started smoking "a lot more than I should," she said, while she was in the Martinique. "Three packs a day"—far more than she'd ever smoked before. "It was the goddamn tension there. You could cut it with a knife. It seemed like almost everyone was smoking. If they couldn't buy a pack, they'd bum a couple cigarettes from someone on their floor."

The cigarette relaxed her. She fell into a reminiscent mood and started a long story about her older brother, who'd been wounded in the war in Vietnam and died a few years later in New York. Her recollection of his death, however, was not elegiac or funereal. Instead, there was an almost antic unreality about the way she spoke of this.

She said that someone at the hospital in which he died had "put a sheet over his head" and rolled him down a corridor "to put him somewhere where they put a body when it's dead." But, she said, "You know what the hospitals are like these days. I guess they didn't label him correctly. So then they couldn't find him.

"My mother called me from the hospital and said, 'Come quick! We've got to find your brother!' So I went there to the hospital. And we had to hunt around with someone from the staff and we kept on asking everyone we met whether they had seen an extra body on a stretcher and they asked us, 'Is this body dead or living?' We said, 'Dead.' At last we found the stretcher and my mother said, 'That's him.' And so we made arrangements for the funeral and then we buried him."

She told me other stories like this, some of which I thought she was elaborating for the pleasure that she took in spinning out a narrative. Typically, they'd begin with something rather serious but then take on a comical momentum. It was as if the facts themselves existed only to provide her with the evidence of life's irrationality. Enjoyment of absurd improbabilities was frequently the glue that held these narratives together.

She told me once about a group of men who beat her up and robbed her on the street, not far from her home. One of the men pushed her down. Another kicked her. A third man grabbed her shoulder bag. The shoulder bag was later found, she said, by "an old lady who was watching" as the men ran up the street. "They emptied it of all my stuff," she said, "then tossed it in the trash. . . .

"I'd been wonderin' a couple years before if I ought to get a gun. Then I thought it over and I thought it was too dangerous and I decided not to do it. Then these bastards beat me up and stole my wallet from my bag. So then I changed my mind again.

"I went down and talked about it with a cop. I asked him, 'Should I get a gun?'"

"He said, 'You should.'"

"What cop?" I asked.

"A New York cop. A sergeant at the precinct that I know. He took me in the back room at the station so no one else would hear. 'Mrs. Washington,' he said, 'if I was you I'd go and get myself a gun and go out to a firing range and take some lessons and learn how to use it. Learn how to defend yourself.'"

"I don't think a cop is s'posed to tell you things like that. He told me, 'This is off the record. I'm just telling you what I would do for you if you was my own mother.'"

I asked her if the officer was black. "No," she answered. "He was Irish. I used to see him on the street. I knew he liked me and he meant it for my good. Still, it frightened me. I thought, 'Hello?! This man ain't no criminal. He's a cop here at my precinct and he's telling me I ought to get a gun!'"

"What did you say?"

"I told him I would think it over—and I did. But then I changed my mind a second time."

She looked down at her hands and shook her head and laughed.

"So that's the end of it. I didn't do it." But she grabbed her key-chain from a corner of the kitchen table and showed me that she had a pocketknife attached. And she made a point of saying, "I know how to use it if I have to. . . ."

Much of her humor, not surprisingly, was at the cost of people far more powerful than she. Over the course of years she would regale me with light-hearted commentaries about stories she had read that described the peccadilloes of the very rich and privileged.

"This one made me laugh," she said one night, pointing to a story she had marked with exclamation points. The story was about the Harvard Club on 44th Street in Manhattan. One of the obligations of employees there, according to their contract terms, the story said, was to clean up "vomit," "blood," or "excrement" when members drank too much and lost their self-control. Whenever this unpleasant chore was called for, workers got ten dollars extra. The story was in the news that day because the workers were on strike to protest several matters, one of which was the decision of the club not to give them extra pay for dirty jobs like this.

"If people who went to Harvard can't control themselves and drink too much," she said, "I think they ought to be grown up enough to clean up their own vomit."

She often spoke as if she was convinced that a persistent self-indulgent immaturity was accepted in New York as one of the entitlements of privilege. She noted, for example, when erotic misbehavior by the very rich was granted absolution by the press that would not be given to the men and women in her neighborhood.

"Another millionaire who didn't bother to get married had another baby," she reported to me once in speaking of a well-known real estate tycoon. "I notice that they never say rich children are born 'out of wedlock.' They never say these babies are 'one-parent children.' If you're rich, you don't get judged the way poor people do."

Her most acidic commentaries were reserved, as in the past, for stories in the press that she believed misrepresented the realities of her existence and those of the other people in her neighborhood. The giddiness of fashion stories, for example, that had no connection with the lives of ordinary people tended to elicit some of her most cutting and sarcastic observations. "Whenever they say, 'Women in New York are wearing such and such these days,' I always wonder who they mean, because I know for certain that they don't mean anyone like me. They do it in this ignorant and excited way as if they didn't know that there are people in New York who have to wear the clothes they bought ten years ago.

"They live within a made-up world. 'Everyone is doing this. . . .' But who is 'everyone'?"

Once, on a steamy Sunday afternoon, she showed me a story in the New York Times that said the heat had been especially uncomfortable for the carriage horses, which are popular with tourists in the midtown area. "It wasn't much of a week to be a horse . . . ," the paper said. "People, at least, have air-conditioning and friends with pools."

Her reaction to the glibness of this sentence was less bitter than resigned. "I guess that puts me with the horses," she said quietly.

Alice, however, was even-handed in the anger and impatience she displayed. She could be very harsh on people in her own community, for instance, when she was convinced that some of them deserved it. Once when she had read a story in the Daily News about a man who'd terrorized his girlfriend and then killed her fifteen-month-old child, she wrote in the margin, "Kill the bastard! Bring back the electric chair!" Another time, when a group of teenage boys raped a woman in her neighborhood, she told me, even before they'd been convicted, "Lock them up and keep them there until the day they die!"

On some occasions, she would later qualify her first response. "Some are arrested who are innocent," she conceded once after there had been a mass arrest of something like two dozen men up on Cypress Ave—one of several mass arrests that took place in that area, three blocks from St. Ann's. "You can't arrest that many men without making mistakes."

She told me of a man she knew, because she used to tutor him in reading, who, she said, was doing time in prison for a crime that she believed, or wanted to believe, he did not do.

"It happens," she said. "Some never go to jail who should, and some who do should not have gone there in the first place."

The man she'd tutored was arrested in a roundup, she explained, after a group of men had murdered someone in the course of an armed robbery. "The murderers," she said, "were friends of his. They were wearing leather coats and leather caps. He dressed the same way they did, and he was always with them. The cops, I think, had had him under observation. So they took him off and booked him."

His mother, she said, was in the hospital the night he was arrested. A friend of hers for many years, "she was the first woman that I knew who died of AIDS. . . .

"When he was a boy, he had a learning problem and his mother tried to help him, but she wasn't educated well and, in fact, could barely read. He used to come to my apartment after school and I would try to help him with his homework.

"He was with his mother at the hospital the night the crime took place. That's what he says at least. His mother told me it was true. She died while he was in the lockup, so he couldn't be there for the funeral. I guess they thought he was too dangerous to let him out.

"He did look dangerous. He had that way of walking, looking at you. . . . Anyway, he got ten years to life.

"I visited him the first year while he was at Rikers Island, in pretrial. I hated goin' out there, but he didn't have nobody else to count on. He used to call me 'Auntie.' He would ask me to explain things. He had a hard time understanding what had happened to him. I sometimes wondered if he was retarded.

"Now he's somewheres up near Buffalo. His birthday's in December, same as mine. I send him birthday cards and write him notes, which I print in big square letters because he can't read cursive writing."

"Can he write enough to answer you?"

"He tries. He writes a few lines but they're hard to understand. He never got the stuff a student's supposed to know in second or third grade. A lot of boys they send upstate never got much further."

It was one of the few times she'd spoken of a man in prison with a feeling of real sympathy.

"He could have lied to me. He could have done the murder. He could have been there and not done it. He could have been with his mother in the hospital, just like he says."

"I get the feeling that you think he may be guilty."

"Some days I do. I go both ways on that." But, she said, "It can't be easy for the cops to know when somebody is telling them the truth. If these boys are goin' to dress like gangsters, walk like gangsters, talk like gangsters, and behave like gangsters, and their friends are gangsters, then they *got* to know that they'll attract attention."

She showed me a photo of the boy before he went to prison. In the photo, he did not look tough at all. He still had a childish look. Alice said she kept it on her bureau.

– III –

One summer evening when we were sitting in her kitchen, Alice talked with me at greater length than usual about her state of health. I haven't spoken of this matter

up to now, except to mention that she'd gone through periods when she felt extremely weak, or feverish, or sometimes
had no appetite for several days and couldn't bring herself
to eat.

There's a reason why I haven't given further information about her medical condition and the likely cause
of her susceptibility to episodes like these. I didn't want
to give the incorrect impression that Alice, in the fullness
of her character—a woman with so strong a spirit and so
many interesting and affirming qualities of personality and
character—could be faithfully portrayed as if she were,
above all else, a person who was weighted down by medical
dilemmas.

The fact of the matter, nonetheless, is that, shortly after
Alice left the Martinique Hotel, she had had a medical
examination and had tested positive for HIV. She told me
this at the time, but we didn't talk about it often. She wanted
it that way. The only reason it came up again that summer
night was that she had seen her doctor about a chest congestion and he had kept her in the hospital in order to observe
her for a couple days and give her a new round of tests.
He had concluded that her HIV was considerably more
advanced than when he'd seen her just six months before.

Alice was, of course, somewhat shaken by this news,
but she was too steady on her feet, too stable in her temperament, to be shattered by the information. She'd already
known that a progression in her illness was to be expected.
She simply wanted me to know what she had learned
from her physician. It was, as I've said, part of our unspo-
ken understanding that we would share our worries about
things that were important with each other. She didn't like
to speak about her health, but she wanted me to know her
doctor's name—she wrote it out for me—and said that she
would not object if I spoke with him from time to time.

HIV, as I was well aware, had swept across the South

Bronx in the preceding years, ravaging entire families, including many women who had, unknowingly, contracted the disease several years before. Quite a few had been infected in the homeless shelters. Alice's doctor, with whom I spoke shortly after she had given me permission, told me that one fourth of the admissions at the hospital where he was treating her were carrying the virus.

Men and women using drugs had frequently been sharing needles with each other at a time when many were not yet informed about the ways the virus was transmitted. Suddenly now, volunteers were setting up "needle exchanges" on the sidewalks of the Bronx—there was one on the sidewalk right outside of St. Ann's Church—where they were giving out clean needles and disposing of the dirty ones that addicts had been using. Nearly 4,000 people in the Mott Haven area—the neighborhood around St. Ann's—were known to be intravenous users at the time.

When she was in the Martinique, Alice told me, she had been recruited by the nurse to work with people who had AIDS and to counsel women on precautions they should take to avoid exposure to the virus through relationships with men who were injecting drugs. Because she was so well informed, it appeared improbable to me that she herself contracted the disease while she was living there.

Still, I knew that she'd had times of loneliness while in the Martinique, and even the most careful and most knowledgeable woman in that situation might have found it difficult in the course of four long years to maintain a wholly celibate existence. The other possibility—one that she believed to be most likely—was that it had been her husband who infected her.

I had little knowledge of the length of time it takes before the consequence of HIV becomes apparent once a person's been infected. Her doctor told me that, unless a person had some reason to be tested, there could be an extended period before the indications of the virus were detected. In any event, he said that he'd been treating her with antiviral medications and that the intermittent sense of weakness and the loss of appetite she sometimes underwent were, in part, the side-effects that commonly accompanied these medications.

The real concern, he said, was not the presence of the HIV infection in itself but that her body now had fewer weapons of defense against other and potentially life-taking forms of illness. He did not want to over-emphasize this point in his talks with Alice because, he said, "Anxiety does no one any good and can be debilitating to the body too." He simply wanted me to understand "the realistic aspects of the situation" and the full dimensions of the danger she was facing.

The next time she and I had dinner at her home, Alice made no reference to our previous conversation or to the information she'd been given by her doctor. It was "there"— a fact that would not go away, a test result, a new reminder of a piece of inescapable reality. But, for Alice, life went on and, that evening, when I came into her kitchen, there was not a hint of grimness or foreboding in her eyes, or in her voice, or in the things she said to me.

She had gone out to the store and picked up some rib-eye steaks and she broiled them and served them, as she liked to do, with vegetables and baked potatoes, cooked, of course, exactly as her mother had instructed her. She made some kind of caramel pudding for dessert, and topped it off with ice cream. Then she brewed a cup of coffee, as she always did, and as she sipped her coffee she asked me what was going on around St. Ann's, and whether I'd seen Martha.

She told me she'd been trying to reach her at her home the night before. "I called and called and all that I could get was that damn whistle on her fax machine. I hate that sound. It's like a train about to leave the station.

"I called her at the church today and told her that she needs to get it fixed. 'You can't just plug it in! There *must* be a book of instructions that came with it. I know they put instructions in those boxes.' I told her that she needs to take a little time and look at the instructions. I know that they don't give you the instructions for no reason. I told her, 'People are supposed to *read* that shit! That whistling sound is awful. Try your phone and see.'"

I asked, "What did she say?"

"She said she's goin' to look at the instructions. But, between the two of us, I guarantee you that she won't. She doesn't take the time to sleep or eat. So how's she goin' to find the time to fix a fax machine?"

"Sometimes," I said, "those booklets of instructions can be hard to understand."

But she did not accept this. "Are you tellin' me a woman with a law degree that went to Radcliffe College isn't smart enough to figure out instructions?"

"No. That isn't what I meant," I said.

But she was so engaged with this idea by now that she would not relent until she'd made a few more comments about people "who do not take time to read instructions" and who therefore force the rest of us to listen to a whistle sound.

When I left, she packed up a box of brownies she had made for me. The air outside was mild and she said she needed something she'd forgotten at the store, so she walked me to the station and, when we said good-bye at the bottom of the stairs, she reminded me to call her when I got to my hotel.

The following day, I was at the St. Ann's afterschool, then flew back to Boston and did not get home until rather late. I went to bed and didn't check my phone until I woke up the next day. When I did, there was a message from her scolding me for having let a day go by without reporting in.

"Did you get home? Are you okay? You didn't call. Did you get any sleep? Did you go and see your mother? Did you eat your dinner? Did you remember to tell Martha what I said about her phone? The answer better be 'yes' to all of the above. Please call me when you get this."

It was in keeping with her authoritative style and her protective nature to talk to me like that, as if she were my parent, even though I was slightly older than she was. More than a year later, in the fall of 1994, when my mother, who was nearing ninety, had to undergo a surgical procedure, Alice went out and bought a card with pink and yellow roses growing on a garden gate in front of a small cottage with a gabled roof and asked if I would give it to my mother. "I know this is a hard time for you and your mother. If I could take away your worries, I would do it with no questions asked. No one lives forever and I know that no one else can ever take your mother's place. Whatever happens, you will always know you have me. . . ."

In the spring of 1995, however, Alice called me on the phone and told me she was in the hospital again. I was lecturing in California at the time and could not be there with her. But she said that cancer cells had been detected in the pleura of her lungs—the protective membranes that lie between the lungs themselves and the tissue and bone structure that surround them.

"They gave me a procedure called a pleurodesis. It was the longest thirty minutes of my life. It felt like somebody was stabbing me."

But three days later, when she called me from the hospital again, she no longer seemed to be in pain, and certainly she didn't sound as if her spirits had been beaten down. As sick as she was, her old satiric sense of the absurdities of certain situations had obviously not abandoned her. She told me, for example, about a man, a patient on her floor, who set off a fire alarm by smoking in his bed. When I asked her how a patient thought that he could get away with smoking in a hospital, she laughed and said, "They do! They do it all the time. If somebody catches them, they just go down the hallway to a room where they don't think that anyone will know. . . .

"You see," she said, "the hospital's not staffed the way it's s'posed to be. You know the deal. Weekend's worst. There's hardly anybody here."

I asked if she was feeling well enough to eat.

"I don't know why," she said. "I am. I had an appetite today. I ate a piece of fish, some beans and broccoli, part of a potato, and some kind of pudding for dessert. . . . Doctor says I'll be here for another week."

The next day, she was sounding energized again and was still complaining about problems with the staff. "They was supposed to give me tests this morning, but it was a madhouse here today, so I think that they forgot. When my doctor comes tonight, I know he's going to break some eggs because he doesn't take no crap like that from anyone."

"Neither do you," I said.

"That's right," she said. "I don't. I never did, and I'm not starting now."

Two weeks later, I was in New York. Alice was home from the hospital but she wasn't strong enough to try to cook a meal, so I bought some things I knew she liked at the market opposite the train. After we ate and after she made coffee, she said she felt like having something sweet, so we had ice cream for dessert.

The following day, when I came back to visit in the afternoon, she was in a much more lively mood. As weakened as she'd been by the pleurodesis, she said she felt like getting out and going for a walk. Once we'd gone a block or two along East Tremont Avenue, she suggested that we visit with Pietro and the girls, whom she had known since they were children in the Martinique.

"They're pretty girls—and gettin' tall. They got those beautiful long legs. Pretty figures. Wavy hair. I meet Miranda at the store sometimes. He tries his best, but you can see she don't got much to wear. . . ."

Grandma and Pietro were at home when we arrived but we didn't get to see the girls because they were still at school. I hadn't told Pietro I was in New York so he was surprised to see us at his door. He joked with me, as he used to do, about the Red Sox, who, as it happened, were doing well at that point in the year. Still, as I've noted, he seldom missed the opportunity to make amusing comments on the rivalry between our teams. It was a bond between us that he very much enjoyed.

Alice remarked, after we had left, that Pietro did an awful lot to try to give the girls a safe and normal life with the little money that he had, but she also noted that he and the children lived closer to the edge of total destitution than any other family in the neighborhood she knew. She liked Pietro. She did many things to help him in the last years of her life. Even when she wasn't feeling well enough to visit him, she would send a message to the girls to come up to her building so that she could take their measurements. Then she'd send the information on to me so that I could buy them what they needed at a store in Boston.

She would give precise instructions too. When cold weather came that year, she said they needed winter coats. "See if you can find them something pretty but conservative. Dark colors. Navy blue or gray in a good woolen fabric would be nice. . . ." She was like that. He was grateful. When she died he wept for her.

* * *

Alice's health appeared to be much better during those winter months, although periodically she would have discomfort in her chest and she saw her doctor several times when she developed a low fever once again. Now and then, she'd have a spell of coughing and would need to use a vaporizer or inhaler of some sort in order to relieve her of congestion. But her appetite was good and, when I called her in the evenings, she would always tell me what she'd had for dinner.

One day when I was there, she told me there was something that she needed on East Tremont Avenue and asked if I would go with her. After we had passed the market next to the train station and crossed the street beneath the tracks, which are elevated in that section of the Bronx, she stopped in front of a boarded building next door to a pizza shop. She had told me more than once that she was smoking marijuana sometimes to relax. Her doctor was not opposed to this, she said, but was not allowed to prescribe it for her legally.

I went into the building with her, where a man with graying hair and wearing red suspenders was sitting at a table in a dingy-looking room, watching a TV. He disappeared into the back part of the building and came back a moment later with a paper bag for which she paid five dollars. Walking up the street after she put the paper bag into her purse, she said, "He's been there in the same spot for as long as I've been living here." I got the sense that she derived a certain kind of satisfaction from the fact that she could do things like this in my presence and had no concern that it would bother me.

As we headed back to her apartment, she indicated other buildings on the street where drugs of different kinds, she said, were usually available. When we approached a group of men who did not look friendly and who partly blocked the sidewalk—there were always men like these, seemingly unoccupied but with alert looks in their eyes— she ran me down on who they were: "Don't worry. They won't bother us. The short one thinks that he's some kind of gangster, but he's harmless. Besides, I know his mother. . . ." As we came up beside them, she said, "Hi!" and "How you doin'?" And one of them nodded politely in return.

She had no hesitation about walking with me in the streets or going to a store with me, no matter what the hour. But if she learned that I was in the neighborhood by myself at night, she'd make it clear that this disturbed her greatly. Similarly, on other nights, if she knew that I'd be up on Cypress Ave or Beekman Ave with one of the families of the children in that area, and if I didn't phone her when I got back to Manhattan, she would tell me the next day that she was up late looking at the clock.

Alice's worries about my safety in the streets, although they were sincere—she did get worried if I promised I would call and then forgot—were, in reality, something of a game she played with me, because I'd walked these streets for years, much as I'd walked the hallways of the Martinique at the time when she was there. Far more important, as I knew she understood, were my worries about her and the problems that I had to deal with back in Boston that concerned my mother and, especially, my father, whose deepening confusions were indications of the rapid onset of dementia. When I was obliged at last to move him to a nursing home, Alice was compassionate for my father's sake, although, as a woman, she identified more closely with my mother, who was now alone at home except for a companion who looked after her.

In spite of all the frightening uncertainties that Alice had to live with, she never lost her generous serenity in helping other people who had problems far less serious than hers. I told her once, after I had visited my father in the nursing home and he asked me wistfully if it was "time yet" for me to take him home, that I had trouble sleeping and found it hard to focus on my work. I told her that I wondered if I ought to see a therapist.

"I don't think you need to see a therapist," she said. "I think you need to spend more time with *me* and with the children at St. Ann's. I always see how much it cheers you up to be with them."

The following day, she mailed me a big envelope containing half a dozen bags of herbal tea and a picture of a sleepy-looking bear, with a red hat on his head, that she had cut out from the box in which the tea bags came. "You don't need no therapist," she wrote. "Drink this tea. Drink it to your heart's content! My love, as always, to your mother. . . ."

A year after she had undergone the pleurodesis, Alice's doctor told her that the cancer for which he'd been treating her, and which had appeared at first to be arrested, had in fact metastasized into a more serious malignancy. Alice's left breast had to be removed. She didn't say a word about this to me in advance. I think it was a matter of her wish to get it done, to bring things to completion, to be finished with the surgery before she felt prepared to speak of it.

"The growth was as hard as a rock," she told me, once she had recovered from the surgery and called me from her home. "It was more than they expected. I was awake. Well, I was half-awake. They call it 'twilight anesthesia.' Then they bandaged me. It's very tight. So now I'm here at home."

I asked if she was taking a painkiller.

"Yes," she said. "They gave me Tylenol with codeine—

and some Percocet." When the pain was very bad, she said, "My doctor said that I could take the Percocet."

"Do you have an appetite?"

"Surprisingly, I do. I ate a lamb chop last night with some buttered sweet potato—piece of melon for dessert."

She complained about the melon, which, she said, was hard and didn't have much taste. "You can't find good melon now. I don't know why. The ones they got are mostly shriveled and look sick. Same with the cucumbers. I don't see why anyone would buy them.

"I wanted to make a salad, but they want too much for lettuce. Lettuce is two dollars. Fresh tomatoes are $1.39. . . .

"So, anyway, I'm trying to take it one day at a time."

Over the course of the next six months, Alice had to go back to the hospital for further treatment as a regimen of chemotherapy began. Each time she was there I could tell when she was starting to feel better because she'd begin to criticize the food that they were serving her. She'd also tell me stories, usually good-natured ones, about somebody that she liked, or didn't like, who was a patient on her floor.

"I got another patient in my room with me right now," she told me one night on the phone. "An elderly woman, eighty-three years old. She's having a hard time. Called for her bedpan for an hour yesterday. When the nurse showed up, she said a couple words I didn't think a lady of her age would know.

"I had to help her open her milk carton for her lunch today. She does pretty good for somebody her age. She tells me that she lives alone. Her sister lives downstairs. She's Jewish—did I say that? Still lives in the Bronx but says there isn't any synagogue up there in her neighborhood no more. You know, Jonathan, there ain't no synagogues around here anywhere no more. . . ."

As almost always, she asked about my mother. I told

her she was doing well. "Give her a kiss for me," she said. "Here's one for you. God bless."

I was traveling again that year and didn't have a chance to get into New York as frequently as I would have liked. But Alice and I kept in touch by phone and I saw her several times when she was at home.

By early winter—it was the end of 1996—bottles of pills, assembled like a military force, occupied almost one quarter of her kitchen counter. More bottles, related to her HIV infection, were inside her refrigerator door. Once, at her request, I copied down the names of all her medications. The list of medicines, with jagged-sounding names including many consonants in awkward combinations and other nearly unpronounceable discordant sounds, took up more than half a page. I'm not certain why I kept this list, or why she asked me if I would. Maybe, for my own part, writing out the list and then updating it from time to time helped me to distract myself from thinking of the reason why those pills were there. But no distraction could suppress my recognition, or her own, that time was getting short.

She was in the hospital again in March, and a second time in May. The second time was longer than the first. When she was home, she sometimes had an appetite. I brought her a broiled chicken once, and smoked salmon and some other treats and good desserts, from a delicatessen on Third Avenue near 42nd Street, and we had a cheerful evening with each other like the ones we'd had before. But there were also times when she had no appetite at all except perhaps for something sweet—a slice of cheesecake, for example, or a piece of honeydew cut up into chunks— "icy cold, the only way that I can eat it now. . . ."

One afternoon near the end of June we went outside, because it was pleasant weather and she said she'd been cooped up in the apartment for too long. We sat in a playground opposite her building and watched the children playing on the swings and slides. She didn't ask about my mother this time. She lit up a cigarette and exhaled it slowly. Whatever damage it might do to smoke a few more cigarettes seemed unimportant to her now.

– IV –

The time came four weeks after that, when her doctor called from the hospital and urged me to get on a plane. He said that Alice was in very poor condition. He didn't know how long she would survive. I flew to New York the following morning and got to the hospital a little after noon. When I walked into her room, oxygen was being fed to her through plastic tubes inserted in her nostrils. Electronic monitors next to her bed were measuring her vital signs. Her arms and cheeks were very thin. Her nightgown only partially concealed the portion of her chest where her breast had been removed.

As sick as she was, she still was eating solid food. She said she'd eaten a little of her lunch but didn't have dessert "because it had no flavor." She told me that she had a taste for something like a piece of cake, something sweet, if I knew of any place around there where they sold it.

There was an Italian neighborhood not far from the hospital. I went downstairs and out to the street and walked around to see if I could find a pastry shop. A few blocks from the hospital, I came upon an old Italian bakery. Two young women were working at the counter and were joking with the customers and with one another.

When I asked them to pick out some pastries for me, since I didn't know what any of these cakes and pastries were called, they joked with me a little too. Then they asked if this was for a patient at the hospital. I said, "Yes. It's for someone who's been very sick." One of the women filled an extra box with cookies decorated with round faces made of colored sugar and she said, "No charge for this," and smacked her fingers to her lips like someone tossing off a kiss in an Italian movie, and then wrapped both boxes in red ribbons.

When Alice opened the first box, then the second, and found cream-filled pastries in one of them and cookies in the other, she tried one of the cookies first and asked me where I got them. I told her about the bakery and the women who had waited on me and the one who gave me all the cookies.

She said, "I bet you liked it when they joked with you."

"What do you mean?"

"I think it flattered you," she said. "A man your age—tell the truth. I bet those girls were pretty."

"It's true," I said.

She laughed, although she was in pain, and took my hand and gave it a slight squeeze. "If they looked as tasty as these cookies I don't blame you in the least!"

She tried one of the pastries and asked me if I knew what it was called. I said I hadn't asked.

"It's got some rum in it, I think," she said, eating a little more.

"Is it good?"

"Delicious."

Conversations about food, or friendly girls, or casual attractions, or all three, remained a pattern for us right up to the end. The last conversation that I had with her did not have to do with life or death, or love or hate, or God or faith, or any of the pain that she was going through. It was about hamburgers.

I was with her in the hospital again that night, about two weeks before she died. She mentioned that McDon-

ald's was engaged in "war"—"a price war," she explained—
against its rival, Burger King. She said she thought that it
was funny that a word like "war" would be employed in
speaking of hamburgers. I thought it was funny too and
made a foolish joke about two armies made up of hamburgers holding little swords and stabbing at each others' rolls.

"Don't make me laugh! It hurts too much," she said,
holding her hand against her chest; but she kept on laughing. That was nearly the last thing Alice ever said to me. I
flew back to Boston the next day to be with my mother. The
next time I came to New York, it was for the funeral.

The funeral was in the Bronx. The burial was in New
Jersey. At the graveside, Martha spoke the final prayers.
Alice's son and her daughters and a number of her oldest
friends were present at the end.

I have not spoken of her children in this story. I never
knew her daughters well. They were nearly adults when
they left the Martinique and had subsequently married and
were seldom present when I visited her home. I was closer
to her son, who was nearly sixteen when they moved into
the Bronx. He completed high school and had an opportunity to go to college but, despite his mother's urging and
my own, decided not to do so. For a while it appeared that
he was drifting. But, within a year or two, he pulled himself
together, found a decent job, and stuck with it through a
series of promotions. He went on to lead a relatively stable life. He's a gentle person, and he seems to be at peace
within himself.

But it is Alice herself, not her children, not her friends
or any other people who'd been kind to her and cared for
her, and would deeply mourn for her, whom I want to celebrate. It is the qualities of character and personality that
she had revealed to me from the first time that we met, and

much more so as we became closer—the courage that she took from small encounters with the odd particularities of life, the vitality of anger and the outrage at injustice that afforded her an outlet for the strong emotions other people in her situation tended to turn in upon themselves in ways that damaged them tremendously—it is these qualities, as well as the generosity of spirit she displayed to me when I was going through some hard times of my own, that render her unique among the men and women I had come to know during their years of homelessness.

When I remember Alice Washington today, I do not think about her as a victim of societal unkindness or as one of many women I encountered in those years who were stricken down by illnesses like HIV and cancer well before their time. Victimhood is not the word that comes to mind. A taste for bagels and smoked salmon, and for garlic bread with butter, and for melons that are ripe (not the "sick" and "shriveled" kind) and the price of fresh tomatoes come to mind. The flavor of cream soda comes to mind.

She empathized with those who were true victims but, in her own case, she rejected victimhood. The details of life and the amusement that she took in dwelling on those details, toying with those details, were her weaponry of choice against the many difficulties that she had to face. New York was a bitter place for women of her class and color in those days, but she did not reciprocate that bitterness. She rose above the meanness that surrounded her. She punched holes in that meanness with her cleverness and wit and with her eye for the preposterous. She laughed a lot. She loved her lamb chops and her baked potato. In the details, she transcended.

PART TWO

A Bright Shining Light

CHAPTER 6

Survivors

These are the children of hope.

These are the survivors.

There are many of them.

For some of the sweetest children that I knew, who found themselves drawn into trouble by the age of ten or twelve and fell into "the life of the streets," as Ariella spoke of it, while in their teenage years, their victories consisted in the fortitude with which they turned their backs upon that life and the dangers that it held. As limited as this victory may seem to some, it was not a small one to their families and the other people in the neighborhood who loved them.

For others, who steered clear of trouble but were drifting for a time in apparent aimlessness after leaving high school, whether they'd completed their degrees or not, victory and vindication, even of a modest sort at first, depended on that moment, never easy to pin down in time, when the hunger for a sense of purpose and direction coincided with the gradual emergence of what theologians often term "a sense of calling," whether it's a call to service or the strong appeal of a particular vocation.

Some of the kids whose lives have been most difficult are struggling still and have yet to find that place of inner peace in which they can start to shape a vision of contributive maturity. But the fact that they are searching for that vision and meanwhile have retained much of the earnestness and elemental kindness I saw in them as children—and do not put up a slick veneer of toughness to disguise their vulnerable feelings—lends them a quality of honesty and innocence that leaves me optimistic for the future.

There are others, an impressively large number of the children who were active in the programs at St. Ann's, who, almost from the time they entered adolescence, had started to perceive themselves as virtually unbounded in their academic goals and were looking to a future that encompassed colleges or universities. In some cases, they'd already set their sights upon professional careers. More than a few have fulfilled those aspirations. I will be speaking of these students too, at great length, and joyfully.

But, even in the case of those who were most successful in their schooling, who went on to colleges and universities and completed their degrees, or will shortly do so, and who tell me that they have their eyes set firmly on vocations, even on specific jobs, I suspect that several will strike out in new directions that they can't anticipate at the present time. That is one of many reasons why these stories will remain unfinished. There will be no hyperbolic endings of the kind we find in unconvincing movies about instantaneous success for someone who climbed out of destitution to dazzle the commercial world before the age of twenty-five or thirty. Success within the lives of those I've known for all these years is as much a matter of their inward growth—in decency, in character—as of their outward victories. And, at the end, uncertainties remain. How could it be otherwise? They still have, as I dearly hope, the best part of their lives ahead of them.

The Boy Who Ate a Giant Bag of Cookies While He Walked Me All Around the Neighborhood, and His Very Interesting Mom

He liked cookies. He was not quite seven. His name was Leonardo. I met him on the first day I visited St. Ann's.

His mother had a meeting scheduled with the pastor at the time when I arrived, so Leonardo volunteered to take me for a walk to see the streets around the church.

It was a warm day at the start of summer in 1993. He was wearing red sneakers, blue shorts, and a jersey with a picture of three gerbils on the front. He had a bag of cookies with him—very big, chocolate chip—and he kept on munching them and asking if I wanted one the whole time that we walked.

At one point we passed a vacant lot and he looked up at the branches of a tree to which a number of stuffed animals had been attached.

"Bears," he said.

But when I asked him why the bears were in the tree, he smiled at the animals but gave me no response.

"Okay," he said after we had walked a while. "I think we need to go up here." We crossed the avenue and went up a long street, with the grimy buildings of Diego-Beekman on both sides, until we got to P.S. 65.

Leonardo was a small boy, with soft brown hair and dark brown eyes. When he got scared at night, he said, "I go in my mommy's bed and crawl under the covers." He was one of hundreds of young children in the area who had chronic asthma. So he stopped for a moment at the top of the hill and took out a small inhaler from his pocket, gave himself a few puffs, then seemed to be okay.

As we turned right on Cypress, he pointed to a small black dog. "Hi, Princess!" Then, to me: "That's Princess." Then: "You see? We're almost there."

After we had walked a block on Cypress, he asked me, "Do you want to go on Jackson Avenue?" I said it would be fine. When we got to Jackson he pointed to another street. "Do you want to go down there?"

I said, "Okay."

He hesitated for a moment. "They're burning bodies there. . . ."

His mother had warned me before we left the church, "He does tell fibs," so I asked if he was telling me the truth. He pretended that he didn't hear. Instead, he munched another cookie and began to hum.

"Come on. I'll take you there. We have to go around this block."

As we approached the place where he insisted people had been "burning bodies"—it was on a street by the name of Locust Avenue—a sour, rancid-smelling odor, drifting from the partly open metal door of a peculiar-looking building with a blue gunmetal top, did become perceptible. When we stood outside the door, the odor became stronger.

"You sure," he asked, "that you don't want a cookie?"

I thanked him but declined.

"I think I'll have another one," he said.

A few moments later, he announced, "The day is coming when the world will be destroyed. Everyone is going to be burned to crispy cookies."

A car stopped to let us cross a busy street. He waved at the driver, who waved back.

"We're out of cookies," he reported. "I ate a whole bag. . . ."

When we got back to the church, Leonardo's mother and the pastor told me that his story about "burning bodies" had not been a fib at all—or was only a slight exaggeration. The building that he'd shown me was, in fact, burning *parts* of bodies, among other objects, and the odor I had smelled when Leonardo and I stood outside was usually more powerful.

As Martha would explain to me, the building was a medical incinerator, burning what are known as "red-bag products," hospital waste, amputated limbs and embryos, hypodermic needles, and the like, which were brought here every day from fourteen New York hospitals. An attempt to build a comparable incinerator on the East Side of Manhattan had been halted when physicians and environmentalists cautioned people living in that area of carcinogenic and respiratory dangers it might pose for children. As a result, it was constructed here instead, within a few blocks of a neighborhood in which at least 6,000 children such as Leonardo were residing and could not escape its emanations. The burner, moreover, because of its high smokestacks, spewed its toxins to a wider population of approximately 40,000 people, virtually all them black or Hispanic families.

"When it's going full blast," Leonardo's mother told me, "the stench is really potent. I have to close my windows, but it gets to Leonardo anyway."

Parents in the neighborhood launched impassioned protests over a period of years, beginning at the time of its construction in 1991. But their pleadings were discredited by the influential New York Times, which supported the construction of the burner in their neighborhood and said that the resistance of the parents was "misguided."

Under the headline "WASTEFUL PROTEST IN THE BRONX," the paper ran an editorial that may have been decisive in the outcome of the question. "It would be a tragic mistake," according to the Times, if "panicky fears" of those who led the protests were to halt this installation.

"Medical wastes are not only unsightly but danger-ous. No one wants them in a residential neighborhood." The "only place for such a facility," the editorial continued, was in "a zone" where construction of residential housing was "forbidden"—a puzzling assertion in view of the fact that Leonardo and I were only about five minutes from his home when we stood in front of the waste burner, but which the paper justified on the technicality that the burner had been built just across the border of an adjoining area, which, according to the zoning laws, had been adjudged to be "industrial."

Leonardo's mother—her name was Anne, but people who enjoyed her feisty personality used to call her "Antsy"—was one of the parents in Mott Haven who had fought most fiercely in opposition to the medical incinera-tor and who was convinced that it would be harmful to the children in the neighborhood. Four years later, in 1995, hospitalizations for attacks of asthma in Mott Haven and in neighborhoods nearby were fourteen times as high as on the East Side of Manhattan. By that time, the pediatric asthma rate in the community affected was, according to a pediatric specialist with whom I consulted, higher than in any other urban area of the United States.

Even before the waste incinerator went into opera-tion, asthma rates in Mott Haven and adjoining areas had been very high. One reason was believed to be the concentration of several other factors known to be injurious to a child's respiration—truck depots, for example, in which eighteen-wheelers would be parked with engines idling, venting their exhaust into the air. Large bus depots added to the problem, as did the lack of proper sanitation and healthy ventilation in much of the housing in the neighborhood. Physicians who were treating asthmatic children in Mott Haven were troubled that the city now had added yet another source of toxins to the air these children had to breathe.

The incinerator was at last shut down by the New York State Department of Environmental Conservation in 1997. A year later, under a consent decree, the Browning-Ferris Corporation, owner of the installation where 500 violations of environmental law and air-pollution law had been recorded, agreed to donate money so that children who had trouble breathing could attend an "asthma camp."

All of this, from Antsy's point of view, was a classic instance of racism gone wild. But, for Leonardo, pulling out his asthma pump to take a puff or two or three when he began to wheeze, it had come to be a fairly normal part of his existence and, to all appearances, he did not let it slow him down or undermine the pleasure that he took in making observations that he may not always have intended to be quite as funny or alarming as they were.

It was only at night, his mother said, that his wheezing grew severe enough for her to be concerned. During the day, his asthma pump and whatever other medication he was taking seemed to keep his asthma under fairly good control. And, with his whimsical and comic personality and his ease at making friends and his popularity among the children at St. Ann's and at his public school, he struck me as a relatively happy little boy and one with whom I always found it fun to talk because, among his other virtues, he was never boring.

He did get quite a lot of satisfaction out of making off-the-wall remarks, some of which I was convinced he must have known a grown-up would find startling. He told me once, when I met him on the street a block or two from where he lived, that somebody—"this man I saw"—had "buried another man back there," gesturing behind him. "The man he buried was alive."

I asked him, "Did you try to dig him out?"

"No!" he said. "It was too gross!" He told me he had asked the man, "'Are you still alive?' But he said no."

He left the story there and, as he often did after saying something that he purposely left incomplete, he began to hum. Then he continued walking in the way that he was heading.

In the years that followed, I spent a lot of afternoons and evenings visiting at Leonardo's home, which was on the fifth floor of one of those buildings, the Diego-Beekman Houses, that Ariella had described. His mother, Antsy, was one of the savvier and more politically acerbic parents in the neighborhood. A very smart and largely self-taught intellectual, it seemed that she had done a great deal of reading in her teenage years and throughout her twenties and had thoroughly immersed herself in some of the writings of prominent black authors who had captured the attention of the public in the last years of the 1960s. One evening in her home, she carefully explained to me the highly conscious strategies by which black and Hispanic people in the Bronx were isolated racially by New York's city planners in the years when white folks who had previously lived there "started their stampede to get as far away from us as possible," and she quoted from an essay of James Baldwin that I had long forgotten.

Like Ariella, she had an investigative instinct and she
knew a bit about the owner of her building—"lives in Massachusetts, your neck of the woods," she said—and she had
a barrel of well-justified complaints about the disrepair her
landlord had allowed and told me of her battle "to keep the
rats behind the walls" from "getting out into my kitchen
area."

Her background, however, was very different from
that of Ariella. She had grown up in the South and came to
New York City with her mother when she was thirteen. Her
mother was a nurse at Albert Einstein Medical School for
twenty-seven years and lived, she said, in one of the nicer
sections of the Bronx that hadn't yet been totally abandoned
by white people, although the trend was underway and the
schools, as a result, had already started their decline. Her
father, from whom her mother was divorced, had moved
upstate to Syracuse and, having had some training in "con-
crete construction," opened his own business and brought
Antsy there to live with him so that she could go to a good
high school in his neighborhood.

She apparently did well in school, studied hard and
graduated but, as she put it, "had no special interest in
going on to college." When I asked her why she didn't want
to go to college, she said that she'd been caught up in "the
whole thing of the hippie era—'Do your own thing,' you
know, Beatles music, Ram Dass, 'wear a flower in your
hair.'" Unfortunately, it led her, as it did so many others,
into being careless about using drugs—"first," she said, "just
smoking weed, doing acid . . . whatever else was on the
scene. But then I started using coke," which she called "a
very bad mistake. . . ."

At some point in her later twenties, she told me that
she fell in love. "A good-looking man, who just happened to
be deep into drug-dealing," although she claims she didn't

know that at the time. Before she got to know him, she said she used to see him from the window of a bus. "He'd wave to me, and I'd wave back. He had salt-and-pepper hair. I thought I was very cool. But when it came to making judgments about men, I was as green as a turnip that fell off the truck. To me, he was the sweetest guy in the entire world."

Within another year or so, the two of them were living together and, in time, were married. Leonardo was born while they were still in Syracuse, but Antsy wanted to be near her mother, so they moved back to New York.

Her husband, she said, was not faithful to her and made little effort to disguise his infidelity. "He'd bring other women here when I wasn't home. One of my neighbors told me, 'Honey, I don't want to shoot your gears but I've been sleeping with him in your bedroom for a year.' I'd kick him out two or three times every month. But you know 'a fool in love'? After I had thrown him out, I'd miss him and I'd go out looking for him in the neighborhood. . . ."

The problem was taken out of her hands when he was arrested and sent away to jail. The timing was fortuitous, since Leonardo now was three years old and Antsy was determined to devote every bit of energy she had to making sure her very talkative and charming little boy had every opportunity to enjoy a happy childhood, and she also was determined to begin his education well before the time when he would enter public school.

"I taught him how to read when he was three or four. I put him into Aida Rosa's preschool"—a reference to my favorite principal in the South Bronx, who set up a preschool on the street where Antsy lived so the children who came into P.S. 30, the good elementary school she ran, would be well prepared.

Like Ariella with her younger children, Antsy had avoided sending him to P.S. 65 but put him into kindergarten at Miss Rosa's school. (People in the neighborhood did not say 'Ms.,' but always 'Miss,' before the names of women of a certain age, followed often by the woman's first name, but they'd use the last name in the case of principals and teachers.) "Then, for no good reason I can figure out, I put him into Catholic school, but the third-grade teacher whipped the kids and so I brought him back to P.S. 30, where he had some of the teachers that you know, like Miss Harrinarine"—a fifth-grade teacher who taught a number of the children who were most successful in their later years.

"He never stops talking," this very strict but good-natured teacher told me once. "But he's so excited and the comments he comes up with are usually so funny that I have to turn my back so he won't see me laughing."

By the time he had completed elementary school, a cluster of Miss Rosa's teachers, one of whom was Miss Harrinarine, had begun a small and innovative satellite of P.S. 30, also run along progressive lines, which extended into middle school. So Leonardo was enabled to escape the so-called "medical" school and the other middle school to which the kids from the local elementary schools were sent.

Antsy was a hustler in the best sense of the term. She grabbed opportunities whenever they were there. She questioned teachers. She went into the classrooms. When Leonardo followed Miss Harrinarine into the experimental school that I've described, the principal told me, "She's always in my hair. She wants to know why we're doing this, or why we're doing that." In the long run, though, Miss Harrinarine said, "I admire her a lot. She asks good questions. Her mind is constantly in motion. I enjoy it when she comes into my room." She said that Leonardo's mother was "the kind of parent every teacher hopes for. I wish that we had more of them. . . ."

– II –

A few years earlier, when Leonardo was in second or third grade, Antsy had begun a baseball team for a group of kids about his age. They played and practiced at St. Mary's Park, which bordered the Diego-Beekman Houses and was "not a place you'd want to go alone at night," she pointed out, "but was safe during the day." As she was talking, she went to the closet and took out a baseball jacket with her name embroidered under the word MANAGER.

Every year, she told me, she organized a party for the children on her team on a street that was adjacent to St. Mary's Park. The street, she said, was part of the province of the Wild Cowboys, the gang of dealers that controlled that side of St. Ann's Avenue. "They'd stand there on the sidewalk selling their own brands of crack, 'Yellow Top,' 'Red Top,' 'Blue Top,' 'Green Top'. . . . 'Tango and Cash' was their brand of heroin. They'd whisper it to people as you were walking past. . . .

"There's a dead-end street partway up off Beekman Ave. There were two small houses next to each other on one side of the block. One was occupied. One was abandoned. That's the one the Cowboys used to hold their meetings and to package up their drugs—you know, little vials with the colored tops for crack and small glassine bags for heroin. Next door to their building was a junked-up lot.

"Jonathan, don't think that I'm crazy, but that's the place I decided we should have our parties. No cars. No traffic. And, besides, I made up my mind that we shouldn't let a gang of hoodlums claim it as their own.

"So I talked with Shirley Flowers, since she lived on Beekman Ave, and she agreed to help me get some neighbors out to help us clean the lot." (Miss Shirley, who passed away three years ago, was a wonderful friend to children in the neighborhood. If it was evening and a mother hadn't yet come home, she'd bring the children into her house, cook them dinner, and, if she thought they needed it, she'd bathe them. During the day, she'd sit outside and keep a close eye on the avenue.)

Without Miss Shirley, Antsy said, she never could have organized the parties. But, as it happened, she got other help as well. "The first time we did it, a week before the party, two of the dealers stopped me on the street. They came right up and said hello. You know me—I say hello to everyone. 'Ma'am,' they said, 'we'd like to help. Is there something we can do?'

"'You can start by helping us get rid of all this junk,' I told them. And they said they'd do it. And they did it, and they did a real good job.

"So Shirley and I cooked up things we knew the kids would like. Hot dogs. Macaroni. Chicken wings. Rice and beans. Somebody brought paper hats. It was a great party. . . .

"I love people," Antsy said. "Leonardo, too. Doesn't matter who they are. We had parties out there every year until he got older."

Life at home in their apartment frequently was like a party too. On the weeknights Antsy kept things quiet because Leonardo had his school assignments to complete. But on the weekends and on summer nights, "the place was full of children." Sometimes, she said, "I had seven kids sleeping over, every place that they could fit. On my bed. On the sofa. On the quilts and blankets that I spread out on the floor. Next morning, get them up, give them breakfast, take them up to Concourse Village, take them to the movies. . . .

"Once," she said, "after I had sent them home, a mother called me on the phone. 'Have you seen my boy?' It turned out her little boy was hiding in the closet. I called her back and said, 'I found him. I'm sending him right now.' Leonardo found this very funny. It turned out the two of them had planned it."

His asthma, she noted, disappeared when he was twelve. "That was the year after the burner was shut down." She could not be dissuaded from her firm belief that the two things were connected, as they probably were. Statistics released by the New York City Department of Health would certainly support her. Once the incinerator ceased its operations, hospitalizations for asthma in the Mott Haven area rapidly declined. The figure dropped by more than half within the next three years. Whether or not this was the reason for Leonardo's freedom from the bouts of wheezing he had undergone since he'd been a little boy, his mother rightly looks upon the termination of the years in which she had to keep her windows closed even on the hottest days as a major victory for people in the neighborhood.

During his years in middle school, Leonardo continued to attend the program at St. Ann's, not only for tutorials but for the creative projects offered by the church and for the atmosphere of unembarrassed intellectuality that was encouraged there. As one of the most successful students in the neighborhood and one of the most outgoing children at St. Ann's, Leonardo now received an opportunity given only to a handful of the children in our inner-city schools. He was recruited by a good New England boarding school when he was in eighth grade, in 2001, to go there for his upper-secondary years.

His mother went with him for his formal interview and to meet some of the teachers and admissions people, whom she questioned closely. It was as if it were they, and not her son, who were being scrutinized to determine if they measured up to expectations. But I knew that, after all her questions had been answered, she would not turn down this opportunity for Leonardo.

Unlike many inner-city kids who are recruited by prestigious boarding schools, Leonardo had no problems in adjusting to the academic pace. "He came into the school at cruising speed," one of his teachers told me; and, with his social confidence, he struck up friendships easily and soon became a leader among students in his class. His friends, as I recall, anointed him "the Mayor," because he seemed to have an easy gift for getting other students to agree to social plans that he enjoyably concocted. Along with all the rest of what appeared to be his relatively effortless accomplishments while he was there, he was also an athletic star, the captain of the football team, even though he'd never played much football in the Bronx.

"He was the only black kid on the team," his mother said, which was "no big deal to him" because "he knows exactly who he is" and, she added, "never had to play those 'black-is-better' games in order to establish his identity." This, she felt, was why he didn't focus much on other students' race or class so long as he could see that they respected him and liked him, which they obviously did.

Leonardo's original recruitment to the school was occasioned by the eagerness, familiar in some of the other well-endowed New England schools, to make a place for "disadvantaged children" in its student population. But Leonardo was not truly "disadvantaged" in the sense in which that term is usually meant by those who also have a tendency to layer on another label, "culturally deprived," in speaking about kids who come from places like the Bronx. In cultural terms, indeed—because of the grounding he'd been given by his mother from his early years—as well as in his psychological development and in his mastery of social skills, he was possibly *less* deprived than many of the economically advantaged kids who were his friends and classmates.

Several of the friendships that he made during those years of school would prove to be enduring. Some of the boys from very wealthy families would later drive down to New York and spend weekends in the Bronx with Leonardo and his mother, hanging out in their apartment. Antsy's home had always been, and it remains, a magnet for young people.

Leonardo went to college in upstate New York. It's possible that he arrived at college with an excess of confidence that did not serve him well at first. In his freshman year, his mother said, "he fooled around too much. His grades were a disaster." His first-semester GPA was 1.50, she recalled. "I told him that it sounds like someone's body weight. I didn't think that it was possible to score so low!"

That first semester "messed him up so much he had to do an extra year to graduate." But he did honors work from that point on and won his degree in sociology "with a GPA of 3.4," Antsy told me proudly.

He had to work for all five years while he was in college to supplement his scholarship—"all sorts of jobs, Barnes & Noble, UPS . . . , and I sent him money when I could to pay for extra college fees and things like health insurance.

"He told me that he missed my cooking so I used to cook a dinner for him every week or two. I'd wrap it up in foil, put it in the freezer, then when it was frozen hard I'd send it up by overnight express." As mature as Leonardo had become by now, she said, "he was still my baby. I had to keep him happy."

Starting in his second year, and more so in the next three years, he told me he had made a point of taking courses outside of his major, including several courses related to psychiatry and to developmental abnormalities. "I'd always had an interest in becoming a psychiatrist, so I interned at a nursing home for people with severe disorders, schizophrenia, deep depression, and advanced dementia."

I asked him why, with his interest in psychiatry, he'd settled upon sociology as his field of concentration. He said it was because he recognized how many years of further study it was going to entail if he studied medicine and, given his financial situation, "I had to wonder whether it was really in the stars." At the same time, "I thought of sociology as something broad enough so that I could take it, if I wanted, in a number of directions."

He also said, "People had been telling me I'm not a bad performer, so I took two courses in performance art." I didn't know exactly what the term implied and asked him if the courses he had taken focused upon theater—acting in a work of drama, for example.

"Not exactly," he replied. He said he wasn't really drawn to "speaking someone else's words." He said he liked to improvise. "That's what I actually enjoy. One of my teachers said that maybe someday I should give it a real try."

Last winter, after he'd been out of college for six months, when I stopped by briefly at his mother's home, he told me he was working temporarily in a clerical and managerial position at the city's major produce market, which was nearby in Hunt's Point. "In terms of salary," he said, "it isn't a bad job for now. And it's kind of interesting, checking out the orders that we send to these expensive restaurants and luxury hotels." But he emphasized that this was "just a short-term thing," a way to earn some money and to buy him time to take the pressure off so he could do more thinking about possible careers.

Meanwhile, he said, he was writing scripts for a stand-up act that he was performing, when he got the chance, in some of the smaller clubs where amateurs were given opportunities to see if they could capture the attention of an audience. He was very organized in explaining this to me: how important timing was, how much planning had to go into working through a script that might end up being less than seven minutes long. "Sometimes, though, even when I've worked for hours on a script, I'll get up there and I'll think, 'What the hell? Why not just say something that I've never tried before?' You know, something that just pops up at that moment in my mind?" Those, he said, were usually the lines that got the most applause.

I couldn't stay there long that day, because I had a meeting scheduled at the church and I'd also promised Ariella I'd come by to talk with her. Before I left, however, Leonardo said there was "some other stuff" he wanted to discuss with me. I told him I'd be sure to plan ahead for us to have a longer talk at a time when neither of us had to rush away. The next conversation we would have was going to open up some deeper and more sober aspects of his hopes, as well as his self-doubts, about the shaping of his long-range plans. But, first, a few more words about his very interesting mother are in order here.

— III —

Leonardo's mother had been through a lot more turbulence and anguish in her life than I had fully realized up until quite recent times. People in the neighborhood thought that Antsy was a ball of fire. With her quick wit, her rapid repartee, her small body moving swiftly (she was barely five feet tall) as she clipped along the streets to go to the many meetings she attended or to one of several jobs she had throughout those years, and with the endless fun she seemed to get from having kids around her in her home, playing with them in her baseball jacket in St. Mary's Park,

I used to think of Antsy like a force of nature nobody could stop. She looked very young; she still does. She's in her late fifties now, but she could pass for thirty-five or forty.

It wasn't until a year ago that she told me she had had a problem with severe depression ("scary feelings," "racing thoughts") for much of the time that I had known her. She attributed the onset of these feelings to the period after she left Syracuse and moved into the Bronx and her husband's infidelity was driving her, as she put it, "up the wall and down again." But I wondered also if her years of using drugs during those "hippie" days, as she had spoken of the period when she was in her twenties, might have been a factor too. "I was trying to find joy," she said, "but it brought me misery."

The problem was exacerbated, in the years when Leonardo was in college, after she was injured in the course of work at a home for people who, she said, were "mentally impaired." Her patients, she explained, were women in their twenties, "a few of them as old as thirty-five," whose emotional and cognitive capacities were those of children in their early years. "Some of them could fold sheets, match up silverware and plates, simple tasks. Some were autistic. One of them didn't talk. Another one repeated everything I said. I thought of them as little girls and I came to love them."

Her injury occurred when she came upon a member of the staff, who she said was poorly trained, "throttling one of the girls with whom I'd been working." The patient was "a twenty-three-year-old with a mental age of seven who was always craving food. Her hunger was insatiable. She'd dig her hand into a peanut-butter jar when nobody was looking. She'd scoop it up and shove it in her mouth and wipe her fingers on her face. It would be all over her. . . .

"One day she was caught. And when this member of the staff took the jar away from her, the patient grew so desperate she slapped the woman in the face. The woman started choking her.

"I walked into the kitchen and I had to force the woman's hands apart and pull her off my patient, who was backed against the wall. When she finally let her go, the patient fell and I fell over with her. I was underneath her.

"I didn't know until the next day that my lower back was hurt and I'd messed up my sciatic nerve. I only knew I had a sharp pain just above my hip. My supervisor said to go and see a doctor but not to tell him this had happened while I was at work.

"So, you know me and my big mouth. I went to the hospital and, of course, I told them everything."

Antsy tried to keep on working after that. "I started reading all my patients' histories. No one ever showed this stuff to me before. Staff members weren't expected to examine the case histories. I told my supervisor: 'There needs to be more information and more education given to the staff.' He said he'd hold a meeting to discuss this. But his main concern was that I would tell somebody what was going on.

"Some of the people on the staff were good. One of them told me other patients had been beaten too. So I told this to my supervisor, and he asked me, 'Have you talked to anyone about this?' I said, 'Yes. I told my doctor and my priest.' I told him, 'You can't treat retarded people like you do.'"

They never got to fire her. She had to quit because she was in too much pain. For a long while after that, she said she found it hard to sleep, or clean the house, or climb into the bath, or go out to the store or to St. Ann's. But the physical pain was "not as bad as the frustration that I felt at being cooped up here in the apartment all that time." She fell, she said, "into the most horrible depression." Even when the medicine her doctor gave her managed somewhat to reduce the pain, "it was a struggle to get up each morning and go out the door."

A surgical procedure and intensive rehabilitative treatment ultimately relieved the pain. Antidepressants got her out the door. "Once I started going out," she said, "my spirits were restored and I didn't need the medications anymore."

People I know who undergo depression cope with their feelings in a multitude of ways, some of which—in Vicky's case, for instance—worsen their depression and isolate them from their friends. In Antsy's case, except for the time when her spinal injury forced her to stay home, she had always compensated for the inward pull—the withdrawal from activity that's familiar to depression—by throwing herself outward into the thick and thin of life, into the streets, into the schools, into the battle for clean air, into the battle to clean out a drug-infested block so she could have a party for her baseball team.

To battle darkness, she was always lighting fires of excitement for herself and Leonardo, encouraging his playfulness, spurring him on to indulge his curiosities, filling her apartment with more kids than it could hold, and, even at the time when she was in the deepest pain, bringing food to UPS so that he could get a respite from the college cafeteria.

The last time I saw her, in the summer of this year, a bunch of Leonardo's college friends were coming there for dinner. Antsy said, "I'm feeling a lot better now. Back doesn't hurt unless I bend way over. Then a twinge, right down here"—she reached her hand around her waist—"and my old friend, Mr. Pain, says, 'Here I am again!'" She kept a heating pad on her sofa, but she didn't sit on it for long. She kept getting up and going to the door or looking out the window to see if Leonardo and his friends were there.

I had to leave before they came but, two weeks later,

I was at St. Ann's again. Leonardo told me, when I called him in advance, that he'd love to talk some more if I wanted to stop by.

Antsy was out when I arrived. He'd been in the living room working on a script he was preparing for his stand-up act. He showed me the first lines, which he said were "very rough." As a joke or as a form of flattery, he asked if he could have my pen, and so we traded pens with one another.

He hadn't yet had much success in finding clubs that would let him do his act on more than rare occasions. But he told me he'd been branching out and looking beyond comedy to see if he could find an acting job and had started showing up at casting calls and asking about agents. His earlier antipathy to "speaking other people's lines" had been, he said, "an ego thing. . . . I like to *perform*. Any way I can." If he could find an acting role, "whether it's a comic role or something very serious," he thought that he could do it and was hoping he would have a chance.

In the midst of these ambitious plans and amidst the friendships he'd developed in the stand-up clubs and at the outer fringes of the theater world, he told me he had kept in contact with some of the friends with whom he grew up in the Bronx. One of the boys he'd always liked, who used to hang around St. Ann's when he was in kindergarten and the first and second grades—an angelic-looking child who was not, in fact, angelic in the least and, despite the pastor's affectionate attention and efforts at protection, had started drifting off into the streets when he was only eight or nine— had ended up in trouble with the law before he was sixteen. He was in and out of jail for a number of short stays while Leonardo was in college.

"When he was not at Rikers Island," Leonardo said, "he liked to stay in our apartment, because he never really had a home to call his own." His mother lived on St. Ann's Avenue when I knew him as a child. I didn't know what problems she was facing, but her life, and that of her son, had always been in some kind of disorder. He seldom had clean clothes to wear to school or sat down to a decent meal unless Antsy or another neighbor fed him. "Even today," Leonardo said, "he feels more at home with us than in his own apartment."

Sometimes, he continued, "when I was home from college for a weekend, I'd bring him back with me to school on Sunday night. He had no purpose in his life. He wasn't doing *anything.* It's hard to do something to help yourself when no one else around you in the street is doing anything. . . .

"When he came to college once, I kept him with me for two weeks. He had to wake up with me every day. He had to come to every class. I told my teachers in advance. In a class on sociology, he asked the teacher questions. The students seemed to like him and they asked him questions too. He would get right into it. He said he didn't want to leave. 'I love it here,' he told me.

"He saw people of his age going to their classes with their backpacks. He was amazed, after class, to see them, with their books and laptops, lying on the grass. 'Wow!' he said. 'You got trees! You got grass!' It wasn't like he'd never seen a tree before—it was the whole setting. Students playing Frisbee. Other students studying. Open spaces. Lots of grass! There was a pond. People looked relaxed.

"The main thing is, he saw people going somewhere with their lives. And he liked what he was seeing. I think that something changed in him. He didn't get in trouble for a long time after that. . . .

"He's still at our house a lot. When my college friends are here, he sometimes seems to think that maybe he's supposed to slip away. I tell him, 'No. You're my friend. We've known each other all our lives. When I go to do things with the other guys, you're going to come with us.' "

He got up to get us cold drinks from the kitchen. I took

that as an opening to shift the ground a bit, because I had a question in my mind that I assumed he must have thought about as well. It was difficult, as he'd said, to break into the world of stand-up entertainment, and he was discovering it was even harder to get into acting. "If, at a certain point, it proves to be impossible. . . ." He nodded at those words before I could finish, and he told me that he'd talked about this with his mother.

He said that if he found he simply couldn't "hack it" in the world of entertainment, he had more or less made up his mind to go back to college for a graduate degree "in something like developmental studies" in order to obtain the depth of understanding and, he hoped, the level of authority that would make it possible for him to find a role in "helping to shape policies, maybe in the government, maybe in some other way, that affect the lives of children." He was, he said, already so involved with young men like the friend he had described that it would be a natural progression "to notch it up enough" to get himself to a point where he could exercise at least a small degree of power in altering conditions that had led so many kids he knew into "lives that have no value to them, and no meaning."

Previously, he said, in spite of all the confidence he'd been able to display ever since his years in boarding school and college, he suspected there had been "some kind of obstacle, some kind of 'wall'" within his mind—"not economic, something else"—between himself and any higher academic goals or aspirations. "Whatever it was, that wall is gone. I know that I can do this if I want."

At those words, I asked him if he ever felt the hankering he'd had some years before in reference to psychiatry.

"Yes," he said. "It's still there."

It had often come into my mind, after he had told me of his internship in college, that with his warm, supportive personality and his relaxing manner, not to speak of his compassion and his easygoing sense of the comedic, he could probably walk into the darkest ward of any mental institution and bring a smile to the most despondent patient in the room. I also thought he had the keen eye and quick intuitive intelligence of a fine clinician. But I didn't say this. I thought that it would push the envelope too far, and so I dropped the matter there.

Leonardo will be reading what I'm writing here. He's mature and wise enough to tell me to "shove off"—although I'm sure he'd say it in much nicer words—if he thinks I've overstepped the boundaries of a friendship between two adults who, in most respects, now stand on equal ground. He's no longer the little boy who introduced me to the streets of the South Bronx and consumed a giant bag of cookies by the time that we got back. Like many people who are fond of someone whom they've known since he was a boy, I see him sometimes through a double lens. Endearing child. Strong and decent man. He'll make his own decisions and his own plans for the future, and he'll do it at the time that's right for him. With Leonardo, as with others who were children when we met, but are not children now, I have to stop myself from time to time in order to remember this.

CHAPTER 8

Pineapple Comes of Age (Part One)

She was in kindergarten on the day we met when I walked into her classroom at P.S. 65. She was six, a bossy little person, slightly on the plumpish side, with carefully braided and brightly beaded cornrows hanging down across her eyes. She wrote her letters in reverse. Her teacher suggested I might try to help her figure out the way to get those symbols facing in the right direction.

But when I leaned across her shoulder to watch her shape her letters, she twisted around and looked at me with stern dissatisfaction. "You're standing on the wrong side," she instructed me and indicated that I ought to stand behind her other shoulder. Once I was standing over her left shoulder, she seemed to be entirely pleased, as if things now were as they ought to be.

We got to know each other very quickly because, at the end of school each day, she came to the afterschool at St. Ann's. So I'd see her sometimes in her class at P.S. 65 and then in the afternoon I would see her wave to me as she and her schoolmates raced into the basement of the church to have their snack before they went upstairs for their tutorial.

Her authoritative inclinations became increasingly robust with every passing year. By the time she was in third grade, she began expressing her displeasure at the nature of my social life—she knew I wasn't married and she tried to fix me up with Miss Gallombardo, a very pretty third-grade teacher at her school. Within another year, she began to comment on the suit that I'd been wearing ever since I met her. It was a black suit, a little on the formal side, from a store in Harvard Square, but she noticed it was kind of shabby and she made it obvious that this did not please her.

"Jonathan," she asked me once, "is that your only suit?"

"No," I said. "I have another suit." But I told her that the other one was virtually the same.

She reached out to finger the lapel the way my mother might have done when I was much younger. We were sitting opposite each other on two metal chairs, so that she was close enough to see the white threads showing through the fabric near the buttonholes and at the bottom edges of the sleeves.

"Jonathan," she said, folding her arms against her chest, as people do when they're sizing up a situation, "I'd like you to look more respectable."

Then, without the slightest hint of hesitation or any fear of impropriety in talking to a grown-up in this way: "Do me a favor. Someday, when you're over there, in Manhattan"—"over there" was a term she used to indicate a nicer part of town—"go into a good store and buy yourself a nice new suit. Will you promise me you'll do that?"

"Maybe," I replied.

A month later, I went to a clothing store in Boston and bought myself a suit I thought was quite respectable. The only problem, from Pineapple's point of view, was that the new suit was a black one, like the ones that I already had.

She sat me down for another conversation.

"Jonathan," she said, "I know that you get sad sometimes. I can tell when you come in." She put her hands on top of one of mine. "But you don't always need to dress in black. . . ."

Pineapple was in love with life. In spite of the ugliness of the building where she lived and the one in which she went to school, she had a buoyant and affirming personality. Even her most serious complaints were usually conveyed within a set of terms that were peevishly amusing rather than self-pitiful.

The problems at her school, however, were severe. P.S. 65, the same school Ariella's older boys had attended several years before, was almost always in a state of chaos because so many teachers did not stay for long. They'd often disappear in less than half a year, and there was a damaging reliance upon inexperienced and unprepared instructors. In Pineapple's second-grade year, twenty-eight of the fifty members of the faculty had never taught before, and half of them left the school by the next September. In her third- and fourth-grade years she had seven different teachers.

She wrote a little essay once describing those who came and went. One, she said, wasn't a real teacher, "only a helper-teacher"—presumably because she wasn't certified to teach but had nonetheless been thrown into Pineapple's class with nobody to guide her. Another was "a man who liked us," whose name, she said, was "Mr. Camel," but "he said he needed to earn money, so he found a better job. . . ." A third one, she said, "had a mental problem" and used offensive language in chastising the children. "Sit your A-S-S-E-S down," Pineapple quoted her, spelling out the word because she couldn't bring herself to say it. "And she had yellow teeth that looked like fangs. And so they fired her."

Instructional discontinuity was not the only major problem at the school. The overcrowding of the building and its archaic infrastructure did their damage to the children too. When I went to lunch one day with Pineapple's class, the students left their room at twelve-fifteen. But, because the lunchroom was already packed, they had to sit down in a hallway on the floor and wait for thirty minutes before they could file down a dark and narrow stairwell, with metal grating on the side, while another class was coming up the opposite direction. A mob scene developed at the bottom of the stairs. A school official started shouting at the children. Pineapple stuffed her fingers in her ears.

Once they were admitted to the basement cafeteria, they had to sit and wait another twenty minutes before the crowd thinned out enough for them to get something to eat. They were finished eating by around one-thirty, at which point a woman with a megaphone told them to get up and put away their trays. Then they had to go back to their tables and remain there, for no reason that I could discern, until they were at last released to go outside and run around the schoolyard—no grass, cracked cement—before they were herded back into the same filing process as before. At this point, a fire bell rang, so they stayed there frozen in their lines for fifteen minutes more. They were finally permitted to return to class at 2:00 p.m., nearly two hours since they'd filed out.

In the hour remaining before the end of school, I visited another class, then waited outside at dismissal time so I could walk Pineapple to St. Ann's. When she came out she asked if I would stop with her at an umbrella-covered stand on a corner opposite the school so we could enjoy one of her favorite treats (also mine), which the children called an "icie," coconut-flavored, creamy, and delicious, and then, in spite of all her discontents with school, she chattered gaily all the way down to the church.

The apartment building where Pineapple lived—part of the dangerous Diego-Beekman complex—was even less attractive than her school. When I visited her home she'd wait out front and lead me up the stairs. The elevator, which she almost never used, was pocked with bullet indentations because of the gang activity that took place in that building and the ones nearby. One night, when Pineapple was eight, helicopters swooped down, spotlights glaring in the windows of apartments. Seven men were led away in handcuffs from Pineapple's building, charged with selling crack cocaine and heroin.

Pineapple had two sisters. (A brother would be born a few years later.) The oldest was a serious girl named Lara who had a steady sense of sober judgment that Pineapple counted on for guidance. Her younger sister, whom I called Mosquito because she was tiny and seemed forever to be darting here and there in almost constant motion, was eight years old when Pineapple was ten.

As skittery and squirmy as she was when I got to know her, Mosquito soon developed into a quick-witted and perceptive little girl, with incisive verbal skills that often took her teachers by surprise. When she was in third grade, her teacher asked the class to write an essay on Cortez, Magellan, or de Soto. She narrowed it to Cortez and de Soto, then selected Cortez because, she told her teacher, "De Soto stole the Indians' gold, but Cortez stole my people's soul." I wasn't sure how she'd arrived at this distinction, but I was surprised she knew this much about de Soto or Cortez, because there was almost nothing of this nature in the books about "the great conquistadors" that children of her age were given at their school.

Pineapple's mother and father were from Guatemala. She and Lara liked to tell me stories about the people in their family who remained there. They also had many members of their family living near them in New York. I knew some of their cousins from the afterschool at St. Ann's Church and I'd met their mother, who was named Isabella, when I'd walked Pineapple home. But I didn't get to know their father and his brothers and their other relatives until an evening in December of Pineapple's fifth-grade year.

It was, to be precise, on December 31, 1999, when her father gave a party, as he did every year, mostly for their relatives, to celebrate the new year. Pineapple knew that I'd be in New York and apparently had told this to her father, who, she said, had told her I'd be "very welcome" at the party. It took arm-twisting on Pineapple's part to get me to say yes, because I don't go out to many parties (and Pineapple knew I didn't socialize a lot), but after she had asked me several times I agreed to come.

I had another obligation earlier that evening, so I didn't get there until late. It was close to midnight by the time Pineapple, who'd been watching for me from her window, came downstairs to let me in and lead me up to the apartment, which was packed from wall to wall with grown-ups and at least a dozen children, all of whom, she told me, were her cousins. Guatemalan music, which I'd never heard before, was playing in the living room. Guatemalan food was set out on a table. Her father, who was named Virgilio, greeted me enthusiastically, wished me a happy new year, and brought me to the kitchen, where he scooped up from a big glass bowl a rather potent Guatemalan drink made of mango juice and rum, after which he led me back into the other room to introduce me to his brothers and to Isabella's sister.

He told me he was teaching himself English and now and then would ask me if a word he used for something was the right one and would urge me to correct him when he got it wrong. He was a warm, expansive man, tall and slender, with his hair in dreadlocks. While I was standing with him and his older brother, he spoke to both of us in English as a matter of politeness. He'd reach out for my arm from time to time in order to be sure I felt included in the conversation.

Lara and Mosquito and their older cousin Madeline, whom I'd tutored when she was a nine-year-old, were in a bedroom with their mother in front of a TV set, waiting for the lighted ball to drop upon the stroke of midnight in Times Square. Their mother got up to welcome me. The rest of them were glued to the screen and, except for Lara, who gave me a little wave, paid me no attention until the ball had fallen and they all broke into cheers.

When we went back to the living room, the music had been turned up. Most of the children started dancing, girls with girls (the boys were bashful) or else with their parents. Pineapple asked if I could dance. I told her, "No!"—because I knew I was an awful dancer. But she and Madeline insisted that I try. So they took me by the hand and dragged me out into the middle of the room.

They made me dance with each of them in turn, and with their aunt, and finally with Lara. When the music ended temporarily, Pineapple told me, "You did good! You see? It isn't hard to learn. . . ." But my shirt by now had soaked through to the skin, so Virgilio gave me one of his long linen shirts, open-necked and comfortable, and insisted that I have another drink, which he said would help to cool me off.

Virgilio's older brother, whose name was Eliseo, was sitting in the kitchen with Pineapple's mother. Isabella noticed that I hadn't eaten yet, so she made a plate of food for me and, while I ate, Eliseo talked with me about his son, who was a teenager now but whom I remembered as a cheerful ten-year-old who'd been friendly to me when I first came to St. Ann's. He had started getting into trouble while he was in middle school and, by the time he went to high school, he'd begun to get involved with older boys who, his father feared, were using drugs or selling them. So Eliseo recently had sent him back to Guatemala, where he knew he would be physically secure and would be cared for by his relatives.

At the end of the evening, I had a quiet conversation with Pineapple's mother. She spoke to me, with Pineapple translating or paraphrasing for her—she did not know English yet—about her job as an afternoon and night attendant, taking care of children who had HIV. She also told me of her husband's job at a Manhattan restaurant—washing dishes in the basement, even though, according to Pineapple, he had been a chef and had run a restaurant in his town in Guatemala. Since her mother worked so late, Pineapple said, it was her father who often got them up and made their breakfast and sent them off to school with their books and backpacks, and made sure they had their homework papers.

Pineapple's parents recognized the serious deficiencies of P.S. 65. But their visits to the school and the questions they would ask were, her mother told me, repeatedly rebuffed by those in the office to whom they'd be referred when they sought a meeting with the principal. And because, English fluency apart, they were not familiar with the jargon and the acronymic phrases that were often thrown at parents by officials at the school, they came away most often with the sense that nothing that had worried them was likely to be changed.

This, at least, was the impression I received in those final moments in the kitchen with Pineapple's mother. But more important, when I thought back on that evening in Pineapple's home, was the recognition I had gained of the energy and joyfulness and collective reinforcement of her sense of affirmation that she was receiving from her par-

ents and their relatives. Amidst the grimness of the building
and the neighborhood around them, her mother and father
had created in their home an island of emotional security
and warm congeniality that any child, rich or poor, would
probably have envied. I hoped that this would prove to be a
bedrock of stability from which she'd be able to pursue the
opportunities that were now about to open up before her.

– II –

Pineapple's years at P.S. 65 were nearly at an end. During the spring, the pastor of St. Ann's began to probe the possibilities of winning her admission to a private day school
in New York to avoid the middle schools that had proven so
destructive to the adolescents in that neighborhood.

Martha talked with me at length before she did this.
She was somewhat torn in making the decision. Both of us
were strong supporters of the public schools—not of demor-
alizing places such as P.S. 65 and the local middle schools
but, on a larger level, of the whole idea of public education
as something that was elemental to American democracy.
Still, when a child, as in Pineapple's case, had been short-
changed so badly in her first six years of school, Martha
was not willing (nor was I) to let her be denied the opportunities that lay beyond the options the city had prescribed.

In reaching out to build support for programs at St.
Ann's, Martha had developed close affiliations with a number of the affluent and more progressive churches in New
York, some of which ran private schools, attended for the
most part by children of the privileged. One of these schools,
which was situated on the Upper West Side of Manhattan
and which had some dedication to the value of diversity in
class and racial terms, was willing to admit Pineapple and

provide her with a scholarship, even with the recognition that it would be hard for her to catch up with her peers.

"It will be a struggle," the principal advised me when, at Martha's urging, I got in contact with the school before Pineapple and her parents came to a decision. "But we like this little girl and we'd like to make this work if the child is willing." I shared this with Pineapple and her mom and dad and, because of what they knew by now about the local middle schools, they told me they were eager to move forward. Martha, as I recall, helped them to fill out the application.

Pineapple's acceptance at the school was conditioned on her willingness to repeat a grade because she was far below the academic level of the sixth-grade students at the school—and, as it turned out, below most of the fifth-grade students also. The run of transient teachers at P.S. 65 had done its greatest damage to her literacy skills, a degree of damage that she could not easily reverse even in a school that had the means to offer her the individual attention that had been impossible at P.S. 65.

In this respect, Pineapple's situation was entirely different from the one that Leonardo had confronted when he went to boarding school. For Leonardo, as we've seen, the transition had been easy. For Pineapple, everything from this point on would be an uphill climb.

As early as the winter of her first year at the school, her principal and teachers, in the letters and reports that they were sending on to me, noted that the difficulties Pineapple was facing went beyond her deficient writing skills and reading comprehension. They also recognized that she had never learned the whole array of study-skills that students who had had the benefit of reputable elementary education had mastered long before.

Many students at the school had been there since their kindergarten year, and quite a few, when they entered, had already had as many as three years of preschool education in one or another of those rich developmental programs that were known to upper-class New Yorkers as "the baby ivies." So, in this respect as well, Pineapple found herself competing on a playing field in which the odds were rigged against a child of her background from the very start.

Her science teacher noted that, while he had given her an honors grade for class participation and for laboratory work, her final grade for fall semester was an Incomplete because she didn't take a make-up for a test that she had failed and then missed a more decisive test during the marking period. He added, however, that her oral presentations frequently were very good and he said he was convinced that, in the second term, she would progress more rapidly. In math and English, her grades at the first marking period were also in the failing range, but here again her teachers said that they were hopeful she would pass both courses by the end of spring semester.

Her social studies teacher, on the other hand, was more censorious and less optimistic. On the basis of a stern report she wrote about Pineapple in December, she struck me as a person of unusual rigidity who seemed to be unwilling to make any alterations in some hopelessly outdated lesson plans in order to adapt to the social differences among the children in her class. Pineapple, she said in one of her more annoying observations, "was perfectly capable of writing journal entries from the perspective of a Medieval noblewoman," which was the topic she had been assigned. "She made one or two attempts, then gave it up entirely." It came into my mind that Pineapple might have shown more zest for this assignment if she'd been allowed to write, not from the perspective of the noblewoman, but from that of somebody who had to wait upon the noble-woman—which I thought, given the subservient positions that her mother and so many other women in the South Bronx had to fill, might have had more meaning for her and perhaps elicited some of that spiky sense of "where it's at" that might make her entries in a journal actually quite interesting.

The principal noted, nonetheless, that "socially, she is much beloved, especially by younger students. I love her. And most of her teachers do." As spring arrived, she suggested that tutorials during the summer months with a member of the faculty might be a good idea and asked if I could help to underwrite this.

The teacher who took on this job told me at the start of August that Pineapple had been working hard and had made up most of a year's work in science by that time and was getting better at note-taking in her other subjects. ("Note-taking is hard for her, because her spelling is so poor. It also seems that she was given almost no instruction about punctuation in her elementary years. We've made up for some of this. . . .")

August 9: "Last week was a good one. We worked on syntax. Also run-on sentences. She's learning how to break them up and punctuate effectively. One problem: She sometimes doesn't bother to complete a sentence and answers an assignment only in word fragments. She's also frequently misreading words of similar configuration ('confidence' for 'conference,' for example). We need to do more work on that in our next few sessions. . . ."

August 30: "I think she's made good progress. She's been cooperative and has frequently surprised herself when she's come upon a complicated word she says she's never seen before but has decoded it successfully. All in all, I'm feeling very positive."

Her progress remained gradual that year and the next. "It's still tough," she told me in the winter of her third year at the school, "but my teachers say I'm doing better." And, although she had to struggle even harder in the year that followed—at times, the gains that she was making would come nearly to a standstill as the subject matter in her eighth-grade classes became increasingly complex—she continued moving, almost imperceptibly, closer to grade level.

She had only one complaint about the students at the school. Some of the wealthier girls, she said "stick together all the time. You know, like they're better than the rest of us?" But, she added, there were others "who try to be nice to me." In the spring of that year, one of her classmates asked her to a weekend birthday party at her family's country house. Pineapple was astounded when she and two other girls were picked up in Manhattan in a helicopter.

"Wow!" she said. "I've never seen a house as big as that before." But she said that she enjoyed the party, and all the girls were given presents by her schoolmate's parents.

The school, regrettably, had no upper level. It ended in eighth grade. At that point, the pastor once again began exploring private schools with which she was familiar in order that Pineapple would not lose the gains she'd made and would get the further preparation she would need if she were to realize what was now her stated goal of going on to college—the same goal that her classmates for the past four years regarded as a normal expectation.

Here, once again, Martha's well-developed gift for reaching out to institutions that professed to have a deep commitment to inclusiveness turned out to be essential. An excellent school, not in New York but, as it happened, in Rhode Island, where a group of charitable people had come to know Pineapple in the course of volunteer work they'd been doing at St. Ann's, accepted her enthusiastically and provided nearly a full scholarship to pay for her tuition. An Episcopal church, affiliated with the school, raised extra funds to cover costs that weren't included in the scholarship.

Pineapple knew she'd miss her parents and her sisters—and her little brother, who was three years old by now—but she became excited about going to the school after she had visited and met some of its teachers and seen its lovely campus, which was in a town not far from Providence. Although the school was rigorous in academic terms, it was less internally competitive than what she had been used to in New York. The demographics of the school were also more diverse—"majority white," Pineapple told me, "many Asian, many black, some Hispanic, and some who are 'combinations.'"

She entered the school in 2004 and felt at home there from the start. The white girls in her class, some of whom were wealthy but not at the stratospheric level of so many of her classmates in New York, did not, she told me, "go around in cliques together. It's a different kind of school. Everybody here is nice to one another. It's like—you know?—we all accept each other."

She did confess she missed her family, as she had expected. "I've never been away from home before," she told me in the winter. "So I've had to learn how to adapt to that." But she said with pride that, even though her grades were "you know? not so good?" she didn't flunk any of her courses in the first semester; and she did much better in the one that followed.

One of the special virtues of this school was its quick responsiveness to difficulties students might encounter at the start of a new course or at the introduction of new subject matter in a given course. When she ran into problems, teachers did not wait until she had received a crushing set of grades but intervened before she had to undergo that blow to her self-confidence. "They'd say, 'I'll help you. You come in.' And I'd go in. And right away, they'd sit you down and show you something you were doing wrong. And it was like they knew how to 'unblock' you. And they'd kind of hold your hand until they knew you got the point. And then I'd move right on. . . ."

By her second year, her reading comprehension had "skyrocketed"—that was her English teacher's term—but, with the volume of material her classes were assigned to read, keeping up with those assignments, said the teacher, wasn't easy for her. By this time, however, she'd developed strong attachments to her teachers. She listed several that she said she "liked really a lot." All but one were women. One of them, she said, "is very young and she lives on campus and she helps me to correct my papers, but she doesn't keep reminding me when I have something due. She makes me remind *myself.* If I don't, she says she isn't going to pass me.

"When I talk with her at night? It's not about my work. It's completely different. She's not strict with me at all. She's like a big sister."

In academic terms, that second year became the breakthrough year. Still struggling to perfect her writing skills and needing to read more each night than she'd ever had to read before, still missing deadlines on her class assignments more often than she should, she nonetheless appeared to have emerged from any last remaining doubts as to whether she would meet the school's prerequisites for graduation. "It was that year," she told me, looking back upon this later, "that I knew for sure that I could do it and that I'd be going on to college."

Throughout this time, her older sister, Lara, was in the New York City schools, where she'd been enticed into the same middle school, the same pretended "school for medical careers," that Lisette, Vicky's daughter, had attended also.

I was relieved when a teacher at the school who was impressed by Lara's eagerness to learn made contact with me on his own and told me he believed that he could find the time to give her extra help in order to make up for the historic failings of a school he was too honest to romanticize. Lara had escaped the run of short-term teachers and ensuing chaos that Pineapple's class had undergone at P.S. 65. Her basic skills were well intact; so, with the tutorial assistance provided by her teacher, she managed to get out of middle school with creditable grades.

In high school she again attracted the attention of an empathetic teacher who singled her out as a potential candidate for college. She later told me how important this had been, because the school, as she put it bluntly, was "not a very good one." It was one of the newest generation of heavily promoted but unsuccessful "niche academies," targeted at kids of color, that allegedly had found a way, in the unconvincing jargon that continues to be used today, "to break the mold" of failing schools and, again in the vocabulary more or less expected of administrators in the urban schools, "turn it all around."

If anyone had actually turned this school around, it had not been in a good direction. "We started," Lara told me, "with sixty students in my ninth-grade class. Only twenty of them graduated," she recalled—"and only ten of them deserved to."

Lara had been looking at college options in New York but, by the spring, she told me she'd decided to attend a college in Rhode Island so that she'd be near her younger sister. Pineapple had been on her own for two years by this time. Now, at last, the two would be together.

Lara was awarded a financial package by the college, and the people at the church who had helped to meet Pineapple's costs provided help to her as well. Still, she had to take on a substantial workload to earn enough to meet her personal expenses. Both Lara and Pineapple had to work during the summers too. Neither girl expected to be given a free ride. They also liked the sense of independence it afforded them to be earning money on their own.

At the end of Lara's freshman year in college and Pineapple's junior year at boarding school, I got a startling and excited phone call from Pineapple.

"Guess what?" she said. "My mother and father are moving to Rhode Island!" Her parents, she explained, after having been there several times to visit her, and now with Lara living there as well, had come to the decision to follow them out of New York and look for a home they could afford close to the town in which Pineapple went to school. "Jonathan! They're really going to do it!" said Pineapple.

Things moved quickly after that. In a letter Lara sent me only a month later, she told me they had found a house and that the people from the church had "helped my mother find a job." Her father, she said, had found one on his own.

Isabella's job was in a local nursing home, caring for the elderly. Virgilio talked his way into a culinary job at one of the best hotels in Providence. His experience in cooking at a restaurant in Guatemala was not discounted this time, as had been the case when he was working in New York. The position he was given, as best I understood, was something on the order of a sous-chef in the hotel's dining room.

The modest home Pineapple's parents found was in a waterside community where their backyard faced directly on a walkway, bordered by a biking path, and was just adjacent to a wooden footbridge that crossed a channel leading to the ocean. Mosquito was admitted to the school Pineapple was attending. When he was old enough, their little brother, Miguel, was admitted there as well.

Happily, the distance between Rhode Island and New York was short enough for members of their family to come up and visit them on a routine basis. They'd usually come in Eliseo's van, since he was the only family member who could afford a car. He shared it sometimes with Pineapple's

father, who had obtained a driver's license shortly after coming to New York. As a result, the bond between the children
and their New York relatives continued to be strong.

Pineapple moved in with her family for her senior year.
Academically, things never became easy for her, even at a
school that did so much to bring her up to pace with other
students in her class. But there was no question in her teachers' minds that she would complete her studies in good
order. And, while her grade-point average in the spring
semester of that final year was not as high as she would
have liked, she did get honors grades in two of her five subjects and passed the others with two C's and one B-minus.

Her graduation was a joyful day. A good-sized delega-
tion from the family in New York drove up to the school to
watch her walk across the stage and be handed her diploma.
Afterwards, her parents had a party in their yard, as they
did every time one of their children had achieved a victory
they'd hoped for. According to her father, she was just the
second person in their family (Lara was the first) to graduate from high school.

Three months later, she would be in college.

— III —

Pineapple had gone on college tours with members of
her class. But she had done this dutifully, in order not to be
dismissive of all possibilities, because she had already settled on the college Lara had selected two years earlier. She
had friends there among Lara's classmates. More important, she would have her sister there when she felt the need
for someone to confide in.

Each of them, however, had made divergent choices
when it came to fields of concentration. Lara had begun her

first year as an education major, then switched to "English Lit and Writing" and, she said, "I'm glad I did because I'm reading so much stuff I really love that I never would have had the time to read if I'd stayed on in the program for certification." Pineapple, on the other hand, decided upon social work and she never wavered from this plan throughout the years of college.

Her first semesters were more challenging for her than I think she had expected. She failed two courses, one of them a science class, because she said she didn't realize, when she chose it, that it was "way, way too advanced for me" and there was a basic course she should have taken first. "Bio-science. . . . I didn't transfer out in time."

Still, she was by no means drowning or demoralized. Her letters and phone calls were mostly optimistic, sparked with funny anecdotes and interesting insights into the dynamics of relationships among the different ethnic groups within the student body. In the spring, for instance, when she took a course in urban studies, she told me something that she said surprised her—"and, to tell the truth, it kind of annoys me"—about the way the other students, who were mostly white, tended to defer to her when it came to questions about race.

"Every time something comes up in the class about the inner cities? You know? About the kids who live there? And the problems of their parents? And the schools they go to? And, you know, the bad stuff people think that everyone gets into? It seems like all the white kids in the class turn around and look at me before they give an answer. It's like they want to check things out with me, to ask for my permission. I tell them, 'Go ahead, girl! Speak your mind! If I think you've got it wrong, I'll *tell* you.'"

I was glad that her straightforward and ebullient style hadn't been diminished too much by the struggles she'd been through while she'd been at prep school. I had the impression that her confidence to say what she believed had been eclipsed to a degree during those secondary years. Now, it seemed, her likable impertinence, although with more discretion and maturity, was flourishing once more.

Still, I knew she had her insecurities. In a letter I received in the year that followed from a woman who emerged as one of the most consistently supportive friends and allies to Pineapple and her sisters, she wrote these words: "Brave fronts, soft souls." She was referring to the fortitude the girls displayed when, in Pineapple's second year of college, her parents were confronted with a difficult dilemma that would force the girls to summon up a greater sense of self-reliance than had been required of them in the past. (I will return to that dilemma shortly.)

But the "soft soul," in Pineapple's case at least—an ever-present recognition of her vulnerable status as a student, a quiet understanding of her family's ultimate dependence on the loyalty, and *continuity* of loyalty, of those in Rhode Island who had been there from the start in the role of their defenders—this, along with an inherent tenderness of character, easily wounded sensibilities, emotions that were far more fragile than she would allow the world to see, were always there, as she would confide to me a little later on, just beneath the surface of audacity.

CHAPTER 9

Pineapple in All Her Glory (And Still Bossing Me Around)

On September 5, 2009, I was in Washington National Airport waiting for a plane to Boston.

Text message on my cell: "Happy birthday, Jonathan! Hope you weren't too lonely, far away from home. Miss you a lot. College starts in ten more days. Talk soon. XOXOXOX, Pineapple."

Two weeks later: an e-mail from Pineapple. "Hey Jonathan! Back at college. Here are the classes that I'm taking this semester. Anthropology (Non-western Worlds). We're studying Nigeria and its different cultures. Also taking Intro to Psychology and in this class I'm learning of the workings of the mind and our behaviors. I'm also in a dance class, which I'd like to say is just because I need a daily workout. And I'm in a singing class to improve my voice. I also have an English class, plus tutorial in writing since you know that this has been my weakness.

"I want to thank you and your assistant for sending

me a laptop. I'm able now to type my papers on my own time and not have to count on the computers in the library, which closes way too early. . . ."

September 30: "Hey Jonathan! I heard you're coming to Rhode Island next month for a lecture. Can we do lunch while you're here?"

October 20: She and Lara met me in the lobby of a much-too-fancy old hotel where my hosts in Providence had put me up the night before. I found them sitting on a sofa near the registration desk, looking around them at the huge bouquets of flowers on the tables and an imposing chandelier that hung down from the ceiling.

The hotel had a dining room, a little on the formal side, with dark wood panels and deep leather chairs; but it wasn't crowded and the waitress led us to a semiprivate booth that looked out on a courtyard. I worried that the two of them, whose financial situation didn't ordinarily allow them many luxuries, might feel ill at ease in this elaborate setting; but this was a needless worry. They seemed relaxed and comfortable and were looking through their menus before I opened mine.

They ordered shrimp and scallops with linguine. When the waitress asked what they would like to drink, they asked for passion fruit and mango juice with lime, which sounded awfully sweet to me but which Lara recommended, so I ordered it as well.

They asked me if I liked it.

"Very good. Something new to me," I said.

"It's good for you to try new things," Pineapple said.

At one moment during lunch she noticed that there was an ink stain on my shirt where I'd put a black pen in my pocket, but without the top attached. She leaned across the table so that she could take the fabric in her hands. "It's going to be hard to get that out. You need to be more careful."

After we'd eaten, we stayed there for an hour. It turned out they had waited until now to bring up something serious that was weighing on their minds. Pineapple told me that the immigration service, for reasons neither of them knew, had denied their father's application for renewal of his green card. If this ruling couldn't be reversed, it would terminate his status as a legal immigrant. A lawyer in Providence was helping him to file an appeal.

In the interim, he could not continue working in the restaurant of the hotel, which could no longer legally employ him. Compounding the difficulties that the family now would face, their mother had been laid off from the job she had enjoyed, working with the elderly, and had since been working as a housekeeper at one of the chain motels.

"She's struggling," Lara said. "She's on her knees, scrubbing floors, working full-time-plus." This was all the harder, she explained, because her mother, although she was only forty-two, had premature arthritis. "She can barely make a fist, but the hotel has this rule. You're not allowed to use a mop to clean the floors. You have to get down on your knees and scrub the bathroom tiles with a cloth." Her mother, she said, was also getting stomach pains and headaches, which may have been occasioned by her nervousness about their father's situation.

Both girls told me they were praying for their mother and their father. Both said they believed in God, but, as they explained this, in rather different ways. Lara said that she considered herself Catholic, but she added that she had no close attachment to "any special church" and went to "different churches" with her friends from college. She hadn't found one yet "that fits with my beliefs, where I feel that I belong."

Pineapple did not go to church at all. She told me that she prayed but did not believe in God "as somebody like Jesus—I mean, like a person"—but as "something like a power," "something good," "something that protects you and looks over you." She said that when she spoke of God, however, "I keep on saying 'him' or 'he'—you know? As if it was my father or grandfather."

They had to leave at 3:00 p.m. because Pineapple had a seminar at four. Lara decided they should take a taxi in order to be sure Pineapple wasn't late for class. The doorman stepped out on the street and whistled at the line of cabs. Before I could think of it, Lara handed him a tip. "Thank you for lunch," Pineapple said. Poised and polite, they got into the taxi and headed back to school.

Virgilio's attorney, as I had expected, had no success with his appeal. Pineapple told me, just before Thanksgiving, that he would be leaving in another week to return to Guatemala. Their mother would remain behind to provide a home for Miguel and Mosquito. She and Lara, living in their college dorms, would carry on as they had done before. Their tuition, room and board, and related college costs would continue to be met by their financial packages and the help they were receiving from the people at the church. And they still were earning money from the jobs they did under their work-study grants, some of which they said that they would try to use to help their mother.

If their mother should decide at a later time to follow her husband back to Guatemala, Lara and Pineapple said they had found out they could be their brother's legal guardians, if their parents would agree, so that he could keep on at his school here in Rhode Island. Lara was in her senior year and would graduate in the spring. She wanted to go on and obtain a graduate degree in order to be certified as a classroom teacher. "But if it's just impossible," she said, "I would put it off a year, or maybe two years, so that I could work full-time" and earn enough to function as a back-up for the other members of the family.

After Virgilio left for Guatemala, Pineapple told me that he phoned them or their mother almost every night. Even at a distance, his affectionate protectiveness continued to be comforting, a steady source of consolation for the miles and the border that divided them. Some of the people in Rhode Island, nonetheless, were very harsh in speaking of Virgilio, according to Pineapple. They had not believed him when he said his green card had been non-renewed, or else condemned him retroactively for not taking measures to prevent its cancellation, which they regarded as an indication that he was neglectful in caring for his family.

Pineapple and Lara defended him with fierceness. Lara made the observation that many otherwise enlightened people in the white community tended to be sympathetic to the mothers of black and Hispanic children, but looked upon the fathers, almost automatically, through a lens of stereotype, as lacking in responsibility. These assumptions, Lara said, according to a book she'd read the year before, "have deep roots in history."

February 21, 2010: Mosquito, who was in her final year of high school and would graduate in May in almost the same week as Lara's college graduation, sent me an e-mail about the college that she planned to go to. She had been awarded a financial package of $40,000 by a private college in Connecticut of which I knew very little other than the fact that it was widely known for its athletic programs, but less so, as a friend informed me, for its purely academic offerings.

I wrote to her, "I know I have no right butting in," but I said that, with her nearly perfect academic record, I thought she ought to think this through a little more before she came to a decision.

She replied the next day, "You have every right to butt in, but this is the school I want to go to. They have a department of criminal justice, which is very good and is what I plan to major in. Also, if you're doing studies in the honors program, you get to work with teachers in tutorial relationships, which is something that I like because it's not impersonal. I feel the school fits perfectly with my ambitions and I've been there and love everything about it."

Good, I thought! She knows exactly what she wants. She told me that she wasn't angry with me for intruding. "I know," she said, "you only wanted what you thought was best for me. . . ."

Pineapple wrote to me at the start of April: "Heyyyy Jonathan!! I did not forget you. I'm a little stressed because I'm taking harder classes this semester. Sociology 208. Math 139. Allied Studies, which is s'posed to help me to stay organized. English 100. History of Greece and Rome and the rest of Europe up to something like the Middle Ages. . . . Doing well, but hoping to do better."

She told me Lara's graduation was coming up in May— "May 22," she said.

A month later she reminded me again about the graduation. "We're going to have a barbecue in the afternoon. Starts at two. I hope that you can come. XOXOXOX, Pineapple."

I had to be in Boston the morning of the graduation, so I drove directly to their home and ended up arriving early for the party in the afternoon. There were only about a dozen people who'd arrived before me, relatives who'd driven up with Pineapple's uncle from New York the night before, and a few of Lara's closest friends who were in the kitchen with her mother.

The big surprise for me (Pineapple purposely had not told me to expect this) was that Virgilio was there. He was in the backyard setting up the barbecue when I came up the driveway. He gave me a hug and a terrific smile, like someone who had just performed a magic trick, outwitting all the forces of the immigration service that had kept him from his children. He took off the long white apron he was wearing and we sat together at a table in a corner of the garden so he could explain to me how he had been able to get across the border, and across the country, without any papers.

He had come across the border from Mexico to Arizona, not far from Nogales—not at the legal crossing point but at another spot where people crossed at night illegally. From there, he took a bus to San Diego, where he used his U.S. driver's license to get on a plane for New York City, and then drove here to Rhode Island in a rental car so that he'd arrive before his relatives. In spite of all the condemnation he'd incurred from his critics in Rhode Island who persisted in believing that he'd left his family of his own volition, with the implication that he was deficient in his love for his own children, he had been prepared to undergo arrest—or, given the vigilante atmosphere along the Arizona border, even greater dangers—in order to attend his daughter's graduation.

He said that he intended to remain until he could learn more about the reasons for Isabella's headaches and her worsening arthritis, and then figure out the implications for the children if Isabella did decide, which he said was still uncertain, to return with him to Guatemala. He was less concerned about the girls, who, he knew, were capable of handling themselves in their parents' absence since they'd have each other to rely upon, than he was about their brother.

He didn't want to interrupt the schooling Miguel was receiving but he also said that he did not believe a child who was only ten was old enough to live without his mother. In regard to Lara's and Pineapple's wish to keep him here and function as his guardians, Virgilio, speaking in his measured English syllables, questioned whether they were truly able to assume so much responsibility. As mature as they appeared—and, in the case of Lara, as judicious in her thinking as he considered her to be—he said he wasn't confident that they could fill a parent's role or whether it was fair for him to let them even try to take on that position.

The more he spoke, the more I sensed how carefully and searchingly he'd been thinking through a set of questions he could not resolve but which saddened him tremendously. He reached out and put his hand around my arm and pressed it hard—his hand was strong—and when he spoke about Miguel, I could see his eyes were glistening slightly. It seemed as if he hoped I might have the right advice. But I did not, because I'd never faced a situation like this in the past. I was ashamed of the United States for placing any father in this situation and for the rigidity of policies that would penalize a child, only ten years old, born here in our nation and a citizen by right, by rendering his father an illegal.

— II —

Pineapple stepped out on the porch. Seeing that her father had begun to start the barbecue, she came across the yard and sat down at the table. I asked if she would like to stay outside and talk with me a while until the other guests, most of whom were Lara's friends, had started to arrive.

"I'm in the mood to walk," she said. "Would that be okay with you?"

I said that I'd enjoy that too.

There was, as I've said, a biking trail that started just beyond the garden. So we went off along the path and soon came to the wooden bridge that crossed a broad expanse of water. Families were fishing from the bridge. Young people pedaled past. Older folks were strolling with their children or grandchildren.

"If we walk a little ways, there's a place where we can get a lemonade, or lemon ices, if you want."

"Would you like one?"

"Yes," she said.

I asked if they were like the "icies" that we used to get when she came out of school in the South Bronx.

"Not exactly," she replied. "More like frozen lemonade."

"Can you get *real* icies anywhere in town?"

"Coconut icies?"

"Yes," I said.

"They're real hard to find. They do have them, but not in this part of town. They sell them in *some* neighborhoods. . . ."

The shop where they sold lemonade and lemon ices was, I soon discovered, a good distance from her home. I asked her if she minded if we stopped and rested on one of the benches by the path.

"Jonathan, we can turn back anytime you want. I don't want you getting overheated."

I assured her I was fine.

Pineapple had told me, back in early April, that she had been feeling "stressed" because she was taking harder courses than the year before. While we sat there resting in the shade, I asked her if she'd fill me in some more.

The truth, she said, now that I raised the point, was not so much the difficulty of the work. "The problem is I'm still not organized—you know? The way I need to be?" And she gave me an example of something she had done at the start of the semester, which, however, I was glad to see that she reported, even at her own expense, with a sense of humor.

"I came into one of my classes on the first day of the term and after I'd been sitting there for maybe fifteen minutes I looked around the classroom at the other students and I said to myself, 'These are the wrong students. I know it's my professor but it isn't the right class.'"

"What did the professor say?"

"He didn't say a word."

Finally, she said, "I just got up and took my books and I started heading for the door. When the teacher saw me leaving, he began to smile. He knew I had my schedule wrong.

"I said, 'Oops! Right teacher—wrong class!'"

"He thought that it was funny, since I did exactly the same thing the first semester—and with the same professor!"

"Did you feel embarrassed?"

"Nope!" she said. "I just told myself: 'You still have a ways to go before this part up here'"—she pointed to her forehead—"'learns to get you where you're s'posed to go and when you're s'posed to be there.'"

We headed onward to the store to get our lemon ices, which had lime in them, with pulp, and were cool and tasty. As we were walking back, she told me more about the situation with her family. Her mother, she said, had made a definite decision. "She's made her plans. She's going back to Guatemala by the end of June."

"Is Miguel going with her?"

"Yes," she said.

I told her that her father didn't say that it was settled yet, but she said, "It's settled for my mother. She wants my brother with her."

According to the plan she and her sisters had been making, "we'll be moving out of here and looking for a less expensive place where we can live, probably one closer to my college." All three of them were going to get summer jobs, as she and Lara had been doing all along, which would help with moving costs and with the rent deposit and fixing up the new apartment. "It's important to us. We need to stay together as a family. Where there's a will . . . , we've always found the will before. We've been doing it a long time now."

I told her that I wondered whether all of this was going to distract her from her studies. But she was not concerned by this. "I've struggled for so many years nothing's going to stop me now unless I get sick and die."

We stopped again on the way back, maybe a quarter-mile from her home, and sat in the shade again and watched a freighter moving very slowly toward the ocean. The setting was so pleasant and, despite the news that she had given me, she seemed so much at ease, so utterly serene and happy, that I asked her if she'd ever felt the same kind of serenity when she was living in New York.

"Truthfully? Some of the time I did," she said. "Not at P.S. 65, but when I was with my friends, or at home, or at St. Ann's. I was happy most of the time. A lot of things breezed past me.

"The only times that I got scared were, you know, if there was a shooting? Something like that? Something that was dangerous? I don't think I ever told you that Mosquito once was shot. It happened in our courtyard."

"I didn't know that."

"Yes," she said. "It wasn't with a bullet. It was from a BB gun. They shot her in the eye. She still has the mark there."

"Do you know who did it?"

"It was just a boy is all I know."

"Did he mean to do it? Or was it an accident?"

"Probably an accident. She had just come home from school and was almost at our door. You remember where we lived?"

"Yes, I do."

"And these boys, we didn't know their names or who they were. They were up there on the roof. She didn't feel the pain at first. All she felt was something warm coming down her face. When she put her hand up it was blood. It was coming out right here, just underneath the corner of her eye.

"She had to have surgery. They had to cut it out of her. That's why she has that scar. So that's one thing that scared me. . . .

"But there were shootings all the time—I mean, with *real* bullets—when I was that age. All the way along our street from St. Ann's up to Cypress Ave, right next to the school. It didn't really get to me until they hurt my sister.

"You see, back then, I guess I thought that this was normal because it was all I knew. I had nothing to compare it to. I didn't know when I was ten that it wasn't like this for most other children. I didn't start to think about this kind of thing until I was older, when I went to private school.

"Now I understand it more because I've seen it from both sides and I've read a lot of stuff and I talk about it with my sisters. We understand there needs to be a whole lot of improvement. But for that to happen, other things, *bigger* things, would have to happen first. The entire attitude of white superiority would have to be attacked. You would have to start again from scratch."

"Meaning what?"

"Meaning—when you go into an inner-city school, you see so many children in a class that some of them don't even have a textbook? Or, like me at P.S. 65, you're not allowed to take your textbook home to do your lessons or to study for exams? Meaning books should be distributed more fairly. Meaning schools should look like schools and not like jails and not be smelly places like the one I had to go to. Meaning inner cities should not have been built and need to be eliminated. That's what I mean by 'scratch.'"

I thought to myself: "The entire attitude of white superiority would have to be attacked"!! She was still so very

sweet and innocent in almost every way. But she was looking back upon her own experience with a new perspective
now. She had been immersed in questions about politics
in her college classes. One of her teachers in a course on
sociology—"an African-American, a woman who I love,"
she said—"was really smart about this stuff."

But more important, certainly, as she'd pointed out,
was that she'd been living now for several years in a place
and a milieu so different from the one in which she spent her
childhood. She saw the world through different eyes and,
when she spoke to me about these matters now, there was
an assertiveness and sharpness in her choice of words I had
never heard her use in speaking about anything that went
beyond the personal. The bluntness that was very much a
part of her delightful personality when she was a little girl,
as in her criticism of the clothes I wore, had by no means
disappeared, but it was directed more and more to matters
that went far beyond her own amusements and concerns.

As we sat there on the bench, it occurred to me to ask
her something I'd been asking other students of her age
since Barack Obama was elected in 2008. I started to say,
"Now we have a president—" but she cut me off—"who,"
she said, knowing right away where I must be heading,
"happens to be black."

"Doesn't that mean *something* might be going on? Something in that 'attitude of white superiority'? You don't think
it's changing?"

"Not really," she replied.

"You don't think it means we're getting closer to a point
where we can start to find solutions to at least a couple of
the problems you described?"

"Nope," she said. "Because that's not the reason we
elected him. And if he did the things he should, a lot of
people who elected him, from what I understand, wouldn't
be behind him anymore. A lot of people aren't behind him

even now, and he hasn't done a thing that I can see that will make a difference to poor children and the schools we have to go to and the places where they almost always put us, you know, in the neighborhoods, not just in New York. . . ."

Once she got her teeth into a big and meaty chunk of obvious injustice she'd experienced first-hand, Pineapple clearly wasn't going to hold back. "President Obama didn't have to go to inner-city schools. You know? Where everyone is poor? And everyone's Hispanic or everybody's black? Why does he think it's good enough for other kids, like children in the Bronx?"

Hearing the indignation in her voice, I was reminded of other students I had known—black and Latino students mostly, but conscientious young white people too—who became so wrathful or seemed to be so overwhelmed by the sheer dimensions of the problems they perceived that they tended to give up on many good and useful things they could have done right here and now within the social system as it stands. I recalled a piece of practical advice and helpful exhortation I had heard from someone older than myself some years before: "Look for battles big enough to matter but, at the same time, small enough to win some realistic victories."

"Oooh! I like that!" she replied when I said it to her, and she asked if I would write it down before I left, which I promised I would do.

"You see? That's the whole thing that's been in my mind. That's why I'm sticking to my social work," she said. "I'm going to do whatever I can with my own two hands. Comfort people after something has gone wrong. Help them when they've made mistakes. Help them make decisions that they won't regret. . . .

"I was given so much help when I came here to Rhode Island. One person in particular"—I think it was the teacher that she liked, the young woman who had lived on campus at her school—"made a gigantic difference in my life. Now I want to be that person in another student's life. That's the reason why I picked my major. That's what keeps me going, you know? Even when I make some of the dumb mistakes I make? It's my way of paying back."

I asked her if she'd given any thought up to this time as to where she'd like to work.

"I want to say I'd like to do it in New York, most likely in the Bronx. I think that's where they need it most. But I'm still nowheres near to being sure. I haven't seen the worst of the United States. Well, I don't *know*. I've never lived in any place except New York and here. I'd have to go and look around before I could decide. . . .

"There's one more thing I'd like to say. I've talked about this with my sisters too, and I know that they agree with me. I believe we have a major disadvantage—'we' as in minorities—because we start our lives in debt. And we dig a bigger hole if we stay in college long enough to graduate.

"Like—my parents had no money? So they couldn't help me. Other people helped me, but I know that I'll be starting my career with heavy bills I'll have to pay long after I get out of school. Some kids at my college? Their parents have so much that they don't even need financial aid and don't have to borrow for tuition. So they're starting out a big, big step ahead of me.

"And I think I ought to say it isn't just minorities. So I should correct myself. It's everyone who's very poor and wants to get a college education. And I think the president should change that."

"Do you think he will?"

"Nope," she said. "I just want to say I think he *ought* to."

A boy in a biking helmet pedaled past us very fast. A group of younger children—it seemed as if Pineapple knew them—waved at us and stopped to say hello. The sun was hot, reflecting on the water.

She asked if I was hungry.

"Yes," I said.

"I am, too."

"That walk was longer than we planned."

"It was a good one though," she said. "I'm glad we had this chance to talk. We've never had a talk like this before. . . . Tell me the truth. Were you surprised by what I said?"

"Only a tiny bit," I replied. "Well, actually, *more* than a tiny bit! It's because, when we're having fun together, I still think of you as someone very young."

"I *am* young!" Pineapple said. "Well, you know, compared to you!" Then: "Whoops! That didn't come out like I meant."

"It's okay," I said. "I *am* old compared to you."

But she felt bad at what she'd said. "Jonathan, remember this. If you ever tell me that you need me, I'll be there beside you in a heartbeat. Even when you're really old? Don't forget. You'll never be more than a cell-phone call away from me."

She gave my hand a little pat. Then we got up and went back to the party.

On May 30, there was a text message from Pineapple on my phone: "My mother's going back to Guatemala with my father in three weeks. My brother will go with them. More later. Talk soon. Luv, P."

Ten days later, the pieces of a new arrangement of the children's lives were falling into place. The house by the water was going to be vacated by the end of June. They were planning to move into Providence, where they would live together in the year ahead, so Pineapple wouldn't need to pay for room and board at college anymore. Mosquito would be there with them until the end of summer and then come and stay with them on holidays and weekends once the school year had begun.

Before their parents left, however, there was one last confrontation between their father and one of the people who continued to distrust him.

The altercation took place at Mosquito's graduation, which followed Lara's party by only a few weeks. One of the women who disliked her father, Pineapple reported, stopped him in his tracks close to the commencement stage after graduation, where he had been chatting with the parents of Mosquito's friends.

"I could tell she was going to upset him. I was standing next to him. She told him that he wasn't a good father because he was 'abandoning' his children, and when he tried to answer her, he began to stutter and I saw that he was trembling. We tried to get away from her, but she kept right on and followed us until we got into the car.

"As soon as we got home he went into his bedroom. He was sitting on the bed with his hands over his eyes and he was still trembling. We could see that he was crying. He kept repeating what the woman said to him, that he wasn't a good father. We told him, 'No. It isn't true. We love you.' But he kept on crying."

In her recollection of this incident, which she didn't talk about until her parents and her brother had gone back to Guatemala, she went into detail to explain to me why she looked upon her father as a man of dignity who would never willingly have done harm to his children. "Since they've been gone he's spoken to us almost every night. He taught himself to work on a computer, so we can see each other when we talk. The only nights that we don't talk are when they have a bad storm, because it's the rainy season down in Guatemala now and when it's raining very hard there's no electric power in the town."

She also said that, in the years when they were living in

the Bronx, her father periodically went back to Guatemala because "he needed to check up on a house that still belongs to us." Every time one of the children had been born, she said, he would scrape together all the money that he had to buy them each a plot of land adjacent to the house, "so each of us would know we had a little piece of something of our own. Something to connect us. . . . So, if we ever wanted, we would have a place we could return to."

As purely symbolic as this may appear, it struck me as consistent with their father's longing to be certain that the children wouldn't lose all sense of contact with their place of origin. Since they were young, Pineapple said, he had told them many stories of the village where he had been born, to keep alive that feeling of connectedness. In the winter after he and Isabella had returned to Guatemala, Pineapple went there for a Christmas visit. She told me that the village felt familiar. "I didn't feel as if I was a stranger."

This, then, was the man who did not love his children and deserved to be humiliated and insulted in their presence on a day that should have been a happy celebration. Pineapple said the woman who had hounded him into the parking lot, and then to the car in which he'd taken refuge, had never been somebody with whom she and Lara felt entirely comfortable. Especially as they grew old enough to tell her when they disagreed with some advice she'd given them, the woman would get "very cranky and impatient" with them. "She didn't really 'give advice,' you know? It was more like—giving us 'instructions'? You know, like we weren't supposed to use our little brains to make decisions of our own?"

I don't know enough about the to-and-fro between them to be certain this is fair, but I wondered if this person had perhaps unconsciously arrogated to herself the privilege of judging them according to the values of her class and culture, but without regard for theirs. Most of the people in Rhode Island who had been defenders of the children since they had arrived were too enlightened to deny the girls a sense of their autonomy and too sensitive to make the kinds of statements that no child wants to hear about her father or her mother. These were the people, by and large, who seemed to be the most aware of the dynamics between benefactors and their beneficiaries and most willing, as a consequence, to examine those inevitable biases that none of us can totally avoid.

– III –

Lara and Pineapple showed a lot of ingenuity and practicality in making the transition from the house where they'd been living to the new apartment they had found in Providence. In order to raise money for the rental and the furnishings, they organized a yard sale for belongings they would not be taking with them. Members of the church donated items too. In a single afternoon, they raised $3,000.

"We got the apartment for a good price," Lara told me. "I used $2,000 from the yard sale to pay the landlord in advance toward the first year's rent, which cuts the monthly payments to about $500."

The apartment was small: kitchen, living room, bath, and bedroom. But it had two beds and a pull-out bed and, she said, there were cabinets between them that functioned as dividers and also as bed tables. "We used the money we had left to pick out linens, quilts, and curtains and, you know, all the stuff we needed for the kitchen."

Lara began working at a day care center in July—"ten dollars an hour, until I get more training. I'm putting off my master's for two years because we'll need as much as I can earn. Once Pineapple's done with college, I'll go back to grad school so I can be certified." She still intended to become a teacher.

Mosquito, meanwhile, had been hired as a counselor at the prep school she and Miguel and Pineapple had attended. "Good pay," Pineapple noted. "Next year, she'll be co-director."

Pineapple's job did not pay as well, "but it was the best that I could find, being as I waited for too long." She was doing check-out at a local supermarket. "You know, we need every bit of money we can get."

She sent me e-mails in July and August, most of them light-hearted. "Heyyy, Jonathan! Lara had a party for her friends last night. Stayed up with them really late. Definitely do need sleep. Luckily, it's Sunday." She said her mother's health was "good"—she wasn't having headaches anymore and her arthritis seemed to be less painful than before, perhaps because of warmer weather. Her father was "good." Her brother was "good." But she missed them badly.

Mosquito's job, she told me, would be ending in mid-August, after which she'd be heading off to college since the freshmen had to be there early. "You know? Orientation? Anyway, she wants to be there soon enough to get a single room and there aren't too many. I wish I'd had a single room when I was a freshman."

In September Lara was promoted. "They made her the 'lead teacher' for the younger children," Pineapple said, "so she's making better money than before." Pineapple was getting ready for her junior year. . . .

She kept in touch with me throughout the fall and winter. I saw her once in Providence when I returned there for a teacher meeting. She also came to Cambridge once—it was in the first week of December—to spend a weekend at the house in which my assistant lived and where student interns often stayed a few months at a time. It was a big old-fashioned house, big enough for me to isolate myself when I was immersed in writing, and there was a long and narrow stairway from the second floor to a garret where there were two extra bedrooms for our visitors.

As soon as she walked in, she wanted to check out the house, examine all the decorations and the pictures on the walls, take a peek at every room, and look at all the messages (like "more cheese and brownie mix") taped to the refrigerator door. She was disappointed to observe that I was using wooden crates, turned upside down, for tables in the living room, since I hadn't had the time to furnish it completely. She said that she'd be "more than glad" to go to the store with me anytime I asked to help me find a comfortable sofa and end tables.

She wasn't in a serious state of mind at all. For her it was a holiday. My assistant, Lily, who is only three years older than Pineapple, took to her immediately. The first idea that came into their minds was to take off to a store— Target, of course—that both of them, for reasons I can't understand, regarded as an ideal destination for an early afternoon. They insisted that I come with them but when we walked into the store, they behaved at first as if they had forgotten I was there.

Heading for the section of the store where women's clothes were sold, Pineapple went to work picking out some sporty-looking skirts and jerseys she thought Lily ought to buy. "This one would look cute on you," she'd say. Lily looked at dresses she thought Pineapple might like. They took things down, held them up against each other, and then put them back. Neither of them could make up their minds.

Once we had escaped the women's section, Pineapple took me by the arm and steered me from one aisle to the next as she examined kitchenware and DVDs and table lamps and picture frames and sweet-smelling lotions and bath towels and small scented candles, and then, swerving back into a section for young ladies' wear, she looked at slacks and sweaters and a long bright-colored coat. But when I asked her, "Would you like to buy that?" she kept saying, "No. It's not exactly what I had in mind." And, in the end, neither she nor Lily purchased anything! In the car, I asked if she was disappointed. She said, "Not at all." The whole idea of going to the store wasn't to buy anything particular, as she explained this patiently to me, but simply "to hang out there."

The following day, while I was sleeping late, she and Lily went back to exactly the same store. The only thing Pineapple bought was a set of linen napkins for the kitchen table of our house, Irish linen, lime-colored, "to go with the yellow walls," she said. It was a gracious thing for her to do—she had very little money, and she had bought nothing for herself.

The first night she was there, Lily took her up into the garret, where she'd made a bed for her with new sheets and pillows and a comforter. Pineapple seemed pleased at first, but five minutes later she came down and said it was "too spooky" to sleep up there all alone. So Lily spent the night, and the next one, sleeping on the other bed to keep her company.

On Sunday night, after we had dinner at the kitchen table, she was in a thoughtful mood and talked a little more about her hopes for her career. She reminded me that when she was in elementary school, she used to think she'd "like to be a baby doctor"—or, as she worded it tonight, "go into pediatrics." She said the idea "kind of stuck with me" until she was in boarding school. But when she talked about this with her counselor, he told her that he wasn't sure her science skills were strong enough to do a pre-med major when she went to college. "It was not like he was 'downing' me. If I wanted, he said I should try.

"Then I thought about it more and I explained to him that all I really wanted was to be in a career where I could do something to change the lives of children, to be of *help* to children. And people always used to say I should be a social worker. Long ago! People used to say this when I was a little kid. Back there at St. Ann's. . . ." The counselor, she said, encouraged her in this, and by the time she was in her senior year she'd made up her mind.

I repeated something she had said when we were walking by the water on the day of Lara's graduation. She'd told me that she thought of this as a way of paying back the people who had helped her through the years. But she answered that she'd thought about this more.

"I realize now that I can never pay back everyone who helped me. You can't pay back for something in the past. What I want to do is be able to pay *forward*. Like, you know, Dr. King said this? Or somebody said this. Or something like this? 'Pass the torch along'? That's kind of what I mean: Do it for the younger ones. The ones I left behind. . . .

"So that's what I decided. That's how I settled on my major. And you know it hasn't been too easy. I have to study harder than most students in my class. It's the truth. I'm not embarrassed. It's been that way for me all along. But I know that I can do it. Like I told you, I don't think there's anything that can slow me down."

In the spring she reported that her little brother would be coming back to go to school in Providence. "We're looking for a school that's close to our apartment. We're going to make sure it's a really good one. You know? He's a whole lot smarter than I am. I can say it. He's my brother. I've already told him that he has to go to college."

She also told me she'd be coming back to visit us in Cambridge for another weekend soon. "Heyyyy Jonathan!" she said in one of her e-mails. "Don't be worried.

I won't make you go to Target with me this time. There's other things I'd like to see. Like we're reading Walden now? Is that little house still there? By the way, my grades are gooood!! I can't wait to see you guys.

    "Lots of luvvvvv! Pineapple."

CHAPTER 10

A Life of the Mind
(Jeremy, Part One)

He loved books.

He wrote poetry.

He wrote long stories.

He had a liking for old-fashioned language and inverted phrases.

"Be not offended," he told me once when he disagreed with something I had said.

He was unlike any child I had ever known.

Jeremy was twelve years old when I met him at St. Ann's in 1993. He walked right up to me and offered me his hand. "Sir," he said, "I understand you are an author. I, too, am a novelist." He told me, in fact, that he was working on a novel at that very time.

Shortly thereafter, he handed me a story, twenty-two pages, a complicated mystery, which he said he hadn't yet completed because he hadn't figured out the ending.

"How long," he asked, "does a story have to be for it to
be a novel?"

I said I didn't know if there was a rule about this.

"Is twenty-two pages long enough?"

"That may be a little short."

But I didn't want to spoil his enthusiasm, so I added,
"It's a good beginning."

He seemed relieved to hear this.

Jeremy lived on the sixteenth floor of a badly run-
down twenty-story building, with his mother and his older
brother, five blocks from the church. His mother was very
poor and unable to speak English, but she had a strong and
self-reliant spirit and she made a good home for her children. Jeremy's father, from whom his mother was divorced,
lived in the same neighborhood. His grandmother lived
nearby as well. Jeremy would stay with her when his mother
now and then returned, sometimes for a month or so, to the
town where she was born in Puerto Rico.

The pastor told me Jeremy was more religious than
most children of his age. He read the Bible. He knew his
prayers. He understood the liturgy. He believed in God.
And his sense of faith and his understanding of the mean-
ings of the gospel in his daily life did not, she said, abandon
him when he left the church.

One afternoon, a few weeks after we had met, he took
me for a walk to see the building where he lived. His mother
wasn't home, so we didn't go upstairs. We stopped at a corner store, where I got a cup of coffee, and then headed back
in the direction of St. Ann's. As we were walking, Jeremy
suddenly looked across the street and gestured at a man
with short gray hair staring at a vacant lot and said it was
his uncle, who was suffering from AIDS. The man looked
up when he heard his nephew call his name, but seemed to
be confused and did not react. He stood there on the sidewalk with a razor blade in one hand, carefully held between

his forefinger and thumb, and a cigarette in the other. When Jeremy introduced us, his uncle dropped the razor blade in order to shake hands. After an awkward moment, he nodded and went on.

"Do you know what the shortest verse in the Bible is?" Jeremy asked.

"No," I said. "I don't."

"Jesus wept," he answered.

Jeremy spent his grade-school years at P.S. 30, whose principal, Miss Rosa, was something of a maverick in her progressive views but also ran a tight ship and was able to retain a good deal of continuity within a seasoned faculty. But the middle school he was attending at the time we met was one of those dismal places I've described that would have been shut down many years before if it had been serving a middle-class community. The principal, when I went to meet him, appeared to be annoyed when I asked him about Jeremy and, indeed, he told me that he couldn't find him listed in his records. After he reluctantly went through his files once again, he seemed to remember who I meant.

"Is he the one with pimples?"

Jeremy was mild-mannered—he was not assertive in dealing with his peers—and he was bullied often by the more aggressive students at the school. The principal was not the sort to offer him protection. Then, too, Jeremy stood out from his classmates by reason of the fact that he was an introspective boy and, when he did speak out in class, tended to ask questions that his teachers found obscure— and would sometimes tell him so—which presented yet another opportunity for students to make fun of him.

"He's not like any of the other kids you see around the neighborhood," his older brother said. "He walks along the street buried in one of his books. He goes by these places where the dealers and their friends hang out on the corners. It's like he's in a different world. . . ." Jeremy's brother was seventeen by then and, even though he had not allowed himself to get involved with criminal activities, he was well acquainted with the ones who were.

"I tell them he's my brother and I'll deal with them myself if they ever lift a hand against him."

But within another year Jeremy's mother had become alarmed about the friends his brother had been making and sent him home to Puerto Rico to live with her family there. Jeremy no longer had a brother to protect him. He was beaten several times at school and, when his pleas for help were disregarded by his teachers and his principal, he started staying out of school for three or four days in a row.

This was no great loss to him in academic terms. And, in a kind of prideful indignation, he compensated for his poor attendance by seeking out well-educated mentors who gravitated to St. Ann's and, in particular, a Puerto Rican poet living in the neighborhood who welcomed him into his home and talked with him for hours at a time about the books that lined his wall, immersing him in conversations about Greek and Roman history and reading him some of the famous British authors—John Milton, for example—and others he revered.

After I'd become acquainted with the poet, a distinguished-looking man named Juan Bautista Castro, Jeremy and I spent many evenings with him at his home. At the poet's urging, I began suggesting books to Jeremy that I thought he might enjoy, but the titles I suggested ("young adult books," as they're called) did not seem to interest him, or else he'd tell me he'd already read them when he was in elementary school. When I asked him what he liked, he spoke of Edgar Allan Poe, who was, he said, his "favorite writer" at the time, and he told me Poe had once resided in the Bronx, "somewhere not too far from here." Before long, he was also reading novels of Mark Twain and, soon after that, he told me he'd been "circling Charles Dickens" but could not decide if he was "ready" for him yet.

"My one big problem," as he put it to me, "was that he could find no bookstores near his home, "and for that matter, if the truth be told, there isn't even any bookstore anywhere in all of the South Bronx." The pastor—in those days he spoke of Martha as "the reverend"—had taken him to a bookstore in Manhattan where, he said, he very much enjoyed looking through the aisles for a book that he had heard of.

"'Prowling,'" he said, "is the word that comes to mind" when he wasn't always positive about the book he wanted but liked to look around for something that the poet might have mentioned in their conversations. "Then I'd see it! Then I'd realize that was why I'd gone there in the first place. Check it out! I like to be surprised!"

A year or two later, we began to go together to the Barnes & Noble store that faced directly upon Union Square, in which there were lots of sofas and secluded corners where he could sit and narrow down the books he had collected to the ones he really planned to read. I noticed that he had a rather courtly manner of enlisting the affectionate assistance of people working in the store. Young women seemed especially susceptible to his repeated pleas for help in finding books he thought that he was looking for. And when, as often happened, he asked them for a title he had gotten wrong, or for an author whose name he could not summon up correctly, they seldom seemed to get impatient with him but appeared to take a real delight in helping him untangle his confusions.

When the time arrived for Jeremy to apply to high school, his mother was concerned and uncertain what to do, because she knew the problems of the high schools at first-hand—Jeremy's brother had gone to a school that graduated less than a quarter of its students. He'd been on the verge of dropping out (or, if my memory is right, he may already have dropped out) when she sent him back to Puerto Rico.

It was the spring of 1995. Word was spreading of a newly founded school in the South Bronx, one of the first of the so-called "small academies" that would become, within a few more years, the newest urban answer to the chronic failings of the larger high schools serving concentrated populations of the black and brown and very poor. Martha intervened to win a place for Jeremy, although she did not do so without reservations because of information she and I had both received indicating that the school might not be exactly what its boosters claimed. Still, any school that offered Jeremy an avenue of exit from the kind of large, impersonal, and overcrowded institution that his brother had attended seemed to her worth trying.

The school turned out, however, not to be the richly academic institution it was said to be but was wedded to an ethos of instructional severity at the cost of intellectual vitality, with none of the expansiveness of learning or interest in the individuality of children that would be the starting point of education in a more enlightened school. A narrow emphasis on pumping up the scores on standardized exams appeared, as best I could discern, to be the top priority.

Jeremy's unorthodox mentality was not well suited to this school. The teachers there were not impressed with his precocity and free-roaming intellectuality. His curiosity about the world of history and poetry to which he'd been awakened by the poet who befriended him and the earnest independence that led him into writing lengthy narratives and offering discursive answers to the questions teachers asked of him—none of this endeared him to a faculty devoted to the inculcation of those skills required by test-taking.

He would grow distracted while sitting through a class that asked for no participation from the students other than to spit up predetermined answers. He would daydream often. He'd fill his notebooks with satiric stories or eccentric questions to which he knew that no one at the school would care to give an answer. As a result, he was frequently removed from class and placed in a kind of holding room, which he called "the isolation chamber," with other students whose behavior was regarded as resistant or disruptive and where, he said, they were given no instruction. When important visitors showed up at the school, "they quickly put us back into our classrooms."

When Martha learned of this, she went directly to the school and asked to see the principal. The principal told Martha that, on the basis of his noncooperative behavior and poor performance on examinations, Jeremy was not a likely candidate for college.

Martha was, of course, unwilling to accept this. So she started reaching out, as she had done with other students from St. Ann's, to see if she could locate some alternatives. As a short-term form of intervention, I proposed that Jeremy might benefit from a summer program at a boarding school I knew in Massachusetts that, in the normal academic year, enrolled primarily children of the affluent but, in its summer session, made an effort to enroll more children of low income.

Jeremy's reaction was enthusiastic. His mother, after she had seen the school and met some of the teachers— Martha, I believe, went with her and Jeremy on a day's excursion—gave her full approval.

He seemed to revel in the two months that he spent there. I went out twice, early in July and again a few weeks later, to get to know his teachers. His English teacher had been reading stories he had written and told me that his narrative skills were "far above grade level" and, as

I already knew, that "he reads voraciously." He did note that Jeremy "reaches out for books I should think might be rather hard for him. Sometimes they are. But sometimes he surprises me."

By the end of July, he was in the middle of rehearsals for a play that was to be performed in the last week of the session. I did not confess to him that I had a plan in mind— I did, however, mention this to Martha—that was a bit conspiratorial. I was toying with a notion that went beyond a single summer in New England but might open up another, more ambitious option for the future.

It was too late to act upon this for the year ahead, so in September Jeremy continued at his high school in the Bronx. I urged him, for his own sake, to make a greater effort to conform, for now, to the demands imposed upon him. Meanwhile, he continued meeting with the poet, Mr. Castro. One evening, on Thanksgiving weekend, when the poet's granddaughter was there, the two of them, at the poet's instigation, read lines from Romeo and Juliet to each other. They had a good time playing with Elizabethan phrases and talking in Elizabethan language to one another while they were eating dinner.

Before I left New York, we made another visit to the Barnes & Noble store where he had come to feel at home. He prevailed upon me to buy a copy of Bram Stoker's horror novel Dracula, which, he said, he was "somewhat shocked" to learn I'd never read. I made a bargain with him. I would do my best to get through Dracula if he'd agree to buy Great Expectations and, instead of further "circling" Charles Dickens, would make a concentrated effort to complete it. He conceded to me later that he got the best part of that bargain.

For all his seeming social ease while we were in the comfortable setting of a bookstore, there were certain things he said to me, and certain things that happened to him in the winter of that year, that were sharp reminders of the limits of his confidence. The relaxed and humorous enjoyment that he took in chatting with good-natured grown-ups in the store at Union Square, where he seemed to feel defended and protected by the pantheon of favored books and authors he had gradually created for himself, stood in contrast to his vulnerable status and physically exposed condition in the streets of his own neighborhood. The dangers that surrounded him grew very real to me when he was robbed at knifepoint one night in December.

When I asked him where this had happened, he replied, "In my apartment building."

"In the lobby?"

"No. Between two floors."

He explained that he was walking up to his apartment "because the elevator didn't want to come down to the lobby." When he turned a corner at one of the landings, he found himself surrounded by three men with knives.

"Did you know them?"

"No," he said. "They weren't from our building."

When I asked him what they took, he said, "My Chinese food."

"Did they take your money?"

"Just one dollar. That was all I had."

"Did you tell your mother?"

"Yes," he said.

"Did you report it?"

"No," he said. "That would be more dangerous."

"Did you tell Martha?"

"Yes," he said. "I asked if she would get me something I can use if I get attacked again."

"What did you have in mind?"

"Peppermint spray," he answered.

"I've never heard of that."

He reflected on this for a moment. Then: "I said it wrong. I think the word is 'pepper spray.'"

"Is she going to get it for you?"

"She's still thinking."

"What does your mother say?"

"She does not approve of it."

I told him I agreed with her.

A few months later, he called me at my home with more disturbing news. It didn't have to do with him but with a student in his class who, he told me, was one of the only people at the school whom he regarded as a friend. The student, a fifteen-year-old girl, had been raped and strangled in the hallway of a building not far from her home. According to Jeremy, she was "advanced in all her subjects" and "a very nice person" and, he said, "maybe the nicest person you could ever want to know." The newspapers said the building where the girl was murdered had been nearly vacant and had been infested with crack users.

Murders and assaults, as we have seen, were not uncommon in the South Bronx at the time. A year or two before, I'd counted more than twenty children and teenagers who had died of violence within the blocks around St. Ann's. But the victims of those crimes had not been acquaintances of Jeremy. In this case, it was his friend who was the victim.

Toward the end of April of that year, Martha asked if I'd pursued the notion I had told her I was toying with since Jeremy returned from summer school the previous September. I told her I had kept in touch with the headmaster and had spoken with him, although only tentatively up to now, about the possibility that Jeremy might qualify as a full-time student. He had been reserved at first because he said he'd recognized in the summer session that Jeremy, while he was advanced in writing skills and reading, was well below grade level in most of his other subjects. He wanted to reflect upon it more and discuss with members of his faculty the difficulties Jeremy would face in making this transition.

I called him now and said I'd like to talk with him in person as soon as it was possible. We set a date for the following week. When I came into his office on the day appointed, he told me he'd arrived at a decision.

"The truth is that the school he's now attending has not served this young man well. But we saw a spark in him, an appetite for learning, that we frankly do not always see in students who arrive here from much better schools and have had more thorough preparation at the time when we admit them. I think that he can handle it and, as tough as it may be at first, I can promise you that at this school we don't give up on anyone too easily."

The school, however, did not have a large endowment. He asked me, therefore, if I could assist him in finding a potential donor to provide a scholarship for Jeremy. At Martha's intervention, a generous and wealthy man who had worked in the administration of Bill Clinton agreed to pay for Jeremy's tuition. As in Pineapple's case, Jeremy's acceptance by the school included a condition, set by the headmaster, that he must repeat a grade because the school believed he would need the continuity of three full academic years to graduate successfully.

As summer came, his mother and the pastor made sure he would have the clothes he'd need for fall and the New England winter. The poet counseled him, in his old-fashioned and didactic way, about the effort he would need to bring to bear "to organize" his eager but "undisciplined mentality." When the moment came to leave New York, he packed his bags and favorite books and all his treasured writings, and headed off, still a very youthful-looking boy, with that mixture of excitement and last-minute disarray I pretty much expected.

He didn't call me for about ten days. When he did, I could see that he was calling from another person's number. He said the school librarian had let him use her phone.

"She's sitting here beside me. Would you like to say hello?" Then: "Oh no! She had to go upstairs. . . ."

"Anyway, I have to go, or I'll be late for study hall."

He didn't yet sound organized.

– II –

In the first six months of boarding school, Jeremy bombarded me with voice mails.

"FLASH!" he said one night that fall. "I've been on a roll this week. Check out a book called Tender Is the Night—page 184. Also page 83. Also page 101. . . ."

Another night: "Hey, Jonathan! It's me! If you're there, pick up! If you're not, don't pick up! I'm in my dorm. Writing an essay. I'll be up 'til midnight."

"Actually," he said, when I called him back, "I'm working on two essays. They're for different classes.

"The first one: Why do people pass the blame for things they do to someone else? I started with Adam blaming Eve who blamed the snake who probably blamed someone else. Then Pharaoh blaming the Hebrews. Then Hitler blaming the Jews. I also quoted Jesus, but not as the son of God. I said that, whether you believe in him or not, he was an important prophet and philosopher. . . .

"Essay number two: I wrote about my life at home. You know, about my father? How he's there but isn't there? I tried to do it in a way that will not be hurtful, in case he ever reads it.

"In history the other day we had a talk about the nineteen twenties. I found it of great interest that the Charleston and the flappers with their notoriety and a certain loose-ness, which is not the same as immorality, not necessarily, were all the craze just before the market crash and people jumping out of windows.

"I asked my teacher whether it was okay to say this was ironical."

In November: "A new experience this morning at assembly. We listened to a chamber group. I think it's known as 'an ensemble.'"

"Do you know which group it was?"

"The name escapes me," he replied.

"But you enjoyed it?"

"Shall I speak the truth?"

"Why not?" I said.

"I found it very boring."

On a more respectful note, he told me that his English class had started reading Shakespeare.

"Which play?" I asked.

"Richard," he said.

"Richard the Second?"

"No. The Third."

I told him I had never read it, so he rapidly delivered a summation of the part that he'd already read. He spoke of Richard as "a hunchback—villainous, born premature, dogs howling at his birth because he was so ugly." He said that Richard was "tormented" and "tormenting," "the vic-tim of his own obsession," and connected this with a theme familiar in the writings of his favorite author. "You'll recall The Tell-tale Heart? There's a line there where he talks about his own obsessive thoughts. 'It is impossible to say how first the idea got into my brain, but, once conceived, it haunts me night and day.'

"My teacher says it's good for us to look for these connections. . . ."

In January, he reported, students in his English class did

independent essays. He had chosen "Children's Rhymes" because his English teacher told him that a number of these rhymes originated in events of history.

"'Ring Around the Rosie,' I've discovered, takes us *way* back into history. 'Ashes, ashes, all fall down'—that's about the plague. The one in London, in the sixteen hundreds.

"'Humpty Dumpty had a great fall'—that's King Richard. All the king's men were Richard's men. A king who lost his crown. . . .'"

He also had opinions about certain rhymes he didn't think we ought to read to children. "'This little piggy went to market. This little piggy stayed home. This little piggy had roast beef. This little piggy had none.' Why do we want to rub it in? Why would we want to tell these things to children?

"'Lady Bug, Lady Bug' is pretty awful, too, if you think about the words. 'Your house is on fire. Your children are gone.' Is that the sort of thing we *really* want to read to kids before they go to sleep?

"'When the wind blows, the cradle will rock. Down comes the baby, cradle and all. . . .'

"No wonder children have bad dreams!

"'Itsy-bitsy spider, climbing up the spout. Down came the rain and washed the spider out. Out came the sun and dried up all the rain. Itsy-bitsy spider climbed up the spout again. . . .'

"It's like Sisyphus. He's never going to succeed. You end up feeling kind of sorry for the spider."

I asked what got him into writing about something so unusual.

"Once my teacher set me off," he said, "I kind of kept on rolling. I went to the librarian. She was a great help to me. I found a lot of writing on this subject.

"Anyway, my teacher liked the paper."

In March I drove out to the school so that I could talk more with his teachers. His English teacher made the point that in his essays Jeremy was temperamentally resistant to conciseness. "In his papers he will seldom find the shortest line from 'here' to 'there.' He relies on finding nuggets of excitement to string out his writings, which is what enlivens them but also makes it very hard to grade him."

"Trying to find exactly where he's heading," I remarked, "is something like a treasure hunt."

"At least the treasure's there," the teacher said.

I'd been invited to have dinner at the school, but Jeremy had asked permission to go into town with me to a pizza restaurant that was popular with students. On the way, he asked if we could stop first at a stationery store that was near the restaurant. He said he'd bought a picture as a present for his mother—it was a reproduction of a print by Rembrandt—but that he forgot to buy a frame. We stopped at the store. He had the money crunched within his hand. He picked out an inexpensive wooden frame, and then we went for supper.

We didn't have much time to eat because his theater class was doing a rehearsal of a play—The Inspector General. As we came in, other students filled him in on changes they had made. "Oh no!" he said, but then assured them, "It's okay." I stayed to watch the beginning of the play, then headed back to Boston.

Spring break: He met me in Manhattan. We went to a different bookstore for some reason, not the one in Union Square. When we left and went down in the subway, we got confused and took the wrong train—the Number 5 train, not the Number 6—to go back to the Bronx. We got off at Third Avenue and had to walk for several blocks.

As we walked, he told me of a story he had just

completed for his school newspaper. The story was about the poet, Mr. Castro, but he hadn't turned it in because, he said, he was "having problems" with a couple sentences.

"If you were writing a story," he asked, "and you said a character was 'senile' and 'simpatico,' do you think the person would consider that a compliment?"

"Simpatico," I said, was certainly a compliment, but I told him it would not be flattering to say that somebody was "senile."

"What does 'senile' mean?"

I was surprised he didn't know. When I told him, he said, "Oops! I think I have to fix it."

Rain had started. The two of us were getting soaked, but he seemed oblivious to this and kept on asking questions. "Have you ever heard of people," he inquired, "who walk into the middle of the street and throw themselves in front of cars?"

I told him that I'd never heard of people who actually had thrown themselves in front of cars but that I'd seen stories in the paper about people who would go to court and pretend they had been injured by a car, or on the train, or at the place they worked.

"That's what I had in mind," he said.

"Do you know the reason why they do it?"

"Yes," he said. "I think the word is . . . 'damages.' "

"Damages—for what?"

He reached slowly for the word and finally answered, "Trauma."

"Where did you hear that word?"

"One of my teachers," he replied.

"Did you ask him what it means?"

"He said to look it up."

"What does it mean?"

"Something that happened to you once," he said, "and it affects you later on."

"Is that what the dictionary says?"

"Something like that," he replied. "But right now"—tapping on his head—"I'm giving you my own opinion."

It turned out he wasn't going to his mother's house but was going to sleep over at his grandma's. At the front door of the building, as he was about to press the buzzer, he squinted up into the sky, in which the rain was coming down much harder now. He suggested that I come upstairs to get dried off and "have a cup of soup" and "meet my grandma and my cousin."

I told him that I didn't think I had the strength to get into a conversation with his family at this hour.

"Jonathan, I promise you that 'conversation' will not be a problem."

"Why not?" I asked.

"You won't understand a word they say! None of them speak English."

When I said that I'd feel kind of strange to sit there and not talk to anybody in the room, he looked at the rain again but finally pressed the button to release the door. Even then, he held the door and watched me as I headed down the street in the direction of Brook Avenue. . . .

On my final visit to the school that year, I drove out early in the afternoon to talk with the headmaster. He said that Jeremy was doing "reasonably well," although his grades in math were poor—"marginal at best." He did observe that Jeremy seemed to have "inordinate amounts" of very minor health complaints or "curious small accidents" that coincided closely with the days when he had papers due. "When students pass in papers late, if it happens frequently, teachers sometimes dock them by a grade or two." He said he didn't see this as a matter of immense concern and urged me not to speak of it with Jeremy for now.

I stayed on campus late enough to meet with Jeremy before he went to study hall. We were sitting on the front

steps of the library, with the dorms behind us and the playing fields and countryside below. I took the opportunity to
ask him something that was often in my mind ever since he
had arrived here for the first semester. Beneath the cheer-
fulness that was apparent when he spoke about the friendships he was making and the obvious excitement he was
taking in his literary classes and another theater course, I
asked him if he ever felt displaced at all to be within this
academic setting and this small New England village, so far
from New York.

He thought about his answer before saying, with a prior
qualifier that he often used in order not to give offense,
"Don't get me wrong. I'm happy here. I like my teachers
very much." He said he liked his English teacher in particular. "But there's a certain word you know. . . ."

He said this with a look that seemed to presuppose I'd
know the word he meant, then hesitated, so I asked, "What
word?"

"The word is 'home.' And home, for me, is where my
mother is."

For a moment, he looked very lonely.

I asked him, "Do you ever cry?"

"I've taken a policy not to cry," he answered. "But if
you ever see me weep, you will know that it's because I've
hurt my mother's feelings."

His love for his mother was at the core of his existence.
The fear that she might ever undergo a feeling of abandon-
ment was in his mind continually.

In the fall of 1998, his second year at boarding
school, he told me that his class was doing European history. "Modern history. League of Nations, rise of the dic-
tatorships, Mussolini, genocide in Germany, equivocation

of the French, Ribbentrop and Molotov, Chamberlain, et cetera.... Oops! Sorry! I forgot one other minor thing. The Russian Revolution."

In the spring, he reported, they were doing U.S. history, but he said, "It's not in strict chronology. I mean, it's not in sequence. Like, the teacher wants us to examine certain themes. This month, for instance, we're into race relations, starting from the Civil War and up until these present days.

"And we had a speaker here. Someone that you know. His name was Robert Coles. Dr. Coles, I ought to say. I saw a sadness in his eyes. I went up to speak with him."

I picked up with interest on his words.

"What did that look of sadness mean to you?" I asked.

"A man with nothing false about him," Jeremy replied. "He doesn't hide his feelings. Transparency? Sincerity? Am I using the right words?"

In the same semester he had a course in which his teacher introduced the class to Aeschylus, Euripides—"and, you know, the other Greek tragedians. Then we did some modern authors such as Shaw and Pirandello. Also Strindberg. Also Ibsen and Eugene O'Neill."

Near the end of the spring, he went on, "my theater teacher brought us to New York. We saw three plays, one by O'Neill—it was The Iceman Cometh.

"I don't know what to say. Some of the students didn't like it but, to me, it was like it pretty near destroyed me. . . ."

While he was in New York, he said, "No surprise—you know *me*! I went back to B & N. I was looking at a book about Polanski."

The name had slipped away from me. He reminded me Polanski was a film director—"very controversial."

He said he finally bought the book and went outside. "But then, ten minutes later, I went back and said I'd changed my mind and asked if I could have my money back. The cashier said, 'Is there a reason why?' I told her, 'I just thought that I was ready for this, but I'm not.'"

I asked him if she seemed surprised by this.

"No," he said. "She was sincere. She looked at me with understanding eyes."

He said he had to fill a form out to explain why he returned it.

"What did you write?"

"The same thing I said to the cashier."

"You wrote that down?"

"Yes," he said. "Why do you ask?"

"No reason." I could not explain to him why it struck me as amusing that he'd written out an explanation that was quite so personal. . . .

October of his senior year: The headmaster told me he had no question in his mind as to whether Jeremy would graduate. It was time, he said, to start to think of colleges.

A month later, when parents ordinarily would travel with their children for meetings with admissions officers, or for formal interviews, one of the older teachers at the school offered to drive with Jeremy to several colleges in Massachusetts and New Hampshire. The counselor's home was close to Boston, so he invited Jeremy to stay there with his family on some weeknights and extended weekends, which would make it easier to visit several campuses that were clustered in this area or only a short drive away.

But, in the end, after all his visits to New England colleges, he told me he'd decided that he wanted to be closer to his home. He settled on a college in one of the outer suburbs of New York, about an hour's train ride from the Bronx. Strong letters of support from his teachers and headmaster and a successful interview proved to be decisive. In spite of his uneven grades, he was granted a financial package that included a large scholarship.

Once his college plans had been assured, Jeremy enjoyed his final months at school. His theater group did one last play. His English teacher and his wife took him out to dinner twice. But he was increasingly thinking about home.

– III –

In the weeks after his graduation, he called to tell me he was "catching up on things I didn't know about at home" or "that I forgot to ask about" in the final months at school. Most of them were pleasant things—about his mother and his grandma, and his father's sister, who was visiting from Florida but had left soon after he returned. A cousin that he didn't like had been staying in his bedroom, but he said that he was "very happy to report" that "this unpleasant person has gone back to Puerto Rico."

All the news, however, was not cheerful. One evening in the summer, he called to tell me of some information he'd been given by his mother. His voice was sad. His words were plain. No prefatory ambiguities. No linguistic games.

"It concerns a little boy who has the HIV. I knew this boy since he was born. He's the cousin of my nephew on my uncle's side. . . .

"And there's just one other thing. He's not alone in this. He has an older sister and she has the HIV infection also, and she takes the same three medicines her brother has to take—only he has to take more.

"Their mother has the sickness too. She's in Lincoln Hospital. So they've been living with their old grandmother. Every time their mother leaves the hospital, my mother says she goes back to the street. You know the market at Hunt's

Point? That's where she goes. My mother says that she's infecting other people now."

His mother also told him that the younger of the children was more advanced in illness than his sister. "The doctor said the little boy might only have another year. Jonathan, I *have* to go and visit with this boy. Would you go there with me?"

It was early August then. I told him I'd be in New York for the week preceding Labor Day and promised I would go with him.

We met at 59th Street and took the train that went to Yankee Stadium, which was near the children's home. The boy was standing near the door when we came in, but leaning on a chair. He was wearing shorts and sneakers and a jersey and was playing with a yo-yo, although in a desultory way. Seven years old, a light-skinned boy, very pale, he spoke almost inaudibly. He had been in first grade the preceding year, when he went to school at all. But his teachers didn't feel that he had learned enough, or was well enough, to move on with his class. So he'd be in the first grade again.

The older child, nine years old, who had responded more successfully to treatment, seemed to lead an almost normal life. She liked school, liked her teachers, liked to dance, had a lot of music videos. She said she loved a singer named Marc Anthony, whose salsa music and good looks—"he's so cute!"—had made him very popular with girls and, as I gather, grown-up women too. She chattered gaily about unimportant matters while the grandmother, who was in her fifties but looked older, moved slowly through the living room and dining room and kitchen in a grim and patient way, a solemn and somewhat foreboding figure.

The grandmother opened the refrigerator door, at my request, and showed me where she kept the children's medicines—Retrovir and Epivir were two that I had seen before in homes of other families in the Bronx—and then excused herself because, she said, she had been feeling ill and needed to lie down.

The children sat with Jeremy and me around a table in the dining room. The nine-year-old was talking about things she liked to eat. Her favorite things, she said, were Chinese food, McNuggets, and SpaghettiOs. She said she liked fried chicken too but it was "a mess to eat—your fingers get too greasy," with which Jeremy agreed. The boy said that his favorite things were pancakes and French toast.

"He pours the syrup on!" his sister said, touching his shoulder gently.

She said that he liked Sesame Street, and a program known as Zoom (which has since gone off the air), and he still watched Mister Rogers' Neighborhood—and she said that she still watched it too. The child brightened up when she said Mr. Rogers' name. He whispered in a hoarse but almost cheery voice, "The Land of Make Believe!"

I told them I had visited the studio in Pittsburgh once and saw The Land of Make Believe and got a close look at the trolley. The nine-year-old asked me if I'd also seen the closet in which Mr. Rogers used to put away his coat and shoes and find his sneakers and his sweater. I told her that I hadn't seen the closet but I saw his sweater because Mr. Rogers had it on when I was there.

Jeremy asked the little boy if he knew Mr. Rogers' song about the "neighborhood." The child said he did. So Jeremy leaned across the table to the boy and hummed the song, inviting him to sing. He didn't have the strength to sing so Jeremy sang the words instead. The child smiled and tried to sing the final words himself.

Jeremy had said he viewed it as an obligation to visit with the children, but it didn't feel like something dutiful while we were there. And, once the taciturn and brooding older woman had excused herself to go upstairs, the mood within the dining room took on a little of the normal lightness that is common among children who are relishing the final days of summer before they go back to school.

When we left, we decided not to take the train, and so we walked the fifteen blocks to get back to St. Ann's. Jeremy was quiet. He asked me only a few questions in regard to possibilities he'd heard about that had to do with "cures for HIV"—or, as he quickly edited his words, "not really cures," but "cures that make you almost well and almost like a healthy person for a while."

I told him I believed that he was right. There was no cure for HIV but, as best I understood, there were medications coming out of research that seemed to have had promising results in countering the symptoms that had ravaged HIV-infected people up to now. The nine-year-old, who seemed so energetic that I wouldn't have suspected she was ill if I had not been told, might very likely live for many years—long enough to benefit from these medications. The little one appeared to be less likely to survive because his strength already was so low. Still, as I said to Jeremy, there was no way to know. Perhaps, with one more miracle, one more advance in research, one more medication that had not yet been approved but was in the testing phase for now, he might prevail as well.

Jeremy told me he was thinking of the way the nine-year-old had touched her brother's arm when he said that he liked pancakes and French toast.

" 'He pours the syrup on!' Why do I remember that?"

I told him I was thinking of that too. "Maybe it was reassuring for us to be told that he enjoyed his food, that he had any appetite at all."

"Pour it on!" said Jeremy.

CHAPTER 11

No Easy Victories
(Jeremy, Part Two)

The college Jeremy had chosen was intimate and small, and this made it possible again for him to capture the attention of instructors. It was traditional in its course of studies and had not genuflected to the growing pressure to provide careerist training at the cost of arts and letters, which, of course, appealed to him tremendously, although it would present some difficulties for him when his studies were complete. For now, at least, it seemed that he had made a good decision.

The first semesters were given over largely to the kinds of courses that are introductory in nature ("General Education" was the defining term). For the one elective he was allowed to take, he chose a course on cinema and theater in the modern era.

For several weeks this was all he talked about when he called me on the phone. "Jean-Luc Godard, François Truffaut. . . . Also, Ingmar Bergman, who did The Seventh

Seal. He was Scandinavian. . . . This week, we were looking at René Clément, who made a film called Plein Soleil—
'Purple Noon' in English. We also saw a German film about
an angel who comes down into our world, unseen at first by
anyone but children, but then, of course, he falls in love, so
he decides upon an action of renunciation."

"What does he renounce?"

"The wings of angels," he replied.

"There's a connection here to Brecht, my teacher says.
In other words, this kind of work does not oblige us to sus-
pend our disbelief. The film is just a film. The play is just a
play. That's all it is. You don't need to believe it."

On another night, sometime in October: "There's a
musician named Carl Orff who put on performances in
the Nazi era. He was a collaborator, I am sad to say, but
he interests me enormously. He worked with classical and
medieval themes. He'd find these poems by Latin writers
and he'd turn them into musical theatricals.

"Carmina Burana—that's the title for a series of these
pieces. Wait a minute." He put the phone next to his CD
player and played the section starting "O Fortuna," then
read the lyrics to me. "'O fortune, like the moon, you are
always changeable, ever waxing, ever waning. . . . ' I don't
think you'd ever want to say that to a girl. It might hurt her
feelings.

"The person who got me into this happens to be a student here. She's from Staten Island. I heard her play this
and I loved it and went out to buy it. It sounds much better
if you play it really loud but I'd be in trouble if I did that at
this hour."

In December, he reported he was working on a paper.
"It's supposed to be on something very personal. So I
decided I would do it on the school I went to in the Bronx.
You know, where they put me into isolation?"

I told him I had not forgotten and I said that I would like to read the paper once it was complete. He sent it to me when he passed it in before the holidays.

"At this school I went to," he began, "I felt like a loner, marching, as a certain writer put it, to the piping of a different drummer. There were a group of other students like me who presented a real problem for the faculty, so they developed an unusual approach to annihilate this problem.

"It was five minutes before the end of yet another school day when the principal announced that changes would be made on the Monday that was coming. She avowed, 'Many students will not be admitted to their classrooms. They will be removed and put into a separate room. We should not feel sorry for these students. They are the deviants who do not care about you or about themselves.'

"On Monday, we were cast into a room that displayed the word 'Confinement' on the door. Other students on their way to classes would look in and stare at us. . . .

"As for education, we were given 'sheet work.' It didn't matter to them if you did it. One day I fell asleep and no one woke me up. We had no teacher in the room, just someone to guard us and make sure we didn't leave.

"Finally, I figured out why they were doing this. I think they hoped that some of us would get the message that they didn't want us there, so they could be rid of us, although I'm sure the school would have denied this. Anyway, it seemed as if the principal's new order was having this effect. Students in our little group were dropping out because their parents realized that the school had given up on them. A blemishing malformation of their minds was taking place, or had already taken place.

"The second time I was in confinement, the students who had not dropped out elected me to go and bring their protest to the principal. I realize now that I was quite intemperate. 'You and this cesspool of a school,' I told her, 'will regret this act of malice. The only deviant in this school is you. You should have put yourself into confinement.'

"Not long after that, I left the school and transferred to a school in Massachusetts. I often wondered if I left from anger or humiliation. I now know that I left out of a wish for vindication. I have struggled ever since to show that schools should never write off any student because they regard him as an inconvenience."

In January, just before the end of term, Jeremy developed what he said was bad bronchitis. "The college nurse said I had a temperature of 100-plus degrees. So I couldn't finish up a paper that I had to do for social science. The teacher says that I can turn it in next week. But I'll be docked because it's late."

I didn't want to be unkind, but I told him I remembered, while he was at boarding school, that the many minor illnesses and accidents to which he tended to be prone seemed to coincide with times when he had essays or term papers due. He took this in good spirit. "Yes. I know the way it looks." He said that he "repented" of this and that he'd try harder to avoid these kinds of problems in the next semester.

His grades for the first semester were predictably uneven: A in Film and Theater, B in Sociology, D in Mathematics, B-plus in English I, C-minus in Social Science, in which he insisted he would have received a B if it hadn't been "for turning in that final paper late."

In the second semester he seemed to be more diligent in getting in his work when it was due. "In English," he said, "I'm reading Robert Herrick, Thomas Wyatt, John Donne, Christopher Marlowe. . . . Also Milton. Also Edmund Spenser. . . .

"Oh, I forgot! Andrew Marvell also."

He said he was enjoying what he'd read up to that time, except for Edmund Spenser. "Tell me the truth. Do you think that any student ever felt a thrill go up his spine reading The Fairie Queene?"

In a philosophy course, he said, "It skips around. We start with Emerson, then go back to Plato and Aquinas, Rousseau, Descartes, Kierkegaard, et cetera. I'm writing my first paper for the course on Plato, The Republic. I thought of comparing it to Jefferson—you know, First Inaugural Address? But I've only got six pages. If I let myself get into Jefferson, I know I'll never finish. . . ."

In the second semester of his social science course, he said, the class was having a debate: "'Are the poor responsible for poverty?' I'm taking the positive, just to see if I can argue something that I don't believe. . . . By the way, did I tell you I've been working in the library? Just four hours twice a week. It's for my work-study job," which was part of the financial package he'd received.

In spite of the efforts he was putting in, his freshman year was hard for him. His final grades in two of his courses—math and social science—were not satisfactory. He was allowed to stay on campus and take make-up classes in the summer. He passed them both and began his second year in a hopeful state of mind.

Sophomore year. He didn't call me until mid-October.

"Hello!" he said. "Sorry that it's been so long. I've been through an episode of indecision." He said that he had had to settle on a field of concentration. "I was tempted by European history. Also sociology—it would have been for ignoble reasons. Word on campus: It isn't too demanding. To tell the truth, I found it very 'fuzzy.' There didn't seem to be much focus or direction. . . . Anyway, I made my choice." He had chosen English as his major, as he knew I had expected.

That semester, he was taking British poets of the eighteen hundreds. "Romantic period. Keats and Shelley, Blake and Wordsworth, also the Victorians. You know, Robert Browning? Oh! Also A. E. Housman, who I never heard of. Oxford poet. . . . He reminds me of myself."

"Are you reading Tennyson?"

"Yes," he said.

"Do you like him?"

"Not at all."

"I didn't either," I conceded.

"'Theirs not to reason why! Theirs but to do or die!'"

"At least you know the lines," I said.

"I do, but I repent it."

Instead of a midterm test, he said, students in the class had to do a long term paper—"due in three weeks, beginning of November."

I asked him what he'd chosen.

"'Innocence Interrupted,'" he replied, "because, let's face it, most of these romantic poems, when you come right down to it, are actually about seduction."

He was also taking a two-semester course: "Shakespeare, plays and sonnets. Twelve plays. I don't know how many sonnets." He asked me a question about the Duke of Gloucester, Bolingbroke, and John of Gaunt, and seemed to be disappointed when I drew a temporary blank.

"You wrote your Harvard thesis about Shakespeare? And you don't remember John of Gaunt?"

He apologized right away—"I didn't mean to hurt your feelings"—and went on to tell me of a play that he was doing with a theater group on campus. "Streetcar . . . ," he said casually.

His studies that year and the next blur together somewhat in my memory. I do remember that he called me in the spring to tell me that he planned to stay at college for a second summer to take a class on the modern novel, so that his course load wouldn't be too heavy in the fall. He had chosen a field of concentration that wasn't "fuzzy" in the least, and he knew the work he had ahead of him wasn't going to be easy.

In the winter of his junior year, he had a sad experience related to his friendship with a student in his class he had mentioned to me once before—"the girl from Staten Island," as he called her.

"She was the first good friend I made in my freshman year. She used to cut my hair for me. We used to go for pizza." His room in junior year was facing hers and they made a cheerful custom out of waving to each other from their windows before bedtime.

One weekend, she invited him to come to Staten Island to go to a movie with her and then to a party in her neighborhood. He took the train, the Metro North, from a station near the college, connected somewhere in Manhattan to get to the Staten Island Ferry, and at last, using the directions he'd been given, found his way to the place where she'd agreed to meet him.

"Nothing was bad while we were at the movie," he reported in a somewhat frantic and embarrassed phone call that he made to me very late that night. "But when we left the theater and were walking down the street, I put my arm around her waist, because I thought that was a normal thing to do. And all at once she froze up like an icicle and pushed herself away from me as if I had offended her. It made me feel as if I was some kind of awful monster. She looked at me so meanly!

"She said that she was going home. Or maybe she was going to the party, but she didn't want to tell me. Anyway, she turned away and left me there. So now I'm on the ferry"—that was the first time I knew where he was calling from—"and I'm going to go back and get the train, and then I hope it's not too late to get the Metro North to get me back to college.

"That look in her eyes was like she found me totally repellent. It made me feel like I was unattractive. I needed to tell somebody."

I felt so bad I kept him on the phone until the ferry came into Manhattan.

A short time later, he told me of a story he had written since the night on Staten Island. "I had some trouble with the title. First I called it 'Misery.' Then I thought that might be overstated. Now it's titled 'Shattered Dreams.'" He said this with some humor, which led me to believe his sense of hurt might have abated somewhat by that time, although I guessed that it would be a while more before it went away completely.

Spring break. Late-night call: He told me he had seen a movie, Au Revoir Les Enfants, at a theater in Manhattan earlier that day. He said it was by Louis Malle and asked me if I knew it and I said I'd seen it many times. It was a haunting story about Jewish children who were taken by the Nazis from a boarding school in France where they were being hidden by a Catholic priest.

"The final scene," he said—"you know what's ahead of them—just left me feeling hollowed out inside. . . .

"I know this may seem strange to you but when I see a film like that I feel that, after all the books I've read and everything I think I should have learned by now, I still can't seem to wrap my mind around the evil that we do."

I asked him who he meant by "we."

He said, "The human race."

In April, we had a long discussion about the comprehensives—examinations English majors had to take in senior year that encompassed the entire field. He had looked at the prerequisites and was suddenly aware of a number of works by important authors to which he'd never been exposed.

Knowing his proclivity for running into problems at the final hour, I was glad when he decided once again to remain on campus and enroll in an intensive course on early English authors, prior to the age of Shakespeare, which he would otherwise have been obliged to take during the fall. It turned out he enjoyed it, "especially the Troilus," which he said he liked much better than The Canterbury Tales. He said Criseyde's cruelty to Troilus reminded him of "a certain person you may still recall. . . ."

Senior year: He broke his toe. At least, that's what he thought at first. A week later: "No more cane! They discovered that it wasn't fractured after all."

This time, he didn't let his accidents or illnesses interrupt his concentration on his work. English comprehensives were given in the winter, at the end of January. In spite of all his planning, there were still some items in the guidelines he was given for which he knew that he was not prepared. "Dr. Johnson. Also Dryden. Also Pope—Rape of the Lock. Also Coleridge. Also Yeats. Also Eliot—I never read The Four Quartets."

It was well into October when he told me this. I had to wonder how he could do so much reading in so short a time. Without asking his permission, I picked up the phone and called his college counselor.

"It's a lot for him to do," the counselor conceded. "In some situations like this, we encourage students to stay on an extra year. In Jeremy's case, I've got my fingers crossed. But we need to think of this as another option if we feel he needs it."

As the comprehensives neared, he was staying up late

almost every night, sometimes until dawn. He told me he would fall asleep with his books beside him on his bed. He got permission to remain on campus through the Christmas holidays because he hadn't yet completed reading Pope— "and," he said, "you can guess who, Dryden . . . , ugh!"

I told him what the counselor had said.

"Jonathan, listen to me. I've made up my mind about this. I am going to graduate in June."

He wanted to explain to me how much it would sadden him, and disappoint him in himself, if he had to take an extra year. "In my building in the Bronx, there were many kids—more than half of them, I'd say, maybe closer to two thirds—who didn't finish high school. Even if they did, not many went to college. Or, if they finally got to college, most of them would not remain for long. They'd drop out. Maybe later they'd come back. . . . Of all the children living in that building"—it was a big building, as I've noted, twenty stories tall—"I can't think of more than five who went to college and completed all their courses, and didn't put things off, and graduated with the other students in their class." He was convinced that, if he put it off, it would also disappoint his mother, as well as the teachers at the college who were helping him to finish up his work.

With all these people pulling for him now, Jeremy was resolute not to let them down. As it turned out, he did not. He passed his comprehensives—"not exactly," as he put it, "'trailing clouds of glory'"—but he said his English teachers told him he had done "a reputable job."

At a moment when I should have been relieved, I'm afraid I acted like a nervous parent, worried still that something might go wrong. I felt I ought to caution him about the last few courses he would have to pass.

"Am I crazy?" he replied. "Check it out. The answer is: I'm not." He assured me that he knew he still had a paper to complete and (he wasn't certain yet) either three or four exams to pass. He did the work. No last-minute spills and falls. In the end, he passed them all.

On a day in early June, I sat beside his mother and his father, and Martha and his grandma, and watched him as he lined up with his classmates at the stairway to the platform where the trustees of the college and the faculty and president were sitting. When he was given his diploma, he stood there somewhat longer than he was supposed to, with a slightly sheepish smile on his face, and looked into the audience as if he might perhaps make out his family in the crowd.

His mother brushed her hand across her eyes. Her pride in him was limitless.

— II —

In the pressures of the final months of school, Jeremy had had no chance to look into the future and think about a way he might support himself after graduation. Suddenly now, he had to make some practical decisions.

Thousands of other students every year—unless their college studies have been highly job-specific—face the same dilemma. But I think it may have been more difficult for Jeremy because his fascination with questions of morality and history and the passion that had stirred in him so many years before when he discovered Edgar Allan Poe and then, as he had put it, started "circling" Charles Dickens—the very qualities, indeed, that brought him to my notice and that of his pastor when he was twelve years old—refused to be extinguished on the day he was awarded his degree.

He was writing less, but continued reading deeply.

British history continued to intrigue him. He also grew attracted to the history of Puerto Rico, a subject he had seldom talked about before. He told me of the decimation of the native population, who were known as the Taínos and had lived in Puerto Rico prior to its subjugation by the Spanish, then by the United States. This, in turn, led him into reading more and more about the exploitation of the Caribbean and the Latin nations over the past century by various American administrations.

Contemporary politics in the United States preoccupied him too. This interest had begun while he was still in college during the contested electoral decision in November of 2000. He had since been following political events in New York and Washington more closely. He'd call me now and then, almost always late at night, to tell me something in the news that made him angry or that he found perplexing, or simply something that he thought I might find of interest.

Meanwhile, like a number of the other students who'd been active at St. Ann's when they were much younger, he was working with the children who came to the summer session at the church, a very solid and intensive program in which he was teaching history and reading. Late in the summer, he told me for the first time that he'd started thinking he might like to be a teacher.

I rejoiced to hear this because I'd seen how easily and comfortably he related to the children he was teaching at St. Ann's. And I had not forgotten the very gentle, empathetic way he had leaned across the table to the child who had AIDS and elicited at least a spark of energy and brought a smile to that child's eyes. I also thought the tribulations he had undergone while he was in middle school and high school in the Bronx would help him to identify more closely with young people who had never had the opportunities he'd subsequently received. The problem, however, as in the case of Lara, Pineapple's older sister, was that nothing in his education gave him the credentials to teach in a public school, for which, of course he needed to be certified.

As a temporary measure, after doing some investigation, he found there was an opening into the world of teaching, marginal though it may be, in the form of private programs operated by some corporations that contracted with the public schools to offer children preparation for those all-important standardized exams that were now mandated by the state, and for which a tutor did not need certification.

He got a job with one of these companies, which he, of course, regarded as "the wildest of ironies" since he hated tests like these and, when he had been a student at the high school in the Bronx, before he went to boarding school, had generally failed them. "Whenever I went into those bubble tests," he told me once, "I knew that I was done for. Number 2 pencils! The points would always break. . . ."

Still, he needed money. And, as much as he disliked the single-minded emphasis on pumping test results, he told me he was "slipping in a lot of stuff I'm not supposed to use"— reading children's stories to his students, having them keep journals, helping them write stories of their own—because the programmed lessons he was given were, he said, "so deadly dull" and the supervision was so poor that "no one seems to notice anyway."

He was living with his mother now and used part of the very modest pay he was receiving to help her with expenses and, now and then, to treat her to some luxuries (an evening in Manhattan, for example) that she would otherwise have been unable to enjoy.

One summer day, a year after he'd gotten out of college, he told me he would like to bring her up to Boston because she was fond of music and he thought that she would like to see the Boston Pops performing by the river on the

Esplanade. In the afternoon, he planned to show her the historic sites—"you know," he said, "the Old North Church, Faneuil Hall"—that his class had visited when he was in boarding school.

"We're coming on the Chinese bus," he told me on the night before. (The Chinese bus, a bargain ride, was used by students often when they traveled between Boston and New York.) "Very cheap. Sixteen dollars. We'll be getting in by noon. I'm hoping we can see you."

I met them around five o'clock at the public library, an historic building facing Copley Square. His mother, I was glad to see, had not been as thoroughly exhausted as I had expected by Jeremy's determination to bring her with him all the way up the steeple of the Old North Church to see the spot where the lanterns had been lighted in the famous Longfellow poem about the ride of Paul Revere.

We went for dinner to a place in Cambridge that I thought his mother would enjoy. He persuaded her to have a glass of cool sangria outside on the terrace of the restaurant before we went inside to eat. We ended up talking for so long that Jeremy at last inquired of his mother whether she would mind if they didn't go back into town to hear the concert, even though this had been the major reason why they came to Boston in the first place. His mother said she'd be relieved because, as Jeremy translated this to me, "She says that it's too much for her. The crowds there will be terrible."

So we stayed there at the restaurant and had dessert and coffee, and then I drove them into Boston just in time for them to catch the bus that left at 10:00 p.m. He told me the next evening they didn't get back to the Bronx until after three o'clock. "We had to take the subway. As you will recall, there aren't too many trains around that hour." He said his mother slept until the afternoon.

"It was a good visit. Check it out. I'm glad we caught

you when you were in Boston. My mother's very happy, which is what I wanted."

Throughout this time, he continued thinking about teaching, not in an ancillary situation for a test-prep corporation, but as a teacher—"you know, a *real* teacher"—in the schools themselves. I recommended that he might begin by taking a short course of study to become a classroom aide, "a paraprofessional" in the language of the public schools. But Jeremy resisted this. "I want to be a teacher, not a 'helping' teacher," and for this, he knew, "I need to get credentials."

I admired his persistence in adhering to his ultimate objective. But I honestly did not believe he was ready yet to undertake the concentrated regimen of study this was going to entail. I had the sense, although I didn't say this to him in so many words, that his strictly academic energies had been more depleted than he realized by the final push he had had to make to graduate from college, after having been obliged to drive himself so very hard throughout his years at boarding school.

Nonetheless, he was resolved to give it a good try. He applied successfully to a teacher-training college in New York that had classes in the evening, so that he could keep on earning money in the daytime at his present job. And, at least in the beginning, he threw himself right into it. Before long, new vocabularies and new concepts bubbled up into our conversations. "Piaget's stages of cognitive development. Children learn by imitation. Baby's in her crib. When her Mama waves goodbye, baby starts to understand that this means she's leaving. Then the baby starts to wave goodbye as well. . . . He saw a child moving through four stages. Erikson extended this beyond the childhood years. . . . Now we're going to begin Vygotsky. . . ."

But, at the end of two semesters, he confessed to me

that he found he wasn't in a state of mind to get into the tightly packed curriculum the program called for. He also said the heavy emphasis on metrics in the training program—"measurement of student progress" and the like—had frightened him because he'd never really overcome the math anxiety that had afflicted him since middle school. He conceded in the end that he could not handle it for now.

The disappointment of his premature and unsuccessful venture into teacher education obviously unsettled him and, I know, embarrassed him. He had taken a long journey and had won so many other victories up until this time. Now, after all the hurdles he had overcome, he found that he was locked into a sense of stasis, unable to achieve a goal that stubbornly eluded him.

"I wanted to become a writer," he said to me one evening. "But then I had to recognize I could not make that my career. I still love the theater. I want to be a teacher. All of that," he said, "is still inside of me."

Hearing this, I did my best to steer away from any of those sweeteners that had never been a part of our relationship. I did point out to him that many of the people I admired most, the talented young research aides for instance who help me to complete my books, were typically about his age, and some of them three or four years older, and they still were looking for that moment when their goals and longings, inchoate and disparate as they appeared to be, came together all at once—and frequently in unexpected ways.

But words are easy. And he needed more than words. It was Martha—"the reverend," as he called her still—who understood, better than I, that he needed a specific sense of purpose now, a sense of being "centered" at this moment in his life, no matter what direction he might later go. And she was wise and practical enough to find a way by which to make this possible.

Martha had always been a rock of loyalty to Jeremy. In the time of deep uncertainty he was going through, the church was his safe harbor. She put him to work teaching in the afterschool and, at some later point—I don't recall exactly when—she placed him in a more demanding and responsible position as the manager of the office at St. Ann's. In this role, he worked closely at her side.

For now, therefore, he had a solid job, managed his position well, and intervened effectively when problems would arise, not only at the church but in the community it served. Medical emergencies, warnings of eviction, a child who broke into tears because she'd seen a shooting on the street while walking to St. Ann's, all of this infused the daily fabric of existence at the afterschool and in the neighborhood nearby. When the pastor had to be away, Jeremy would always check with her by phone but, if he couldn't reach her, he was learning to assume and exercise good judgment of his own.

The confidence that Martha placed in Jeremy soon extended into other areas as well. When members of the congregation could not leave their homes, because of illness for example, or if they were in a hospital and perhaps not likely to survive, Martha made repeated visits in which she would hold their hands, talk with them and pray with them, and listen to their hopes and fears. After a while, she began inviting Jeremy to come with her.

"He has a gift for giving comfort to these people. Some of them are elderly," she said. "Sometimes he does this on his own, going back to talk with them, or read to them, or pray with them, or simply bring whatever sense of peace and kindness that he can into their final days. It's not perfunctory for Jeremy. It comes right from his heart and soul. I know that they look forward to his visits."

Beneath the surface of his cleverness with words, beneath his unabated and intensely felt attraction to the literary world and to works of theater that had mesmerized him since his years in school, something new was stirring in him now. Or, more precisely, something that had been there since he was a child, but had been quiescent in him for a good long while, seemed to come to life again.

"You know," he said, "I still have that feeling about teaching. It hasn't gone away. But maybe there are other ways of teaching than the one that takes place in a school. . . ."

Martha had already spoken of his pastoral abilities and had once reflected on whether he might someday be a candidate for ordination. "He has the qualities of character. His sense of theater wouldn't hurt. He'd have to go through seminary first. . . ." I didn't know if this was what was in mind when he spoke of "other ways of teaching." But he left the matter there. And I didn't press him to go any further.

– III –

On a recent evening I was with him in his office at St. Ann's as he was wrapping up his work. It was after six o'clock. The pastor had left. The children were gone. He slipped some messages and memos for the pastor into a manila folder and put them in a drawer. In the silence of the church where we had met so many years before, he was in a mood to talk.

"When I get discouraged"—and, he said, "it happens to me quite a lot—I tell myself to think about the distance that I've gone since I was a child here and you and Martha, in a sense, 'sent me out into the world.'

"The years at boarding school were more intimidating for me maybe than you really knew, because I felt so different from the other kids at first. It was not until I got into my theater group, and even then it took almost a year, before

I felt that I was making friends with other kids, and not just my teachers. And, as I guess you probably knew, I was never positive until my senior year that I would graduate. And all of this became much harder when I saw what was ahead of me in college.

"Theater was my personal protection. I knew that I could do it well. You know what it's like when there's one thing that you're sure of? It was like my fortress. I directed three plays while I was in college, always with a social message. One of them I wrote myself. I don't need to tell you that my grades were not the best, and you'll remember that you wondered whether I could finish in four years. But I surprised myself: I did.

"The disappointment that I felt when I went to grad school and I finally realized it was more than I could do—it could have crushed me. . . . Well, it *did* crush me when I had to give it up. But somehow I was able to get back on my feet, and the reverend helped to make it easier for me.

"Now I've had a chance to work with children here. I was working with the little ones for most of the first two years. I'm always happy when one of them comes upstairs and asks me, 'How you doin', Mr. Jeremy?' I like to think I made a difference in their lives, even though I know that it was just a small beginning. And I think I've come to learn how many other ways there are to make a difference for these kids, and not only for the kids but for their parents and grandparents too. I take some satisfaction in what I've been able to achieve." He leaned across his desk before he spoke again. "But I do not intend to leave it there. . . .

"When people tell me, 'This idea of yours, this thing you have in mind, you will never do it. You don't know the *way* to do it. You don't have the discipline and steadiness to do it. This, for you, WILL NOT BE ALLOWED,' I tell myself, 'I will do it anyway. I will do it someday when I'm ready and I'm strong.'

"Do you remember when I talked with Dr. Coles? I mean, the time he came to lecture at my school?"

"You told me that he had sad eyes."

"Do you remember what I asked?"

"That was a long time ago," I said.

"I asked him whether someone that he wrote about, a little girl in Mississippi—Ruby Bridges was her name—had finally reached her goal in life and if she felt fulfilled. And he said a goal should not be seen as something separate from the journey that a person takes to get there. 'Not the place, but the path. Not the goal, but the way.' That's how I remember it.

"I still believe the journey is ahead of me."

CHAPTER 12

The Killing Fields

A tiny boy.

Seven years old.

Light brown skin. Dark brown hair. A glowing smile in his eyes. Angelo: a mischievous boy. But the teachers at his school adored him.

A little girl named Tabitha Brown, who was in his class at P.S. 30, told me that she sat as far away from him as possible because, she said, "he's bad" in class and says "bad things" to her.

"What does he say?"

"He says, 'Fishy, fishy!'"

"That doesn't seem so bad," I said.

"It's bad! It is! He comes right up behind me when the teacher isn't looking—and he *says* it!"

"Say it again?"

"Fishy, fishy!" she replied, gulping like a minnow at air bubbles as she said the dreaded words a second time. Then she concealed her face in her arms and leaned down on the tabletop and fell into gales of laughter, shaking her head repeatedly.

Angelo posed a lot of minor problems for the people at St. Ann's. He seemed to have decided that he would be "a bad little boy," although the bad things that he did were always fairly innocent—on the scale of "fishy, fishy"—and Martha told me that he had a strong religious side and asked her many questions about God.

Once, according to Miss Katrice, who worked in the kitchen at St. Ann's, "he asked me if I thought that God is powerful." She told him he should go upstairs and ask the priest. Martha, she said, told him that "the Lord makes miracles if we believe in Him with all our hearts." Later, she said, he came back to the kitchen "and he said, 'If God works miracles, how come He never helps me to pick up my toys?'

"So help me, Jonathan," she said, one hand against her breast, "I had to laugh!"

As young as he was, Angelo seemed to do a lot of thinking about God. He didn't doubt that God had power to affect his life, but he believed that he had power too, because he was convinced that his own behavior could determine whether God felt good or bad. God was pleased, he told me once—"He's happy!"—when a child did what he was supposed to do. But when a child misbehaved, he told me that "God cries."

"How do you know God cries?" I asked.

"I can hear God crying," he replied.

"You can *hear* him?"

"Yes," he said.

"What do you do?"

"I go to the priest."

"What do you say?"

"Can you please give me bless?"

"What does she do?"

He told me that she sprinkled water on his head. He called it "whole-fly water," but I had seen her sprinkling holy water on the children's heads so I knew that this was what he meant. The ritual had less solemnity than I had expected. Martha does it in a playful way. But Angelo really did believe the holy water was going to help him not to misbehave.

Angelo's mother was an equable and good-natured woman who worked at the pharmacy on St. Ann's Avenue in the same block as the church. His father was in prison, six hours from New York. He had been in prison almost from the time Angelo was born. Angelo used to say he was away "at school." He told me once his father would be "graduating" soon.

A picture of Angelo, standing in the doorway of the kitchen at St. Ann's, shows a child with a round and friendly face, his hair cut very short, holding a stuffed rabbit under his right arm. Fred Rogers took the photograph, sometime in the fall of 1996. He was in New York to do a lecture with me and then to do an interview for PBS. When we were done, he asked if I would take him with me to St. Ann's so he could see the afterschool and meet the children there.

The place was packed. Angelo was at the far end of the room, but he spotted us the moment we arrived. He headed straight across the floor with his arms spread wide, looked Mr. Rogers directly in the eyes, wrapped his arms around his waist, and reached up as high as he could to kiss him on his face.

After the pastor had welcomed Mr. Rogers to St. Ann's and introduced him to the children and the staff, many of the children left the room to go to their tutorial instruction on the top floor of the church. But she permitted Angelo

and Tabitha and about a dozen of the others to remain
behind to talk with Mr. Rogers, and Miss Katrice brought
out a tray of cookies and little cups of juice.

A few weeks later, Mr. Rogers sent me an album of pictures he had taken, with observations he had jotted down
on yellow stick-on pages. "This one is my favorite," he had
written underneath the photograph of Angelo. "There was
a real light in his eyes, not just a child's normal friendli-
ness," he said. "I won't forget him. . . ."

When Angelo was in first grade, a year before we met,
he misbehaved and didn't do his lessons, and when spring-
time came his teacher said he wasn't ready to go on to second grade. So, on a day in June, Miss Rosa had to tell his
mother that he couldn't be promoted.

It wasn't until September of that year, when he was in
the first grade for the second time, that I got to know him at
St. Ann's, and it wasn't until he was in the second grade that
I started visiting his school.

His teacher, an African-American woman in her fifties
by the name of Frances Dukes, had taught at the school for
fifteen years. She had twenty-nine children in her room, but
she had a firm old-fashioned style that enabled her to keep
a class of children under good control without the need to
raise her voice when they misbehaved. She would simply
fold her arms and give the class a disappointed look—the
way their grandmas might have done—and order and
respectfulness would be restored.

"My children are grown up," she said. "I live alone.
These children are my family."

I could tell she had a special feeling of protectiveness
for Angelo. "Even when he's up to mischief in the room,"
she said, "there's something in his personality that makes it
easy to forgive him. I'd love to take him on a holiday someday. I think it would be fun to take him to the South and
show him where I lived when I was growing up."

Once, when I was standing with her at her desk, Angelo came up to us, put his arm around my waist, pressed his head against my side, and looked up at the teacher. "He's been trying very hard this year," she told me, looking down at Angelo. "But he does talk out of place in class . . . , and we're working on this, aren't we?"—to which he, of course, agreed and nodded eagerly.

Angelo's birthday that year came on the final day of school. Another child's birthday would be one day later. The teacher asked them to come up and stand before the blackboard while the class sang "Happy Birthday," after which everybody got a slice of birthday cake with yellow frosting that she'd made for them the night before.

Angelo had a tennis racquet on his desk: a present from the principal, Miss Rosa. When he brought it up to show Miss Dukes, she asked him if he knew that she played tennis too.

"You do?" he said.

"I do."

She surprised him even more by telling him that she knew how to Rollerblade. The children smiled at the thought of their teacher, who was so respectable and proper, spinning along the sidewalks of the town in which she lived, which was in New Jersey, riding on her Rollerblades. . . .

– II –

The years at P.S. 30 were happy ones for Angelo. In third grade and fourth grade he was very fortunate to have other teachers who were rigorous and seasoned, like Miss Dukes, and who also treated him protectively but firmly. In fifth grade, he had Miss Harrinarine, a wonderful teacher I've described before.

His "bad boy" inclinations had been softened to a large degree by the time he left the school. But they resurfaced when he entered middle school, the same chaotic and unhappy place that Jeremy had attended earlier. The starkness of the contrast between the safe and warm environment of his elementary school and the anonymity and impersonality he encountered at his middle school brought out a combative quality in Angelo. Outbreaks of violence were common at the school. The toughest boys were the ones who set the norm. They clustered in the corridors and teased and threatened students whom they knew that they could scare. Angelo said, "I wanted them to think I was as tough as they were, so they wouldn't mess with me. . . ."

He learned to be a fighter. And, even though he felt that he was fighting in his own defense, he was suspended three times in one year. At that point, his mother moved out of the neighborhood into a part of Spanish Harlem that may not have been as rough as the streets around St. Ann's but, as he told me later, had "big problems" of its own, including a drug culture. His mother enrolled him in a school near their apartment, but his growing tendency to take extreme offense at disrespectful statements other students made at his expense, and the sudden waves of fury with which he'd defend himself, led him soon to be expelled.

He was now assigned to yet another school, which the principal himself described to me as "a dumping ground" for kids that "other schools don't want." The school was one of several of those so-called "themed academies" with pretentiously imposing acronymic names that had been newly founded in New York. But it was academic only in its name. Class size averaged thirty students. (I walked into one class that held thirty-one, another that held thirty-two.) Thirteen of the fifteen teachers were not certified to teach. Supplies were scarce. "Three of my classes don't have textbooks," said the principal. "I have to fight and scratch for everything I get."

The school was only about a dozen blocks from the overwhelmingly white Upper East Side of Manhattan, but more than ninety-nine percent of students at the school were black or Hispanic. I met a single white girl in the hours I was there.

I asked a mathematics teacher how he happened to be teaching there. He told me he had been in business but—presumably, he had lost his job—needed to find other work. "A friend said, 'Bring your college transcript in,'" The next day, he said, he was teaching at this school.

"If we had the money, ideal class size for these kids would be fifteen to twenty," another teacher said. But, even if they had the money for sufficient teachers, the principal observed, "we wouldn't have the space." He opened a door that led into a storage closet. I went into the closet with him. There was scarcely room for us to turn around. "This," he told me, "is our social studies office. How would you like to have your office here?"

I had met the principal at an education conference seven months before. The topic of my lecture had been inequality in funding and resources in our urban schools. I noticed him nodding in agreement when I made a reference to New York. After my talk, he had taken me aside and told me he'd be grateful if I'd visit with his teachers and his students when I had a chance. At the time, I didn't know that Angelo was there.

After the principal brought me to an English class and a rudimentary mathematics class, we came to a room with social studies posters (two of them, to be exact) taped across one of the walls. The other walls were bare. Before the principal could introduce me to the teacher, Angelo stood up in the middle of the class. He came directly to the door. He was much taller than when I had seen him last, but he still had a boyish look and gave me one of those big and un-embarrassed hugs he used to give when he was a child at St. Ann's. I explained to the principal that Angelo and I had known each other since he was a boy. So he invited him to come out to the corridor to talk.

As it happened, at the moment when we left the room, there was an uproar taking place outside the classroom door. A very tall Hispanic boy, bleeding from a wound above one of his eyes, came tearing down the corridor and shoved all three of us aside to try to catch up with another boy who, apparently, had given him that wound. The other boy, however, had already disappeared through a doorway to the stairwell at the far end of the hall and had likely left the building by this time. The one who had been injured was in a state of wild rage. A teacher in the hallway did his best to calm him down.

The principal brought us to his office, where he had a sofa and some comfortable chairs. He put his hand on Angelo's arm. "This is one of the students here who makes me feel it's worth the job. He's trying hard to do his work. He doesn't create problems for his teachers. He tries to keep away from students who would like to cause him trouble, like the boy that you just saw, who is almost out of my control."

He sat down on the sofa next to Angelo. I pulled up one of the chairs in front of them. Then he turned to Angelo and asked if he would like to tell him how it happened that we knew each other. Angelo told him how we'd met when I had come to St. Ann's Church and how I used to visit in his class when he was in the second grade. And he talked about Miss Rosa and Miss Dukes, nostalgically and warmly. He said he wished he never had to leave Miss Rosa's school, because he'd been happy there and the years that followed had been so much harder.

The principal listened to him carefully. When he was finished, the principal, who was an Hispanic man and told us he had grown up in New York, talked to Angelo about his own unhappy years while he was in secondary school. He told him he had been a high school drop-out and that it was several years before he found the motivation to return to school. When he got to college, he resolved to find a way to be of help to other kids who were going through the kinds of troubles he himself had known. This, he said, was why he had decided to become a teacher. Later, he explained to Angelo, he received a graduate degree that qualified him to become a principal.

I was impressed that he was speaking of these matters right in front of Angelo. But it also came into my mind: "He knows what he's doing." I thought that he was doing this in order to create the basis for a sense of reciprocity between the two of them and to break down any sense of hesitation Angelo might feel to look upon him as a friend he could confide in freely as well as an older man he could rely upon with safety.

After Angelo went back to class, the principal said he wished he had more students like him at the school. "I'm sure you can see that I identify with Angelo. I *like* this boy tremendously. But he isn't out of danger. His feelings are hurt easily, and he has a temper. I think he's warring with himself to keep that temper under wraps and not permit it to explode."

He also made the candid point, which he'd alluded to before, that the very scarce resources he received could not provide these students with the caliber of teaching and the close attention and support he knew that they deserved. "All I can offer here is a very meager level of instruction." It was, he said, "a mockery of what a kid of any race or economic class is going to require to survive in this society."

I left the school with a mixture of reactions. The principal's words had hardly been encouraging and had simply reinforced what I'd already seen. At the same time, for all the school's self-evident deficiencies, Angelo had a principal who was going to watch over him and would not abandon him and would do his very best to reinforce his confidence and keep him out of trouble by helping to develop his self-discipline.

Angelo, in any case, had been enrolled already in two other middle schools, the one that had expelled him and the one that had repeatedly suspended him. It seemed unlikely that any other middle school would be willing to accept him; and any school that did would probably be no better, and might be even worse, than the one he was attending. I hoped for the best, but I could not easily dispel a feeling of foreboding.

– III –

The years in middle school for too many children in the Bronx, as in other troubled sections of New York, have proven to be killing fields in academic terms, as well as psychologically and socially. Thousands of students in other cities too, even when their elementary schooling has been relatively good, come out of their middle schools and go on to high school with severe impairment of their basic skills. Whatever assets they've acquired in the elementary years seem to be transmuted into deficits by the time they enter the ninth grade.

High school was a time of misery for Angelo. As hard as he tried, he could not keep up with the subject-matter content of the courses students had to take in their ninth- and tenth-grade years. In September, 2006, when he expected to begin eleventh grade—he was seventeen by now—he was told he hadn't been promoted, because he'd failed so many courses in the year before.

Humiliation, injured pride, placed him in a state of mind in which he found it difficult to focus on his lessons and pay attention to his teachers in the classes he was taking for a second time. Like many other students who are held back from promotion twice or more before they are eighteen, Angelo had lost the motivation to keep on. Early in October, he dropped out of school.

I had not seen Angelo for two years at the time—it would be another two years before I caught up with him again. This was in part because my mother, then my father, passed away during those years and there was a period when I didn't travel to New York at all. When I did begin to go back to the Bronx, I found myself preoccupied with students, or with former students, who were still in the South Bronx and still associated somehow with St. Ann's.

I knew that Angelo was still in Harlem, but I never knew exactly where he lived or if he had a phone. As has often been the case, I kept in closest contact with those of the students who were easiest to reach or who called me on their own to tell me when their phone numbers were changed. When I inquired about Angelo, nobody around St. Ann's seemed to know what he was doing now. Ariella said she'd seen him once or twice in the streets around the church but that he was with his friends and didn't stop to talk with her.

The next time I saw him was in 2009, by which time his mother had moved back to the Bronx. We met on St. Ann's Avenue as I was coming up the block from the corner store. He made it obvious that he was glad to see me—as always, a hug, right in front of everybody passing in the street—but he also looked concerned. We went up to the garden on the hill behind the church. It was early evening. We sat down on the grass.

He told me right away he'd been in trouble with the law

and had been arrested something like a dozen times since he had left middle school. In seven of these cases, he was taken to the Tombs, a complex of detention centers in Manhattan where detainees can be held while their case is being processed and while waiting for arraignment. In theory, they must be arraigned or else released within one day but, because of court delays, this sometimes can take longer.

When I asked him what he'd done to end up in the Tombs, the reasons that he gave me seemed of such a minor nature that I had to wonder if he was leaving something out. Once, for example, he was on the subway platform waiting for a train when a group of young, unruly men about his age created a disorder that led to their arrest. The transit police apparently believed he was part of the same group and asked to see his ID card, but he said, "I didn't have it with me." So they arrested him as well. He was released to his mother, with no charges, early the next morning.

Another time, he had used his Metro card to go through the turnstile—legally, correctly—but after he went through, a man behind him who, he said, looked very poor ("I thought that he was homeless") asked him, as a favor, if he would swipe him through. Only a week before, Martha had done the same for me, since I had no Metro card, when we were going through the turnstile at Brook Avenue. Martha, of course, wears the collar of a clergywoman, and she's a white person, and I was dressed in my suit and tie from Harvard Square.

Not so with Angelo. A transit officer apparently was watching him and, he said, "beckoned to me with his finger," and informed him that it was illegal to do what he had done. "He checked my record and he saw my previous arrest. I also jumped a turnstile once when I was younger, and that was in my record too." So that was the second time he was taken to the Tombs.

Yet another time, he'd been standing on a corner,

somewhere in East Harlem, close to a street where a robbery had taken place a short time before. A police car, he said, swerved up on the curb. The officer said he "fitted the description"—"light-skinned Hispanic male, white T-shirt, close-cropped hair"—of the person believed to be the perpetrator of the crime, even though the same description would have fit at least a dozen other men or teenage boys who were in the neighborhood at exactly the same time.

Again, however, a visit to the Tombs. . . .

When I said that Angelo told me he had been "in trouble with the law," I did not intend by this to indicate that he had committed crimes, or crimes of any magnitude, like the crimes, for instance, that Christopher committed and for which he'd been convicted to a term of seven years. But the simple fact that Angelo was standing on that corner for no apparent reason, or no reason that he could explain, and probably the more important fact that he was often hanging out with boys who *were* committing crimes, exposed him to suspicions on the part of the police that were easily predictable.

In at least one situation that led to his arrest, his role was not as innocent and passive as in the other cases, but involved an element of participation on his part that, as he conceded to me later, was "my own stupidity."

"I was on 110th Street, near the gate to Central Park," he told me, when a wild fight broke out among the boys that he was with. One of the boys, a friend of his, was being beaten by another boy who, he said, had thrown him to the ground and then "was kicking him" and "stomping him" with heavy cleated boots. Angelo jumped into the fight and struck the bully who was beating up his friend with a knuckle-punch that nearly knocked him out.

The entire group ended up in court. Two of the boys, who, he said, had weapons on them when they were arrested, got seven months in jail. Angelo, the youngest of the group, was ordered to return to court for a separate hearing. When he returned, he was released without being charged, but was lectured by the judge, as he knew that he deserved to be, for letting himself be drawn into the fight.

Throughout the years since he'd dropped out of school, Angelo told me, he'd been looking for a stable job. None of the jobs he found, however, lasted very long. One was with a construction firm for which, he told me, he was "doing stock," but it was a seasonal job and ended in four months. Another job, one he said that he enjoyed, was for a man who was renovating brownstones in a part of Harlem in which gentrification by white families had begun. But this, too, was a temporary job and, like the other, "off the books," and it ended shortly.

Every so often when we met, which we did more often now, Angelo would tell me he was "going back to school" and, every time he told me this, he would sound entirely earnest and sincere. But there was a terrible naïveté, as I would repeatedly discover, in what he had in mind when he spoke of "school" and what he believed the schooling he was thinking of was going to deliver.

He was easily attracted by profit-making firms that offered a degree or some other document, which, as prospective applicants were told, was going to prepare them for occupational employment. One of these firms, called "TCI"—which stands for Technical Career Institute— advertised "associate" degrees or "associate occupational degrees," for which it charged $6,000 for each of four semesters. What Angelo had no way to know was that the attrition rate at TCI was a catastrophic 81 percent. Fewer than one in five of those who had enrolled in TCI learned enough, or stayed with the program long enough, to receive degrees in what the catalog issued by the institute described, in an obscure location, as "150 percent of the normal time. . . ." How many of that 81 percent who did not receive two-year degrees by the end of three years may have done so after four or five or more years was not stated in the catalog, which leads one to suspect it was very few.

Angelo knew none of this. I didn't, either, until somewhat later. All I knew was that he talked about it constantly, and with the highest hopes, over the course of several months. Suddenly, he never spoke of it again.

Another time, he was attracted to "a school," as he mistakenly described it, which, he said, would prepare him for a job (guarding municipal buildings, I believe), give him a certificate, and arrange for his employment. He saw the advertisement in the New York Daily News.

When he told me of his interest, I asked my assistant to see if she could locate any information about this institution. The only source of information she could find, after an extensive search, was a consumer website in which former clients of the firm, some of whom were from the Bronx or Brooklyn, issued warnings to potential applicants.

"Beware," said one. "They prey on your desperation," said another. "The training is a joke. . . . You get a fake certificate and they send you on your way. . . ." "I tried to get my money back," but the company "refused." "It needs to be shut down."

What comes across from all of this, as I look at notes I made on the intermittent conversations we were having in New York, is the high exhilaration that would lead him every time to think that any of these programs would represent a magic key to open up whatever door appeared to stand in front of him. At one point—he was not yet twenty-one—he told me that he'd signed up for a program to obtain a GED. But, as he belatedly discovered, and as my assistant was able to confirm, the instructors in the program were not licensed teachers, had no experience or background in remedial instruction, and had not been given the pedagogic training they would need to give a student who had little more than elementary level skills the preparation it would take to get through the exams.

One of the questions that obviously comes to mind is why he kept on wasting time looking into programs that never led him anywhere, instead of turning for advice to someone well informed who was right there on the scene and who would have guided him—Martha could have done this—to any of a number of good nonprofit agencies that could offer realistic preparation for the world of work or for the GED that he was hoping to achieve.

Once, when he was seven years old, another child at St. Ann's, an older girl named Stephanie who sometimes helped the younger ones, asked Angelo, "What grade are you in?"

"I had to repeat," he said.

"What grade did you repeat?"

"First grade," he replied, looking up at Stephanie. "How do you pass first grade?"

"It's hard," she answered, trying to be kind to him.

"Yes. It *is*. It's hard," he said. "All that work! And now I have to do it all again. . . ."

Thirteen years had passed since then. But, as grown-up as he was and as tough as he believed that he could be, it seemed as if the puzzled seven-year-old boy in him remained. How do you do it? How do other people do it? Why are these things so difficult for me when other people seem to find them easy?

Sometimes, when he told me of his feelings of perplexity about a goal he thought he was about to reach but which once again had slipped away from him, I found that I was thinking of a child's toy, a little boat without an anchor, spinning in a circle as the currents drew it off in one direction and then pulled it in another. Unfortunately, one of the strongest of those currents was his unwise and persistent loyalty to a circle of acquaintances whose unhealthy patterns of existence, as he should have known by now, were not good for him. His inability to rid himself of these acquaintances was now about to lead him into making an unfortunate mistake.

– IV –

In the summer of 2010, Angelo was standing with a friend outside of a corner store in Harlem—he called it "a loosie store"—where people could buy cigarettes for fifty cents apiece and where, he said, the owner of the store was working with drug dealers for a portion of the profits—and possibly also for his own protection.

Angelo's friend was dealing drugs, which Angelo insisted unconvincingly that he did not know before that time. Like many other dealers in the Bronx and Harlem, Angelo's friend did not keep the drugs that he was selling in his own possession. Instead, he left them stashed inside the store.

"A Puerto Rican guy," said Angelo, "comes up to my friend and asks him for *manteca*," which is a term, in Puerto Rican slang, meaning dope or heroin. Angelo's friend— whom he calls "this idiot"—"isn't thinking fast. He wants to make the sale. He tells him, 'Go inside that store.'"

His friend, he said, waited outside for a moment, then asked Angelo, "Come on with me into the store," as if this were a casual matter, which it obviously was not. This is the point where Angelo, as he was about to learn, made the worst misjudgment of his life.

"I followed him into the store. . . ."

His friend, as it happened, was under surveillance by narcotics officers. The man who asked him for *manteca* was an undercover agent. "He slapped the cuffs on both of us." Angelo was brought to court and charged with sale of heroin. He was sent to Rikers Island while awaiting trial.

His attorney—he was fortunate to have a good one—cautioned him that if, as Angelo intended, he insisted he was innocent, it could be as long as twelve months, even more, before the prosecution was prepared to bring the case to trial. During that time, unless he had the large amount of money it would take him to make bail, Angelo would remain in prison. If he was found guilty when he finally went to trial, it was possible, because of his prior record of arrests, that he might face a sentence of as long as four to seven years.

The attorney convinced him to agree to a plea bargain, one in which he pleaded guilty, but to a lesser charge than the sale of heroin, and with the understanding that the prosecution would reduce the sentence it would seek for him. The prosecution, it appears, accepted his plea bargain. As a result, he was released from Rikers Island on the day before Thanksgiving with the date of sentencing set for eight weeks later. On January 20, he was sentenced to six months in prison and five years of probation.

The court gave him credit for the four months he'd already spent at Rikers Island and an extra two months because of "good behavior," so, as it turned out, the sentence he was given had already been served. He would, however, be obliged to meet with his probation officer on an intensive basis. This, I knew—at least I hoped—would make him far more wary about going out at night with people who were using drugs or selling them or, for that matter, who were simply living, as he had done for several years, along the outer edge of criminality.

There was an unexpected benefit in the months that Angelo had spent at Rikers Island. The prison runs a number of education programs, some of which I've been able to

observe. Excellent instructors from the New York City public schools deliver Adult Basic Education to the lowest-level
learners—those who never learned to read and write when
they were in school. For inmates at a more proficient level,
the prison also runs a program for the GED. Angelo seized
upon the opportunity and took advantage of the preparation he was able to receive in classes that were half the size
of those he'd had in middle school and high school.

In the months that followed his release, he finally
passed the GED in social sciences and high-school-level
English language skills. He's studying now to pass the GED
in math and science also.

Angelo is a very different person now from the injudi-
cious boy who went into that corner store and, in so doing,
walked into the arms of the police. One of the major reasons is a happy alteration in the make-up of his family and,
as a direct result, the nature of his life at home.

Angelo's mother decided to remarry about seven years
ago and, soon after, she gave birth to twins—a boy named
Timothy, a girl named Violeta. When they were born,
Angelo was still caught up in the behavior that led him into
problems with the law. It was only after he came home from
Rikers Island—the twins were nearly six by then—that he
began to stabilize his state of mind enough to take a healthy
and constructive role within the children's lives.

Their father is an older person, now in his late sixties.
He has a heart condition that has recently required surgery. For these reasons, and perhaps for others of which I'm
unaware, he has not become an active presence as a parent
in their home. Angelo has, in effect, become the father of
his younger siblings.

He wakes them up. He gives them their breakfast. He
walks them to their school. He comes back to wait for them
at the end of school. If his mother's working late, he cooks
their supper. He puts them into their pajamas. He sits beside

them while they do their homework, and he helps them with their homework, before he lets them watch TV—but "only for an hour." Then he puts them into bed and reads to them before they fall asleep.

One night this year when I was there, Violeta said she had a dream the night before. It was about Angelo. "He was in my room at school, and he and I were exactly the same size, and there was a dog with brown hair and white spots in between our chairs. The teacher said, 'If the dog knows how to talk, he can stay. If it's not a talking dog, he will have to leave.'"

Angelo scooped her up and held her in his arms and swung her in a circle all around the room.

Timothy told me that he had two teachers at his school. One of them, he said, was named "Miss Chicken Pea"—Angelo said the name was "Chicopee." The other was "Miss Song." He and Angelo took me in to see the bunk beds where he and Violeta slept. He climbed up to the bed on top, then swung around gymnastically and landed on the bed below. "You can call me Spider-Man," he said. Angelo tickled him on the bottoms of his feet. Violeta came into the room. She wanted to be tickled, too.

Angelo works in the hours while the children are at school—a part-time job, "a restaurant job, around the corner from my home"—but he says he misses them until he picks them up at four. The sweetness of the evenings that he spends with them at home functions as a counterforce to whatever anger other young men in his situation often feel—at themselves or at the world—after they have undergone so many troubles for so many years. And he's not embittered by the insufficiencies of education he encountered after he had left behind the good years he had spent in elementary school, although it's possible he has a right to be.

– V –

In September, Angelo and I were having dinner in the Bronx at a place called Camaguey, a small Honduran restaurant—four tables on one side, a counter and six barstools on the other. While we were eating, Angelo stood up from his chair and stared very hard at an attractive woman who was wearing denim shorts and sitting at the counter having a cold beer.

My first reaction was that he was hoping he might capture her attention. But, after he sat down, he leaned across the table and asked if I remembered who she was.

I told him that I had a distant memory that she was somebody I might have known before. It was the soft configuration of her jaw and the deep expressiveness within her dark brown eyes that made me think I might have met her once. But I wasn't sure.

"Remember when you used to visit in my second grade? There was a student in my class that I liked to tease and Miss Dukes had to scold me? And she seated her as far from me as possible?"

I remembered that he used to tease a bashful little girl, but I told him I could not recall her name.

"Tabitha Brown," Angelo replied.

At the mention of her name, the woman turned halfway around, hesitated for a moment as if she wasn't certain whether it was Angelo, then got up, came over to our table with the cold beer in her hand, said hello to Angelo in a warm and friendly way, and took a chair from another table and sat down.

Angelo told her that I used to visit them in the second grade. She did not remember this, but she was polite and poised and held out her hand to me and spoke to me respectfully. She smiled when I said how much I liked Miss Dukes.

"I loved Miss Dukes," said Tabitha. *"This one"*—she gave a nod at Angelo—"gave her a hard time."

Angelo said not a word.

"He was a wicked little boy," she said. "He teased me without mercy."

I asked if she remembered other teachers at the school and, not to my surprise, she spoke of Miss Harrinarine. She said she was "forever grateful to that woman" because "she was the first teacher that I ever had who made me realize I could go to college. She kind of held me by the hand, and, later on, when I was in high school, I would ask for her advice. If I called her after school she'd always call me back. . . ."

Tabitha said she knew that she was fortunate because her parents did not let her go to middle school or high school here in the South Bronx. After P.S. 30, she had gone to school in a suburban district where her aunt and uncle lived. From high school, she had gone directly into college, but was taking off a year to work and save up money for her senior year.

She struck me as a confident and serious young woman, not at all the bashful child I remembered from so many years before, and, when she joked with Angelo about his schoolboy days, she did it in an amiable but very grown-up way, as if she felt much older than he was. When she left to head out to the street, Angelo watched her with, I thought, a hint of something like intimidation in his eyes.

The following day, he told me he was thinking about Tabitha. She had done "so much," he said, and had gone so far beyond the point where both of them had started out. She had gone to college—not some kind of "institute" that advertised for customers in the Daily News—and she made it very clear that she planned to graduate. He did not sound envious of Tabitha, but he seemed to be subdued.

I reminded him that Tabitha had some big advantages that neither he nor many other children in the neighborhood had had. In view of all the disappointments and the years of misdirection he had undergone, I told him that his own achievements were impressive too. I said I thought he should be proud of the calm and steady life he was leading now. I hope that he believed me.

When friends of mine who take an empathetic interest in the lives of children of the very poor try to picture what "success" might represent for kids who grow up in those sections of our cities where poverty and racial isolation are the norm, they tend to gravitate to the iconic narratives of children such as Pineapple and Jeremy, and others such as Tabitha, whose victories seem indisputable because they are recognizable in familiar academic terms. "They struggle hard. They get into college. They graduate from college. They contribute to society." And, in Jeremy's case, and Pineapple's, and that of her sisters, all of this is obviously true. I still feel a sense of wonderment at what those three young women have accomplished up to this point in their lives.

But "success," an arbitrary term at best, takes a wide variety of forms, some of which do not glow so visibly. Angelo did not have the opportunities that Jeremy and Pineapple received. He never had the conversational exposure—to history, to books, to questions about ethics, and to challenging ideas—that Jeremy was given by the pastor and the poet and his other mentors. Nor did he have the very strong parental backing that Pineapple knew she could depend upon. His father, it will be recalled, had been in prison from the time when Angelo was born. His mother, kindly woman that she is, did not have the temperament or determination to oversee his education and could not help him to control the furious defensiveness that erupted in him in his adolescent years.

But seven sessions in the Tombs and four months at Rikers Island have not destroyed the qualities of decency and earnestness, and persistent innocence—that "real light in his eyes" that Mr. Rogers noted when he took the photograph of Angelo that now hangs here on my wall. He isn't slick. He isn't glib. He isn't cruel. He isn't mean. He's a kind and loving human being, which is not the case with many of the more sophisticated people that I know who have been to college or have multiple degrees. To me, those qualities of elemental goodness in his soul matter more than anything.

CHAPTER 13

Number Our Days

This is about my godson. I saved his story for the last, because it was the hardest one to write.

Benjamin lived on Beekman Ave in one of the Diego-Beekman buildings owned by Gerald Schuster, the slumlord and political contributor. The Wild Cowboys ruled the street when Benjamin was growing up. "Crack and heroin," he recalls, "were everywhere."

Benjamin's mother died when he was twelve, in 1992. She had five children. Only two are still alive.

His oldest brother was shot dead when Benjamin was eight. He had been a drug dealer in Brooklyn.

A second brother, Edward, whom I knew to a degree because he begged for money in front of a coffee shop and pizza place where I used to go with Jeremy, was a ghostly figure, wasted by addiction and frequently arrested. He choked to death on his own internal fluids while in the custody of the police.

A third brother disappeared after his mother passed away and, having never reappeared, is "presumed dead," in the language of the law.

Benjamin has a sister who is his elder by twelve years. Addicted to crack at seventeen, she has been convicted countless times for sale of drugs, use of drugs, robbery, and gun possession. She has spent more of her life in prison than she has on the outside.

Benjamin was raped at the age of nine. It happened in his own home on his mother's bed. He was raped by Edward, the drug-addicted brother whom I used to see on the corner outside of the coffee shop.

When he was ten, he began to steal as a way to bring home money to his mother. She was very sick by then with the cancer that would kill her two years later.

With his mother's passing, and no father in his life (he scarcely knew his father, who was an alcoholic), there was no one in his family left alive or capable of offering protection other than his sister when she was not in prison, and what she could offer by way of protection was not without entanglements that endangered him still more. Benjamin was on his own or, at least, he would have been had it not been for the fact that Martha had already come to know him by that time.

Martha was not yet the pastor of St. Ann's when his mother became ill, but she was familiar with people in the neighborhood because of the years in which she was a lawyer and had done pro bono work in the community. Later, when she began her preparation for the priesthood, she did her fieldwork at the church as a seminarian. Once she was ordained, she returned there in the role of an assistant priest. It was in that year, prior to the time in 1993 when she was appointed to be pastor, that she and Benjamin had become acquainted with each other.

"One day," she said, "Benjamin came into the church

and asked me for a job. He was all of eleven years old. I didn't really have a job that I could give him, but I liked him right away and could see he wanted someone he could talk to. After that, he began to come here every Sunday. Then he asked if he could be an acolyte, and the first Sunday when he stood there at the altar was the day I met his mother. She was in enormous pain, but she got up out of bed and came here to the church, because she wouldn't miss that day for anything.

"At that time," Martha said, "Benjamin's mother was living in the kind of destitution that most people who don't live in neighborhoods like this one could not easily imagine. In the four years prior to the time we met, she never had the money to cook Thanksgiving dinner for him in their home. They had to line up at soup kitchens and hope to get their dinner by the grace of charity." There were days, she said, when they had no food at all—apart from what Katrice and Martha packaged up and sent home with Benjamin.

"He'd often come to church on Sunday mornings in the winter without a pair of socks, so we'd have to look into the boxes of donated clothes to find a pair of socks to keep him warm." Sometimes he would come "in clothes that were still damp, because he'd put them in the washer but didn't have the money to put them through the dryer. . . .

"After I met his mother at the church, I began to visit her at home. When she went into the hospital, I would go with Benjamin every day to be with her.

"In the last weeks of her life, she asked me several times if I would take him in and be a mother to him after she was gone. But I hesitated. He was a boy, twelve years old, and he was maturing quickly. My apartment's small. I didn't know if I could do it. I could not decide.

"Then, as she was dying, Benjamin's father showed up at the hospital. He said he wanted custody so that he could get the right to live in the apartment, even though he'd never been there at the times when he was needed and had never shown a bit of love for Benjamin. He appeared to be inebriated. 'I'm not stupid. I want that apartment.' That's when I made up my mind."

Before Benjamin's mother died, Martha promised her that she would take custody of Benjamin. In the fulfillment of that promise, Benjamin's life and that of the soon-to-be-selected priest of St. Ann's Church would be transformed forever.

Martha's apartment in Manhattan was not in an expensive building, but it was a safe one and was in a neighborhood where Benjamin could go outside without the risk of danger and without exposure to the street life of Mott Haven that had led his two surviving siblings (his brother Edward did not die for several years) into lifetimes of addiction. But bringing a boy approaching adolescence to share so small a space with her was not an easy matter.

It may have been a trifle easier for Martha, because of her patient and adaptive personality, than it was for Benjamin. He'd never lived in any place like that before, where residents, although modest in their means by the standards of the East Side of Manhattan, and certainly not among the highly affluent, might have seemed as if they were to a boy who'd lived for his entire life in the Diego-Beekmans.

Simply adapting to the habits of another person—a priest, moreover, and a woman he revered—was, he said when we talked about this later, "a really big personal thing that I had to figure out and learn how to live with." Then, too, "there were times when I had this fear that it all could end somehow. It was too good to be true. Why me? Not my sister? Not my brother, still there in the street? He was so far outside of the world he barely seemed to know I was his brother when I saw him on the corner. He was out there from the time my mother died until he died in 1998. I was safe in Martha's home, but there was no way for me to pull him into safety.

"When he died, Martha heard before me. Some people in the neighborhood who would bring him in sometimes for a shower or a meal told Martha he had died in jail. The medical examiner said that he had had a kidney failure. That was what had caused the fluid back-up that had choked him. Martha and Miss Katrice took me to the morgue. I didn't have to see the body. I was shown a photo to identify.

"The sun came out while I was looking at the photo. The light from the sun passed across his face. I remember hoping that he was in peace, but I also felt relief that I wouldn't have to see him on that corner anymore."

Meanwhile, his sister was calling him from prison, "asking me to send her things. She'd call me four times, five times, in a day. She'd already been in prison seven years when my mother died. They brought her to the wake in handcuffs. They would not allow her to attend the funeral. . . .

"When she was out, it was worse. She wanted to have money in her pocket. She always wanted to buy clothes. 'Fly' clothes—you know what that means? So this would lead her back to stealing and, sometimes, drug-dealing. And I was grateful to her in one way, because she did try to protect me from my brother when he had molested me, and from other threats as well. Every time she called me now, I would get down on my knees and pray. I was afraid she'd kill herself, which she used to threaten she would do if I didn't give her something that she asked for."

When Martha saw the guilt that he was feeling she found a therapist for Benjamin, but he told me that he "didn't find it easy to connect with him" because he was, in Benjamin's words, "a downtown psychiatrist who couldn't put himself into my situation." And he started stealing things again, including a few precious things that belonged to Martha, in order to get money for his sister.

But he told me that he stole for other reasons, too, not all of which were wholly altruistic. He told me this, I think, because he did not want to make excuses for himself that would oversimplify a pattern of behavior that had started, as we've seen, when he tried to help his mother but, in the years that followed, took on a momentum of its own.

"I also think," he said, "that, at one level, I was testing Martha, trying to see how far I could go before she would give up on me and send me back. It was like I wanted to provoke her. I still did not believe that I deserved what she had done for me."

But, in that one respect at least, he did not know Martha yet. She had more sticking power, more tenacity and loyalty, than all his provocations would be able to break down. Besides, she loved him deeply by this time, as deeply as she would have loved a child of her own—"even more," she told me, "if that's possible." And there was that promise to his mother.

– II –

Benjamin's life, since his mother passed away, was so closely linked to Martha's that it seems important here to say a little more than I've said before about the obligations she was undertaking at St. Ann's while also doing everything she could to relieve the anguish Benjamin was going through and to keep him out of danger.

Before Martha had become the pastor of St. Ann's, the church was in a state of instability—poor financial management, questionable use of funds, an afterschool that was in its doldrums, poorly run, amateurish in its offerings, and meagerly attended.

The priest who was the temporary pastor at the time was a person of Hispanic origin who seemed to use ethnicity in a divisive manner that left black people—who were roughly half the congregation—with the feeling that they were not wholly welcome at St. Ann's. He was a passionate man in the defense of his identity and culture but may have lacked the will, or else the capability, to reach out to people whose ethnicity was different from his own, even though they all were living in the same community. The diocese was desperate to find someone to heal the wounds and keep the church from being shut down altogether.

When Martha was appointed, her predecessor organized a campaign of resistance, based upon his confidence that he was entitled to be the pastor of St. Ann's and that the failure of the diocese to keep him in that role was unrelated to the question of his own effectiveness. He was supported by a small but highly vocal group of people whose hostility to Martha, as it was conveyed in signs and posters they were waving in her face, had no apparent basis other than the fact that she was a woman who happened to be white and, for this reason, ought to be rejected by a parish in the heart of the South Bronx.

People in the neighborhood came to her defense and rapidly accepted her, not in a pro forma way but with affection and tremendous confidence. Many knew her well by then because of the work she had been doing there since she was a lawyer and a seminarian. They'd seen the warm attachment she'd developed to families that were going through the throes of illness or were simply trying to survive amidst the many crises and periods of instability that accompanied their poverty. Once she was appointed to be pastor of St. Ann's, they were thankful and relieved when she made it clear that her first priority would be the education of their children.

But the turmoil she had undergone at the time of her appointment—the hostility of those who were offended by her race and, perhaps, even more so by her gender—was one of the added burdens that she had to bear at the time when Benjamin came into her home and as she was setting out, with all the strength she had, to address the many urgent problems he was facing now.

Benjamin had gone to P.S. 65, two blocks from his mother's home. Between the well-known problems of that school and the sense of constant crisis he'd been going through at home, he graduated P.S. 65—the school "just pushed me through," he said—not knowing how to read. At the time his mother died, he was starting middle school at the place that called itself a "school for medical careers."

"Martha made me go to school, but I hated it," he said. Like many other kids who were channeled to that school, Benjamin learned almost nothing there. But, unlike those who, at least, could read and write by the time they left fifth grade, Benjamin had nothing to sustain him, nothing to hold on to from his elementary years. The "killing" years had nothing to kill off in him. He was illiterate when he started middle school and illiterate when he left there two years later.

Martha pulled him out of school in the South Bronx and enrolled him in a school in Harlem, called The Children's Storefront, an innovative school with a good reputation, run by a poet with whom I was acquainted by the name of Ned O'Gorman. The school had been successful with other children who had grown up in poor neighborhoods, especially with those who had started there in preschool or in the early grades of elementary school. But Benjamin was an adolescent now and the gulf between his literacy level and that of the other students of his age presented an intimidating challenge for himself and for his teachers.

He stayed at the Storefront a year and a half but made no academic gains that Martha could perceive. After that, she put him into an expensive private school on the West Side of Manhattan, which specialized in serving kids who were disabled academically. He remained there "a year or two," as he remembers this, but his learning gap was now so great that it confounded every effort that his teachers made to bring him up to competence beyond a third-grade level.

"P.S. 65 had been my ruin—then those years at middle school," he said. "I was scared that there was something wrong with me. I didn't think that I could ever learn. I *did* try. Martha helped me every night. But I'd freeze up when I went to class. And, even when I thought that I was learning, it's like it slipped away from me. It didn't stay. And I was always back where I began."

He reminded me that he had started stealing when his mother became ill, and that he continued stealing and had stolen things from Martha, even though he was getting an allowance from her and had no need to steal. This remained a problem at the school he was attending. He was also slipping back to his old neighborhood at night to be with friends, some of whom were using drugs and some of whom were selling them. Sooner or later, he'd return to Martha's home. But he could not fail to realize that he was tormenting her when he came home much later than he'd promised.

Finally, Martha came to the decision that the only way to break the pattern he had fallen into was to send him to a boarding school—not the kind that Jeremy and Pineapple attended, but a school that placed at least as great an emphasis on discipline as it did on academics. There's little point in speaking of this school, because he didn't last there long. He was expelled for stealing.

Martha quickly found another school, this one in the Berkshires, in the western part of Massachusetts close to the border of New York, that had a reputation for coping well with students who behaved defiantly or self-destructively. A therapeutic system of behavioral conditioning was at the center of the ethos of the school. Although he stayed for two years and was not expelled this time, he told me he learned very little there and that the Skinnerian agenda had no enduring consequence in changing his behavior.

"I'd run away," he said. "Then I'd go back. I'd be penalized by being taken down a level"—levels of advancement or demotion were part of the incentive system at the school—"and then I'd run away again."

I asked him where he went when he would run away.

"I'd go to people in New York I knew."

I asked him who these people were.

"Different people. Usually I went to the family of a friend. He had been my closest friend. . . ." He hesitated briefly, and he sounded guarded. Then he said, "His parents were drug dealers. They still are. My friend is dead. . . .

"Too many deaths," he added.

But Benjamin continued to place himself in danger. He soon began hanging out with a group of people, most of them teenagers or in their early twenties, who had formed a kind of club that met in the evenings in the home of an older man who, as Benjamin described him, was "sort of the club leader." The man was old enough, he said, to be the father of most of the kids who came to his apartment. But, in a scenario reminiscent of a novel of Charles Dickens, it seems that he was something of an artist at manipulating younger people and, said Benjamin, encouraged them in acts of criminality.

"Drugs were part of the scene," he said. "and I got involved in that. But mostly, it was 'boosting.' Stealing clothes and other stuff from expensive stores. Fashionable labels like Gucci and Armani. . . ."

When Martha learned of this, she knew what she had to do. She went directly to the house and confronted "the club leader." I don't know how many people would have wished to walk into that house at night with no one at their side. But Martha is a fearless woman and, when it came to someone whom she loved, there was nothing that could stop her.

"Martha brought me home with her," he told me. "By the grace of God, she hadn't given up on me."

But his troubles were not over. He continued stealing. His use of drugs continued too, and this soon intensified. He didn't tell me until recently that he'd grown dependent upon marijuana—but, as he explained this, not just any common kind of marijuana. "It was sprayed or mixed with something else to increase its potency," and "I found it overwhelmingly addictive. It threw me for a loop. I needed it when I woke up. I needed it right through the day. I needed it at night. I couldn't cope without it."

He knew he'd started using it, he said, "to run away from my emotions." Ever since his brother died after begging out there on the corner all those years, he said that he had been consumed with even greater guilt than he'd felt before. "Now it was only my sister and myself, and she was far gone into drugs." He worried, with good reason, that he might be heading in the same direction.

"I was seeing a therapist again, but it wasn't getting through to me. Same problem as before. I had seen three therapists by then, but none of them were able to connect with me."

His drug dependence and his stealing finally caught up with him when he was arrested one night in Manhattan and taken to the Tombs. Martha could have paid his bail the next day so that he could be released, pending his time of trial. "But," she said, "I thought it in his interest to delay for a few days." Then she paid his bail—"it was a thousand dollars"—and she brought him home.

Benjamin agreed to enter a plea bargain. As in Angelo's case, this allowed him to remain at home while awaiting sentencing. At the sentencing, he was fortunate to be given nothing worse than a year's probation. If he stayed away from drugs and kept out of trouble, his guilty plea would later be expunged, so that his record would be clear. Staying away from drugs, however, was not going to be easy. His need for them, by this time, was physical, he said, as well as psychological. He realized he could not get over his addiction on his own and solely by willpower.

A moment of decision had arrived for Benjamin. Traditional psychiatry had been unsuccessful in addressing his addiction on an outpatient basis: talking for an hour with a therapist, then being free to go back to the places and the situations where the problem had begun. As tough as it would be, he knew what he had to do. "He had some inner voice," said Martha, "that *told* him what he needed. It was a remarkable internal quality. And it was this quality that ultimately saved him."

Benjamin entered Odyssey House, a residential program for the rehabilitation of addicted people. It was a long struggle for him, hardest at the start, but he stuck it out and didn't try to run away. And he didn't use excuses to steer away from his responsibility. Harking back to the world of drugs by which he'd been surrounded in the first twelve years of life, or to his mother's early death, or to the lives his older brothers and his sister led—none of this could help him now. He had to look into himself. And he did so, bravely.

I've wondered often why it is that so many adolescents and young men—Vicky's son, for instance, and Miranda's brother, and Ariella's oldest boy—never found it possible to search into themselves, even though all three of them had support available at the time when they were courting their self-ruin, while Benjamin was able to look piercingly into himself once he went into recovery. Martha's love and loyalty surely had a role in this. More important, I believe, was the model of determination he had seen in her, starting in her first year as the pastor of St. Ann's. He told me he was "at her side when that group was waving posters at her on the front steps of the church"—"NO WHITE WOMAN WANTED HERE"—and he saw the way she moved right on "to do the work that God intended her to do." He's told me many times that her example of persistence and relentlessness throughout the years he'd lived with her "helped me find the strength inside of me I didn't know I had."

But, in the long run, Benjamin's recovery depended on his own ability to dig out of the nightmare of his early years and see enough potential value in himself to turn his back upon the past, look hard at the present crisis he was in, and then begin to shape a set of goals that would give some meaning to the future. "He was one of very few in the group that went into the program with him," Martha said, "who went through it all"—it was, she said, "a kind of twelve-step program"—"and who completed it successfully."

In the final stages of the program, as Benjamin explained it, those who had progressed the furthest were expected to assume a leadership relationship to others who were finding it more difficult or were on the verge of dropping out. It was the evolution of this sense of leadership in Benjamin that led him in the years to come, and up to the present day, to take responsibility for other groups of drug-addicted people, either in recovery houses or in settings such as neighborhood centers, for example, in which he ran or supervised programs of his own.

Working with other people in recovery, Benjamin believes, has helped to reinforce his own willpower too, because "the process of 'recovery' is an ongoing thing that isn't over when you finish with a program. When I work with people who are fighting their addictions, I don't speak about myself as 'a recovered addict.' I say that I'm a person in *continual* recovery."

Meanwhile, he was back in school, in individual tutorial instruction. In the role of leadership and mentorship he was assuming now, he had a stronger motive to bring up his academic skills than he'd ever felt before. His use of language was increasingly adept. His analytic gifts in sorting out "the pieces of the puzzle," as he called it, in addicts who relied on him, as well as in himself, were more and more insightful and mature. At the church, where he was present often as an unpaid volunteer and, along with Jeremy, sometimes filled the role of surrogate for Martha when she had to be out of the office for a time, he became unusually effective in calming stormy waters when a staff dispute occurred. Developing his literacy skills, so that he could read with ease and develop a degree of mastery in his use of written words, was a natural progression for him now.

His sister continued to lead a troubled life. Three years ago, he says, he brought her into Odyssey House. "She stayed there almost for a year until she threw a pot of scalding water at a man who said something she didn't like. They had to throw her out. . . .

"I try to numb myself emotionally in order to protect myself from sudden shock because I still believe it's possible that she could kill herself or do it unintendingly by provoking someone else to kill her. I think that's more likely. . . ." But, he says, "this sense of being powerless to bring my sister back is part of what is driving me. When I can help other people, it's as if I'm doing it for her, or maybe for my brother. I know that isn't very clear. It's something I'm still working through, to try to understand. . . .

"You know?" he says. "My sister has a heart of gold

when she isn't messing up her mind. She's helped a lot of other people. But she cannot help *herself.* No matter how I try to dull myself—because I simply cannot live with so much guilt for what I don't know how to change—I cannot abandon her. I never will."

– III –

"Lord . . . , teach us to number our days, that we may apply our hearts to wisdom."

The twelfth verse of the ninetieth psalm has come to be especially important to Benjamin and Martha. Benjamin has been obliged, more forcefully and frequently than most of us, to look into the face of his mortality. The sheer amount of death he's had to witness, not only when he was a child and teenager but up into these recent times as well— the many funerals, at which he's served with Jeremy as one of Martha's acolytes, for people who have passed away all too early in their lives—might easily have left him with unhealthy feelings of foreboding or morbidity. Instead, it's had the opposite effect of teaching him to value life with all the greater thankfulness because he's come to recognize how fragile it can be.

Meanwhile, the call to service that he feels and the sense of calm that he can bring to others, and now to himself, have given him the kind of dignity that elevates his life far above the level of obsession with his own concerns at the cost of those around him.

"Every bit of sorrow he's been through," Martha said in a reflective moment when we had some quiet time together earlier this fall, "all the anguish, all the deaths he's seen first-hand—I wish this could be said for all of us—has, I think, intensified his wish to do as much good as he can within this world in the years that God allows us. The words of the psalm, 'to number our days,' are not an invocation to presentiments of death but to use the days that we are given wisely."

Benjamin's religious faith, which became important to him as a child when he walked into St. Ann's and knocked on Martha's door and, soon after that, began to stand beside her as one of her acolytes, has never left him through the years. But it deepened greatly and became essential to his sense of hope when he began the process of recovery from his addiction. "It's a guiding force within my life today," he says. "God had a role in sparing me. Everything I'm doing now, I like to think that this was part of His intention."

He moved into his own apartment seven years ago, but he says he speaks with Martha three or four times every day, "and I see her all the time when I stop by at the church, and every Sunday, when I'm there for mass. She and I went to hell and back—sorry for my language!—when she took me in. I couldn't bring myself to call her 'Mom' at first because, I'd think, 'God gives us only one Mom and I've buried mine.' Now I think of Martha as my mother. I simply couldn't say it until something in me had been healed. I think I'm even closer to her since I moved out on my own."

Now and then on Sunday afternoons, not as often as I'd like, they drive up to New England, to a seacoast town, and stay over a few nights. Martha's work is too intense for her to let herself relax on more than rare occasions, but when they're here we have a chance to go out to a restaurant and reminisce about the kids I first encountered at St. Ann's when they were very young, and still very innocent, and sometimes very funny—Pineapple and Angelo always seem to come up in our conversation—and they bring me up to date on the newest programs at the afterschool.

Benjamin's cell phone rings at least a few times every evening that he's here. "Someone who's not feeling well," he'll say, or "someone who's a little scared. . . ." He'll take the phone outside to talk. When he comes in, he sometimes has a worried look. His worries (I have the same problem too) go right to his stomach and he'll wait for a few minutes for the flurries to subside so he can enjoy his meal.

His life is full. He has a wide circle of friends. He goes to class to complete his education in the mornings and goes to a gym to exercise and swim for his health and relaxation in the afternoons. Meanwhile, almost every evening of the week, he leads a group of people in recovery. He's often with them until ten or twelve at night. This is his true vocation.

What always strikes me when we talk or get together now is the sense of warm protectiveness he brings to bear, not only in the work he does but in the lives of everyone who's close to him. When he knows I'm home alone, he'll call me on an impulse. If I'm out, he'll leave a message on my phone. "Hi, God Daddy! Thinking of you. Give a ring when you have time. God bless. Take good care. . . ."

Benjamin's birthday and my own come on the same day in September. We always try to talk the night before. He very seldom speaks of any problems he may have. He may tell me just a bit about some of the tribulations in his work. Mostly, he fills me in with cheerful details about somebody that he knows I care about. "Miss Katrice was in the hospital, but she's feeling better now. . . . Angelo's keeping out of trouble. He's still got that big wide-open smile. . . . Jeremy's been just terrific in the job he's doing at the church. The afterschool, by the way, is going beautifully this year."

He likes to bring me good news from the Bronx.

Pineapple Has a Few More Things to Say

There are people, I believe, who will look at certain children in this book—those whose lives have been most difficult, those whose lives were cut off at an early age—and will see these outcomes as the consequence of circumstances far beyond society's control. Vicky's son, like Pietro's, and like Silvio, seems to have been driven to pursue his own destruction by forces in his character he could not understand. Angelo, as he would now agree, repeatedly made errors of poor judgment that compounded the external obstacles he faced. Benjamin, too, had more than a minor role in deepening the troubles that his family history had handed on to him.

But society also had a role in darkening these children's lives. Three of these boys underwent the miseries of places like the Martinique at ages when they were the most susceptible to the pathological conditions that surrounded them. Angelo came of age at a time when criminality was raging in Mott Haven. So, too, did Benjamin, who saw his siblings drowning in the river of narcotics that flooded Beekman Ave. Why would any city put a mother and her children in a place like that to start with?

The word "accountability" is very much in fashion now. Children in the inner cities, we are told, must be "held accountable" for their success or failure. But none of these children can be held accountable for choosing where they had been born or where they led their childhood. Nor can they be blamed for the historic failings of their schools. Nor, of course, are any of these children responsible in any way at all for the massive unemployment, and the flight of businesses and industries, that have put so many young men on the corners of the streets with no useful purposes within their daily lives. ("Visitors," Martha told me at the time of the recession of 2001, "are asking if the economic crisis has taken a high toll on people in our parish. I tell them that we've always been in a depression in Mott Haven, so it's hard to see a difference.")

The question might be reasonably asked: If all of these externally determined forces of discouragement had not been present when these kids were growing up, would some of them have fallen into turbulent and painful lives in any case, or forfeited their lives before they even grew into maturity? There's no way to know, but I suppose the answer would be yes. Unhealthy and self-destructive inclinations are not the "special illnesses" of young men and women who grow up in inner-city neighborhoods. I recall, from my father's sixty years of practicing psychiatry, that he treated many affluent young people who seemed "hell-bent," as he put it, "on finding any way they can to ruin their own lives," and some of them attempted suicide repeatedly.

But, for the children of a ghettoized community, the pre-existing context created by the social order cannot be lightly written off by cheap and facile language about "parental failings" or by the rhetoric of "personal responsibility," which is the last resort of scoundrels in the civic and political arena who will, it seems, go to any length to exculpate America for its sins against our poorest people.

The question of exceptionality needs to be dealt with here.

Pineapple, as I've noted, lived in the Diego-Beekman housing and trudged up the street to P.S. 65. That was where she had the teacher she called "Mr. Camel," one of the seven unprepared instructors who came and went throughout her third- and fourth-grade years. Jeremy lived in a tower of decrepitude where he was robbed at knifepoint, as we've seen, and sometimes had to walk the stairs to get to his apartment when the elevator, as he put it, didn't "want to come" down to the lobby. He was fortunate to go to P.S. 30; but he was often beaten up and bullied when he was in middle school.

Yet both these children, as well as Leonardo and Pineapple's sisters, and Tabitha, and several of the others I was close to at St. Ann's rose above the problems and the perils of the neighborhood, finished their schooling in a healthy state of mind, went on to college, and are now envisioning the range of opportunities their education will allow. Benjamin, meanwhile, without the benefit of college, has been able to carve out a beautiful vocation of his own.

The point I need to emphasize again is that all these children had unusual advantages. Someone intervened in every case, and with dramatic consequences. In Lara's situation, it was a devoted teacher in a failing middle school and, again, a teacher at an otherwise unsuccessful high school in New York who "spotted" her as a gifted student and gave her individual tutorial instruction that enabled her to have her choice of colleges. In Pineapple's case, and Jeremy's and Leonardo's, it was either Martha or someone from outside the Bronx, or a group of people from outside New York City altogether, who shepherded these children into avenues of exit from the damage they'd already undergone, or would likely undergo, in the schools of the South Bronx. Other children from the Bronx and similar communities have been given access to good education through programs like A Better Chance, which serves children nationwide, or Prep-for-Prep, an institution in New York that looks for highly motivated students in minority communities and helps them gain admission to some of the most exclusive prep schools in the city.

All of this, however, depends upon the charitable inclinations of a school or philanthropic donors, and charity has never been a substitute, not in any amplitude, for systematic justice and systematic equity in public education. If any lesson may be learned from the academic breakthroughs achieved by Pineapple and Jeremy, it is not that we should celebrate exceptionality of opportunity but that the public schools themselves in neighborhoods of widespread destitution ought to have the rich resources, small classes, and well-prepared and well-rewarded teachers that would enable us to give to every child the feast of learning that is now available to children of the poor only on the basis of a careful selectivity or by catching the attention of empathetic people like the pastor of a church or another grown-up whom they meet by chance. Charity and chance and narrow selectivity are not the way to educate the children of a genuine democracy.

– II –

Much has changed in the St. Ann's neighborhood and other sections of Mott Haven since the days when Benjamin and Jeremy and Pineapple were young. But much remains the same.

The changes are self-evident in physical respects. Many of the vacant lots in between the large apartment buildings have been filled in by attractive single-family and two-family houses, constructed since the last years of the 1990s, with small front lawns or gardens and a place to park a car, most of them protected by wrought-iron fences. An entire row of these wooden houses has been erected on St. Mary's Street, opposite St. Mary's Park, close to the end of Beekman Ave. Initially intended for families living in the neighborhood already (or so those families had been told), these houses at the present time sell for upwards of $200,000 and are owned or occupied by individuals or families whose incomes are at least three times the average family income in Mott Haven.

What these houses represent, Martha Overall believes, is a modest early stage in a gentrification process that may be seen as well in a narrow stretch of streets ten or twelve blocks to the south and west of St. Ann's Church, close to a bridge that leads into Manhattan. In this area, warehouse structures or buildings that were occupied in decades past by manufacturers and industries have become the studios and living spaces of artists and photographers. There are also a number of new-looking buildings on these streets, with signs that advertise "lofts for rent," and, nearby, a handful of antique shops and a couple restaurants that have the look of bistros. When Martha and I spent some time walking through the neighborhood earlier this fall, the owner of one restaurant told us that he doesn't do much business yet but sees the money that he's spent as an "investment in the future."

On other streets, also in the sections of Mott Haven closest to Manhattan, a number of brownstones that might have housed low-income families in the past have been renovated to attract a clientele the New York Times describes as "adventurous and relatively prosperous." According to one of the newer residents cited by the Times, Mott Haven brings to mind a formerly black neighborhood in Brooklyn that has since become "this really expensive place to live. . . . It has that feeling of something about to happen to it."

Those words may be taken in several different ways. If Mott Haven were someday to become a "really expensive place to live," none of the families that I know would be able to remain there. And their continued presence in the neighborhood might, indeed, be seen as an impediment to the growth in value of the new or renovated housing, which those who purchase them are counting on.

Optimists may be willing to believe in the promise, perennially made to inner-city residents by promoters of development, that a community of racially mixed and economically diverse mixed-income housing will evolve, in which the benefits in public education and other public services that generally accrue to neighborhoods in which substantial numbers of the affluent or middle class reside will go to poor people as well. I would like very much to believe that this could happen, although it hasn't often been the case in any other city that I know.

In most cities, "development" unfortunately has also meant "displacement." I have in mind, for instance, the old South End of Boston, where I lived for many years among my students' families. Once realtors and investors discovered its "potential," because of its good location (close to Copley Square) and the brick and brownstone buildings that could be purchased cheaply at the time, the predominantly black and Hispanic population was shunted off into other and more isolated sections of the city. Within a decade, houses that were purchased for $50,000 were selling for $500,000. (Many today sell for upwards of $2 million.)

I doubt that anyone, including the developers, believes that this will happen in Mott Haven, if it ever happens, for many years to come. In the aftermath of a deep recession, and with the presence of vast public housing towers, in which the city has its own investment, any imminent displacement of large numbers of poor people from Mott Haven seems to be improbable.

As things stand, despite the artists and photographers and occupants of new or newly renovated houses, Mott Haven remains the poorest neighborhood in all of the South Bronx, which remains the poorest congressional district, out of 435 such districts, in all of the United States. The median household income in the South Bronx as a whole is less than $24,000, according to the Bureau of the Census. In Mott Haven, according to figures released by New York City in 2011, it's less than $17,000. The federally established poverty level for a household of five people is $26,000. Families of five are common in Mott Haven because of the doubling-up of relatives taken temporarily into an apartment where a mother and her children and, frequently, a grandmother are already living. Often, too, there may be a grown-up son who has a wife and children but who can't obtain a rental subsidy and cannot find employment.

Unemployment in the Bronx continues to be the highest in the city. The U.S. Bureau of Labor Statistics places the figure at just above 14 percent. When thirty-five jobs at minimum wage, with no benefits, opened up at a sneaker store close to Yankee Stadium in September of 2010, "more than 300 people showed up," according to one press account, out of their desperation to find any work at all.

But even the figure of 14 percent for the borough of the Bronx understates the jobless rate in its poorer areas. The Bronx encompasses middle-class and working-class communities in its northern and northeastern areas and the wealthy, semi-suburban neighborhood of Riverdale in its northwest corner. When unemployment figures are broken down by neighborhood, and when we add so-called "discouraged workers"—those who have given up looking for a job and are not included in government statistics—the actual unemployment rate in the St. Ann's area is certainly a great deal higher than in the borough as a whole—and, according to people on the scene whose estimates have always been reliable, may well be twice as high.

Those who can't find honest jobs are not inevitably drawn into illegal ways of making money; but the temptation is certainly intensified. And dealing drugs is one of the surest ways of making money in a neighborhood where drug-addiction rates, as Benjamin can testify, continue to be high. In the immediate St. Ann's area, Angelo recently pointed out a building, only three blocks from the church, where he said, with all too much apparent knowledge, that a heroin market presently was based. It turned out to be the building where Miranda, Pietro's daughter, had been living. Angelo became concerned when I told him I'd been spending afternoons and evenings in the building, talking with Miranda and her little boy. He cautioned me not to go there after dark. (Miranda, I'm glad to say, has just moved out and found a new apartment in a better building.)

"Things are quieter on the surface," Ariella says. "The drug trade is less blatant now. The market has gone underground." Crack cocaine "is still the inexpensive drug of choice, but heroin use is on the rise." And, she says, "these are not just old-time addicts who've been using it for their entire lives, but much younger people, eighteen, nineteen, in their early twenties. This is something relatively new. . . . Also pharmaceuticals such as Oxycontin," which, she says, "they crush and snort or liquefy and shoot."

One of the reasons drug sales are less evident, she says—and may, in fact, have been diminished somewhat in the neighborhood—is a greater watchfulness on the part of the police. "There's a watchtower," she told me in September, "set up by the police, close to the corner of Beekman Ave, almost in front of the building where Pineapple used to live. It's a portable structure with a camera on the top. One officer sits inside and operates the camera. Another sits in a patrol car at the bottom of the tower. I think it's helped to calm things down."

But the watchtower soon was moved away—"over to Brook Avenue," she told me, where more shootings had occurred. "That's the problem. The police are trying really hard, but the dealers move from place to place." She asked if I had seen a story on a gang of dealers that had been controlling sales in a thirty-block-long section of the Bronx. "They were finally busted. It was a big story. I saw it in the Daily News." According to the story, the gang had been collecting something like a million dollars every week from the sale of crack cocaine and cocaine in powdered form. On the same page of the Daily News, the paper also ran a story on a drug lord in East Harlem, in the area where Angelo was living when he got into trouble while he was in middle school, a short ride on the Number 6 train from the St. Ann's neighborhood. The drug lord was arrested for running yet another major operation, this one also marketing cocaine. On his bedside, the Daily News reported, the drug lord kept a photograph of Al Pacino in his role as "Scarface."

Silvio's hero.

Twenty years before.

* * *

It's difficult, after talking to the people whom I've trusted most and known the longest in the Bronx, to come out with a balanced picture of the present situation. On some evenings, when I'm walking by myself in familiar neighborhoods, there *is* a sense that things are calmer and that life is safer for the children in these neighborhoods today. Then, all at once, another grim event takes place that darkens the spirits of people at St. Ann's. A week after Ariella spoke to me with more optimism than she'd ever voiced before, the sixteen-year-old son of the woman who had been director of the education programs at St. Ann's was shot and killed while walking in the street. "No reason!" Ariella said. "Two people stopped him and asked him a question. They didn't like his answer, so they shot him fifteen times. . . ."

Jeremy, who'd been working with the mother of the victim on a daily basis at St. Ann's, was shaken badly, as were other people at the church. "Don't get me wrong," said Jeremy. "Many things"—he qualified this: "other kinds of things"—"are much better now. We have more stores. They've built a mall over there, near the bridge, close to the Grand Concourse. There's a Target, Best Buy, Staples, and Home Depot. I haven't found a bookstore, but that may be next. . . .

"But, then," he said, "something like this happens, and it brings back all the fear. I still do *not* like walking around Beekman Ave and Cypress. To me, it's still a scary place. I don't go there if I can avoid it."

The building in which Jeremy lives is somewhat safer than before—although he told me just two weeks ago that he'd been awakened in the middle of the night when he heard six bullet shots outside his apartment. "When I come down on the elevator on my way to work, I have to be careful where I stand. This morning, there was fresh blood on the elevator floor." The elevator, he noted, "still doesn't like to come down to the lobby. Or else it does, but then, going up, it often stops between two floors. Last time it happened, I was at the tenth floor, or actually just below the floor. It simply stopped. There was a pregnant woman with me. The fire department finally came and helped us to climb out."

I told him that the building looked good from the outside.

"Outside, yes. Go inside—it's not."

The Diego-Beekman complex, on the other hand, has undergone a sweeping transformation in the past eleven years. In 1999, after years of protests on the part of tenants and a number of investigations and reports by government officials, the federal Department of Housing and Urban Development made a series of demands to Mr. Schuster and his co-investors in Continental Wingate. The company decided it would be in its financial interest to reject the government's demands and, instead, give up the buildings altogether.

By this time, HUD already had begun investing public funds to make improvements in the buildings because, according to an agency official, "conditions . . . were horrendous." And, after negotiations with the tenant leaders and those who were advising them, the government agreed to transfer ownership of the entire complex to the board of a nonprofit corporation that included tenant representatives but also, at the government's insistence, several other people, one of whom was Martha, who had had experience in financial management.

Martha is circumspect in speaking of the progress that has since been made. Drug dealers, she says, still attempt to force the locks or get into the buildings by breaking down the doors. But repairs are made more quickly. Security is better. And, in the buildings I've revisited last winter and this fall, the stairways and lobbies are much cleaner than before. Garbage and human waste no longer pile up on the basement floors, which are no longer breeding grounds for rats and vermin. Parents and their children, and the many older women living in these buildings, are no longer subject to the loss of self-respect they had to undergo when their rental payments and their housing subsidies went to a landlord in another city who seemed to be unburdened by a sense of basic decency. Instead, that money pays for a degree of dignity in their daily lives. By any standard, this is no small victory.

The news about the schools is less auspicious. In spite of the efforts of many very good and innovative teachers who have a deep commitment to the children of the area, it would overstate the case to argue that the schools in which they work have been dramatically improved.

At P.S. 65, a number of principals have come and gone since I started visiting. Each of them did what they could to bring improvements to the school, but these incremental victories soon would wash away. Part of the building has been taken over by a charter school, which often makes things harder for the faculty and children of a public school by creating rivalries for space. There is one good piece of news, however, for the children at this school. The newest principal, appointed very recently, is the former fifth-grade teacher, Miss Harrinarine, who taught at P.S. 30 when Miss Rosa was the principal and whose class I liked to visit as often as I could—the teacher Leonardo used to entertain and whom Tabitha adored. If she cannot work a miracle at P.S. 65, I doubt that anybody can.

Aida Rosa retired from P.S. 30 in 2002. After her departure, the school went through four different principals in a single year. A fifth principal, who began in 2003, has now moved on. A new principal was appointed earlier this year. The school is rated very high for its academic progress over recent years, but parents say that P.S. 30 no longer has the intimate and protective feeling that Miss Rosa—"Mama Rosa," as some of the little ones and their mothers used to call her—was able to engender. Here, too, a charter school now occupies a portion of the building.

There are several other elementary schools serving the same neighborhood or neighborhoods nearby. Some are doing fairly well. Others, unhappily, are not. At one of these schools, not far from St. Ann's, 60 percent of students failed to meet the minimal literacy standards of the state last year. At another, 77 percent were in the failing category. All in all, there has been some very modest progress at the elementary level in Mott Haven, but it is uneven.

Meanwhile, there are the charter schools, like those now sharing space with P.S. 65 and P.S. 30. Some of them, allegedly, are coming up with better scores than the larger public schools within the same community. But questions are inevitably raised as to whether they are offering higher levels of instruction or, as in the instance of the small academy that Jeremy attended for two unhappy years, simply drilling students more remorselessly on the narrow slice of subjects that are measured by the standardized exams. All of these schools, in any case, in the Bronx as elsewhere in the nation, serve only a small fraction of the student population, and students who do not conform to what the charter schools demand are frequently encouraged to go back into the public schools they came from.

The middle schools of the South Bronx continue, with a few exceptions, to be disaster zones. At one of the middle schools somewhat to the north and west of St. Ann's Church, only 11 percent of students have passing scores in English, and 14 percent in math. Another middle school, only eight blocks from the church—one that was highly rated, with good reason, in the 1990s when I looked at classes there—has subsequently lost the glories of its past. Only 21 percent of students now have passing scores in English, and 28 percent in math.

Some comfort may be derived from the news that the

violent middle school Jeremy attended was shut down in 1999. Two smaller middle schools now occupy the building. But the new schools apparently have problems of their own. At one of them, only 14 percent of students are reading at grade level—at the other, 12 percent. None of these schools, large or small, is offering the kind of education that the children of the neighborhood deserve.

High schools in the Bronx continue to suffer from catastrophic noncompletion and nongraduation rates. The numbers for black male students are particularly bad. City-wide, 72 percent of black males entering the ninth grade have dropped out of school before the end of senior year or, if they remain in school, do not gain the academic competence to graduate, according to a 2010 report from the respected Schott Foundation for Public Education. That, it's worth repeating, is the figure for New York as a whole. The failure rate for black males who go to high schools in the Bronx may be even worse.

So long as very poor black and Hispanic children continue to be locked into nearly absolute racial isolation in underserved and underfunded schools, the innovative efforts of successive mayors and their appointed chancellors to create "successful" separate and unequal education in New York will likely be in vain. That, at least, is the lesson history has taught us ever since the benighted ruling in *Plessy v. Ferguson* was accepted as a proper guideline for the education of our children—which, in spite of its reversal in *Brown v. Board of Education* in 1954, is still effectively accepted and almost never questioned by those who run the New York City schools.

I had a momentary glimpse of unrealistic hope when I heard about the artists and photographers and others who were moving into buildings on the southern fringes of Mott Haven. I wondered whether they would send their children, if they did have children, to the public schools attended by black and Hispanic students in the area. Figures from the New York City Board of Education indicate no such optimistic possibilities for now. Last year, at P.S. 30, zero percent of students were Caucasian. The same was true at P.S. 65.

"You've been back to P.S. 65," Ariella says, "You've seen the children coming out the door. Do you see white children?"

– III –

More than half a year has passed since I saw Pineapple last when she came back to visit us in Cambridge in the spring, but she's kept in touch with me. In recent months she's had a hard time with her health. Her phone calls and the texts and e-mails that she sends strike me as remarkable because they've been so cheerful and so optimistic, even while some of the news that she's been giving me has not been good at all.

At the start of August, she told me she'd been tested by her doctor, because she'd been feeling weak and had some other symptoms that concerned him, "and he found out from the tests that I'm pre-diabetic." But, she said, in a voice that didn't sound alarmed at all, "he told me what I need to do, and I'm workin' on it so I can be healthier."

Two weeks later, after she had further tests, the preliminary diagnosis was revised. "I have diabetes. I have to begin with my new medicine tonight."

The new medicine was not insulin, she said, but an oral medication—"I have to take two different pills, each of them once a day." She'd been shown how to use what she called "the strips and prickers. . . . I have to do it twice a day to take a sample of my blood, but I can use the prickers twice. So I only have to use one pricker every day."

I would have thought most people would be knocked flat or, at least, disoriented for a time by the information she had just received. But she sounded organized and calm and seemed to have the regimen ahead of her under good control.

I asked about her health insurance, which I more or less assumed would be provided by her college. But she told me, not without embarrassment, that she'd opted out of it a year before, "because it's so expensive" and she didn't think she'd ever need it at her age. The people at the college said she could apply to Medicaid for now.

A week later: The social security office, she reported, had informed her that she didn't qualify for government assistance. "Guess why?" she said. "Because I'm a college student! And, besides, they told me somebody with diabetes of the kind I have isn't actually 'disabled.'" So, she said, "in other words, they turned me down."

Pineapple was too dignified to ask for my financial help in getting through this crisis. But I told her right away I could take care of the monthly costs she faced until the next semester, when she'd be permitted to get on the college plan again. She sent me about seven e-mails to express her gratitude. I assured her that the money didn't come from me but from readers of the books I'd written about people like herself when she was a child. So she was only getting back what was intended for her and the other children she grew up with in the Bronx.

Pineapple is not naïve about the changes in her life—eating habits and the rest—that her diabetes will entail. But she keeps her head up high. And, in the midst of all of this, she hasn't missed a day of class and she says she likes the courses that she's taking this semester—"except for biology, where I've always had a problem. But I'm learning fast!"

She tells me that Mosquito finished freshman year in college with a 3.8 grade-point average and is working this year as a resident assistant, and is playing basketball for her college team, on which, it seems, she's something of a star. "She goes off almost every week for games with other schools."

Her brother, Miguel, she reports, "has made a lot of new friends here since he got back from Guatemala. Lara takes good care of him. She does more than I do, since I have to study hard and keep up with my classes." He's in the seventh grade at the school in Providence that they selected for him.

Lara, meanwhile, "is doing really well." Pineapple didn't tell me whether Lara's at the day care center still, but she says that Lara's earning enough money to support her brother and herself and, Pineapple adds, helping me with college stuff when she can afford to." She's making plans, as she had intended, "to go back to school next year to get her certification as a teacher."

It's not so much in the long and substantive messages she sends, or in the thoughtful updates on the status of her family, but in the lively little texts and e-mails she's been dashing off every couple days, that I can see that old familiar joyfulness and affectionate good nature that appear to be impervious to any kind of serious discouragement.

"Heyyy Jonathan! I hope all is well. How's the new book going? School is going fine for me. Still having troubles in my bio class but I'm sure I'm going to pass. Hope I get to see you soon. Just wanted to say Hi!"

"Good morning, Jonathan. How ARE you guys? Just wanted you to know I'm real exciteddddd by the English class I'm taking. Also Poly Sci. Also in the process of looking for a second job. Miss you tons. Luv, P."

"Heyyy Jonathan! I hope all is going good. I tried to reach you yesterday, but I had no luck. I know you're working on your book. Hope it's coming along okay. Pleeez make yourself take off some time to have a little fun. . . ."

"Dear Jonathan, I am NOT mad at you for not call-ing back. I just got worried when I didn't hear. Lily told me that you're crashing on your book. Believe me, I can understand. Late nite papers. . . . Okay! Got to get to my new job. . . ."

"Hi you guys! I had a nice weekend with my brother and my sister on her birthday. Except for a couple bumps, of which I will say no more. My father says HELLO FROM GUATEMALA."

Pineapple's good spirits help to bring me back to solid ground when I'm having difficulties with my work. As always, she gets peevish about maddening frustrations like the problem that she had about her health insurance. But she doesn't often fall into the grim and gloomy moods that afflict so many other people who receive disturbing news. Or, in any case, she doesn't let herself stay grim for very long. Soon enough, she climbs out of those moods, like someone in a running race who may stumble and fall down but springs right up again and thrusts a fist—"I'm not beaten yet!"—way up in the air. And, at those times when she can tell I'm in a gloomy mood, she reprimands me properly.

When I spoke to her last week, she detected instantly a sound of weariness within my voice and asked me whether anything was wrong.

"I'm fine," I said. I explained that I was simply having trouble finishing my book. I said I wasn't sure how much had changed back in the neighborhood where she and I had met, but I told her I kept going back and forth on this, because I didn't want to end up on a dreary note.

"Jonathan," she said, "I want you to think positive. Lara and I are going to go back and help to change things once we both have our degrees. You know? Make little changes that we can? If lots of people do that, then the changes won't be little anymore."

I said, "I'm going to steal those words."

"Do it!" she said. And she asked if I remembered something that I told her once when we were walking by the water near her parents' home. "You know? Picking battles that we have a chance to win? And not getting frozen up and flustered in your mind by things that are too big for you and me to change, not at least for now. Which isn't any use to anyone at all."

I said, "I think I'll steal those words as well."

"Do it!" she said a second time. "You're the one who said that to me anyway. I'll give it back to you for free." She laughed. "I'm only teasing you. . . .

"Wow! You know? It's been too long. Once you're finished with the book, I'm coming back to visit you. And I think I'd like to stay a few more days than last time. I know that sounds a little pushy, but I like to hang around there in the kitchen with you guys. And, besides, we've got a lot to talk about. You know?"

An Invitation to the Reader

The small discretionary fund that has helped Pineapple and some of the other children and a few of the adults portrayed within these pages was established many years ago as a nonprofit charitable foundation with support from readers of my books. Those who would like to learn more about this fund, or to help sustain it, are invited to contact the Education Action Fund, 16 Lowell Street, Cambridge, Massachusetts 02138. Readers who would also like to be updated on the efforts of my colleagues, and myself, to bring about the changes in our public schools that would render philanthropic interventions marginal in their significance by providing equal opportunity to every child in this land, and on a nonselective basis, are welcome to write to the same address, or to visit our web page at JonathanKozol.com/EducationActionInc.

Acknowledgments

In the course of working on this book, I have had the wonderful experience of being able to enlist many of the children who grew up in the Bronx as my active partners and researchers as I tell the stories of their later lives. Pineapple and her older sister, Lara, have helped me with a multitude of small corrections, and some very big ones, throughout the stages of this writing. So, too, did Jeremy, who updated me repeatedly on events that he observed first-hand and changes that he saw emerging in the streets around St. Ann's. Lisette and Miranda have generously assisted me as well. The young man I call Angelo and my godson Benjamin have also helped me greatly in areas that draw upon their own awareness of the dangers they have now escaped but which continue to be present in the lives of those around them.

The woman I call Ariella Patterson has also been unusually meticulous in helping me to check elusive details—time-factors, for example, and physical locations of various events, when I was in doubt. She's also had no hesitation about leading me to reconsider the thematic emphases of certain portions of the early manuscript and the final version of this book, especially those narratives in which I try to understand the formative distortions that predisposed a number of the young men I've described to fall into the patterns that destroyed them.

To all these people, young and old, and others whom I have not named, who trusted me to tell their stories and then became my colleagues in describing the entire context of the world in which they came of age and live today, I owe a debt of gratitude.

I also want to thank two bright and energetic college undergraduates and literary scholars, Jacey Rubinstein and Julia Barnard, who studied this book with eagle eyes, and helped me to reconceive several of its chapters, when they came to Cambridge to work with me as interns. Jacey has continued to assist me long after she completed her internship. My thanks, too, to Amy Ehntholt, who's worked with me on earlier books and gave me her kind assistance on this book as well.

Reverend Martha Overall examined all the sections of this book that portray the children with whom she's remained in contact since the years when they were very young, as well as the sections that describe the details of her own career. I have, as in my other books about the children of the Bronx, been grateful for the absolute integrity and unflinching candor with which she has advised me and for the enduring dedication that she brings to bear in every aspect of her service to the disenfranchised and the poor.

Steven Banks, the Legal Aid attorney to whom I've turned repeatedly beginning in the years when families in the homeless shelters were in need of his assistance, has helped me understand the workings of the courts and the legal status of young people in New York when they were arrested, or detained, or awaiting sentence. I'm grateful for the time he took in clarifying aspects of the penal system in which Angelo and others were entangled.

I'm particularly indebted to my publishers at Crown for their kindness and forbearance in waiting all this time for a book I promised to them more than seven years ago. My special thanks to my intuitively sensitive and supportive editor, Vanessa Mobley.

In writing about the inner lives and outward struggles of people who have trusted me for many years out of a sense of faith in my discretion and my loyalty, I have relied upon a gentle and judicious friend who had the rare capacity for guiding me through delicate decisions. Lily Jones came to work with me in Cambridge at the moment when I was about to launch into this book. From conception to completion, she has been not only a remarkable researcher and painstaking editor, the kind of ally every writer prays for. Even more important, as I was working on the stories of those children and adults who underwent the greatest tribulations or suffered most profoundly for the loss of those they loved, Lily has repeatedly uplifted me by her gift for seeing the redemptive aspects of their lives—an affirming quality not unlike the one that drew her to Pineapple.

Young as she is, but wise beyond her years, Lily has been instrumental in the writing of this book and has brought a wealth of blessings to this author from a heart of gold and a soul of selfless generosity. Words cannot express my gratitude.

NOTES

CHAPTER 1: THE JOURNEY BEGINS

3 NUMBER OF CHILDREN AND FAMILIES IN THE MARTINIQUE HOTEL, CHRISTMAS 1985: Interviews with Thomas Styron, Robert Hayes, and others working at the National Coalition for the Homeless in New York, December 1985; *New York Daily News,* December 24, 1985; "Monthly Report," Center for Immigration Studies, October and November 1986, June 1987.

4 REFERENCE TO AUTHOR TEACHING IN THE BLACK COMMUNITY OF BOSTON: I described this in *Death at an Early Age* (Boston: Houghton Mifflin, 1967).

7 ASBESTOS IN THE MARTINIQUE HOTEL: According to the *New York Daily News* (June 19, 1987), "A mountain of cancer-causing asbestos—illegally packed in open containers—was uncovered yesterday in the Martinique Hotel. . . . Dangerous asbestos-coated pipes were also found in the hotel's lobby and on the sidewalk." Also see *New York Times,* June 19, 1987.

A RELATIVE OF ONE OF THE TWO OWNERS AND HIS ABUSIVE TREATMENT OF WOMEN IN THE BUILDING: The social workers told me this with confidence, on the basis of their conversations with the relative, and indicated it was common knowledge. Several female tenants in the Martinique confirmed that it was true. The social workers who introduced me to the young man did not tell him, I assume, that I was a writer.

8 GARBAGE BAGS TO COVER HOT PLATES: Families were told by the hotel to hide their hot plates in drawers, but garbage bags were provided for those that would not fit. I describe this and other practices of the hotel's management in *Rachel and Her Children* (New York: Crown, 1988).

9 AUTHOR'S BOOK ABOUT THE MARTINIQUE HOTEL: *Rachel and Her Children,* cited above, was initially published in *The New Yorker* as *The Homeless and Their Children* on January 25 and February 1, 1988. The *Nightline* episode featuring the Martinique aired on March 21, 1988.

9–10 MANAGER OF MARTINIQUE CARRIED PISTOL ON HIS ANKLE: Many residents of the Martinique spoke to me with apprehension of Sal Tuccelli's gun, which I saw on one occasion. He usually carried it in an ankle holster or, according to the tenants, sometimes on his waist. See *Rachel and Her Children,* cited above, and my more

recent book *Ordinary Resurrections* (New York: Crown, 2000).
Also see *Village Voice*, April 1, 1986.

10 JOURNALISTS WERE NOT WELCOME IN THE BUILDING: Although
they were not officially forbidden—CBS got into the building
with a camera crew in 1986 (*New York Times*, April 21, 1986)—
journalists faced resistance and hostility on the part of the guards
and manager. Residents who spoke critically of the hotel to members of the media placed themselves at risk. According to a city
employee, it was "an accepted understanding" that the hotel
would find a way to justify the eviction of such tenants. See *Rachel
and Her Children*, cited above.

$8 MILLION YEARLY FOR 400 FAMILIES: See *Rachel and Her Chil-
dren*, cited above. Investigative reporter William Bastone noted
in the *Village Voice* (April 1, 1986), that $1,800 was "an accurate
estimate" of the city's monthly cost for housing a homeless family
in the hotels controlled by the owners of the Martinique. The cost
of housing the 400 families in the Martinique was in excess of $8
million yearly.

10–11 WHEN THESE HOTELS WERE FINALLY CLOSED IN 1988 AND 1989: In
the last few weeks of 1988, according to the *New York Times* (December 27, 1988), families were "hurriedly moved out of the Martinique . . . as the Koch administration rushes to empty one of the
largest and most troubled welfare hotels in the city by the end
of the year." Conditions at the Martinique, as in the other large
hotels being used to house the homeless, were, by this time, "a
national scandal," according to the *Times*, and "the city had been
threatened with an imminent cutoff of Federal funds to pay the
hotel bills." Also see *New York Times*, March 9, 1988, September 5
and November 11, 1989.

11 AMONG THE HIGHEST RATES OF PEDIATRIC ASTHMA IN THE NA-
TION: I was told this repeatedly by pediatricians and family-
practice specialists familiar with the most impoverished sections
of the Bronx. I was also given evidence that the rate within these
neighborhoods was by far the highest in New York. According to
a zip-code breakdown of hospitalizations statewide in New York
shown to me by Dr. Robert Massad of Montefiore Medical Center in the Bronx, the rate of admissions for asthma at the start
of the 1990s was 2.5 per thousand for New York City as a whole
but 6 to 7 per thousand in the South Bronx neighborhoods in
which much of this book takes place. In the same neighborhoods,
hospitalizations for asthmatic children were fourteen times as
high as in the wealthy East Side of Manhattan by 1995, while
the rate of death from asthma for people in the Bronx was nearly
nine times higher than in Staten Island, which is the whitest borough of New York. See *City Limits*, April 1998. Also see "Poverty,
Race, and Hospitalization for Childhood Asthma" in *American
Journal of Public Health*, Vol. 78, No. 7 (July 1988); "Inner-city
Asthma," *Chest*, June 1992; "Variations in Asthma Hospitalization and Deaths in New York City," *American Journal of Public*

Health, Vol. 82, No. 1 (January 1992); *Newsday*, October 10, 1993; *New York Times*, October 10, 1993.

POOR CONDITIONS, NEEDLESS DEATHS, LOSS OF ACCREDITATION AT LINCOLN HOSPITAL: *New York Times*, October 28, 1988. For more discussion of conditions at this and other public hospitals in New York City, see *New York Times*, October 7 and 11, 1986; April 7, 1991; May 6 and September 23, 1994; March 5, 6, 7, 1995; *Healthweek*, November 1, 1991. Also see my book *Amazing Grace* (New York: Crown, 1995).

CHAPTER 2: ERIC AND HIS SISTER

14   PRINCE GEORGE HOTEL OWNERSHIP: According to information I was given at the time by the Coalition for the Homeless, the family that owned the Martinique Hotel owned the Prince George Hotel as well. Another source told me that Sal Tuccelli, manager of the Martinique, also claimed to have a share of ownership in the Prince George, while a third source stated that the hotel at one point was owned by South African investors. To add to the confusion, documents filed in 1985 with the New York City Register—an agency that records ownership of properties—bear the signature of a man named Monty Hundley, a general partner in a corporation to which the property apparently was leased a year or so after Vicky moved there. Hundley is known to have made a large fortune as part-owner of more than a hundred hotels, the purchase of which was financed by loans that he did not repay. In 2005 he was sentenced to eight years in prison for bank fraud (*New York Times*, April 20, 2005). For more information on the ownership of the Prince George and its surreptitious change of hands, see *Village Voice*, April 1, 1986. Also see *Rachel and Her Children*, cited above.

MARTINIQUE MANAGER'S ROLE AT THE PRINCE GEORGE: *New York Daily News*, March 20, 1986.

14–15   ON-SITE ADMINISTRATOR OF PRINCE GEORGE HOTEL: Kumar Singh was employed at the Prince George after having been convicted of child neglect in 1984, according to journalist Bob Herbert (*New York Daily News*, March 20, 1986). Singh's daughter, reported Herbert, "who had been abused before, was placed in a foster home."

15   FOUR OR FIVE FIRES IN A WEEK: Fires in the Prince George, as reported by Bob Herbert, occurred with "astonishing regularity." The three-year-old boy was killed in a fire that took place in October 1985. See *New York Daily News*, March 20, 1986.

VICKY AND HER CHILDREN LEAVE THE PRINCE GEORGE HOTEL AND MOVE TO THE BRONX: Families were moved out of the Prince George during the last months of 1989 (*New York Times*, September 5, 1989).

POOREST NEIGHBORHOOD IN POOREST BOROUGH OF NEW YORK: Nearly twenty years later, this remains unchanged. According to the City of New York's "Community District Needs" report for the Bronx, Fiscal Year 2011, "The Mott Haven area has the highest percentage of people in poverty, 65.3 percent more than in the entire City of New York."

19 $8,000 FOR A YEAR'S SUBSISTENCE: The *New York Times* gave the median household income of Mott Haven two years earlier as $7,600 (*New York Times*, November 5, 1991).

CHAPTER 3: PIETRO AND HIS CHILDREN

53 CHILDREN IN THE MARTINIQUE PANHANDLING IN TRAFFIC: The Martinique was on the corner of West 32nd Street and Herald Square. Broadway and Sixth Avenue were the major thoroughfares.

56 "APARTMENT FIRE KILLS BRONX BOY" AND OTHER HEADLINES: *New York Daily News*, April 6, May 4, 5, 6, 1994.

60 CHRISTOPHER SENT TO JUVENILE DETENTION, HIS SUBSEQUENT SENTENCES AT RIKERS ISLAND: Children in New York younger than sixteen are brought before a family court and, if the judge so determines, may be sent to juvenile detention. On rare occasions, children thirteen to fifteen years of age who commit very serious and violent crimes may be tried as adults, but Christopher's early offenses never warranted his being tried in adult court. Christopher was eighteen, or nearly so, before he began the first of his several sentences at Rikers Island. (Information on court disposition of youthful offenders according to their ages and severity of the offense is provided, under the heading of "New York City Family Court," on the website of the New York State Unified Court System, in a posting dated January 31, 2008.) Attorney Steven Banks, at Legal Aid in New York City, verified my understanding of this information. Also see note for chapter 4, p. 97.

61 PRISON WHERE CHRISTOPHER SERVED THE LONGEST PORTION OF HIS SENTENCE: The prison, in the town of Alden, which is called Wende Correctional Facility, is nearly 400 miles west of New York City. He had also served a briefer part of his sentence at a prison called Great Meadow in Comstock, New York, which is about 200 miles closer to the city.

62 DEMOGRAPHICS OF NEW YORK PRISONS AND FINANCIAL BENEFITS TO AREAS WHERE PRISONS ARE SITED: There have been no significant changes in the racial make-up of the prison population in recent years. According to the New York Department of Corrections and Community Supervision, in a document titled "Profile of Inmate Population Under Custody," dated January 1, 2011, the state's male prison population is 22.4 percent white, 50.5 percent African-American, and 24.9 percent Hispanic. See the New York State Department of Corrections website for a list of prison facilities and their locations. For a troubling examination of the economic value these penitentiaries have held for the communities in which they have been built, see "The Prison-Industrial

Complex" by Eric Schlosser in *The Atlantic*, December 1998. New York State has closed many prisons since 1999, when Christopher's sentence was nearly at an end, and is now attempting to create new employment opportunities for those sections of the state that have long depended upon prisons as the main support for their economies. This, at least, is the recently declared intention of Governor Andrew M. Cuomo, according to a press release from his office, June 30, 2011.

63 "A SCENE OUT OF DICKENS": Former New York Governor Mario M. Cuomo used this term in speaking of the Martinique in his book, *The New York Idea: An Experiment in Democracy* (New York: Crown, 1994).

69 "SO MANY PEOPLE COMING THERE": Pietro was referring to groups or individuals who might have been bringing food or clothes or other gifts for children, most commonly in the weeks preceding Christmas. These visitors, in general, were not permitted or encouraged by the management to go up to the floors on which the residents were living.

CHAPTER 4: SILVIO: INVINCIBLE

82 RESTRICTIONS ON VISITORS: See note regarding journalists for chapter 1, p. 10.

84–85 DIEGO-BEEKMAN HOUSING: See *New York Times*, March 25, 1973, May 7, 1978; *New York Daily News*, November 11, 1993, February 4, 1993. Also see notes for Epilogue, p. 311.

85 DIEGO-BEEKMANS OWNED BY OUT-OF-STATE CORPORATION: The Boston-based company was Continental Wingate (*New York Times*, March 31, 1999). Its primary owner was Gerald Schuster (see below).

85–86 GERALD SCHUSTER'S NOTORIETY IN BOSTON AND HIS POLITICAL CONTRIBUTIONS AND FUNDRAISERS: *New York Times*, March 31, 1999; *Village Voice*, December 14, 1999; *Boston Globe,* May 9, 1998; July 1, 2011; March 10, 2012.

86 BERNARDO RODRIGUEZ'S DEATH: *New York Daily News,* January 16 and February 4, 1994.

87 AVERAGE INCOME IN MOTT HAVEN, 1993: See note for chapter 2, p. 19.

97–98 A BOY OF TWELVE OR THIRTEEN BROUGHT BEFORE A FAMILY COURT: As explained to me by Legal Aid attorney Steven Banks on April 6, 2011: "There is always a pre-petition hearing or a remand/parole argument prior to detention, where a court hears 'evidence' and makes a determination regarding detention (unless it's a situation in which the police have taken the child into custody after court hours and the child is admitted to a detention facility overnight," in which case the hearing is held the following day). "It is not common for a child to go into detention; more kids go home than to detention."

99 FOUR OUT OF EVERY FIVE KIDS DID NOT COMPLETE MONROE
    HIGH: The school had a well-earned reputation for violence and
    for consistently abysmal graduation rates at the time Armando
    attended. Over the next decade, the high school was divided into
    six smaller schools with student populations of 375 to 490. Fig-
    ures from the New York City Public Schools Annual School Re-
    port for 2002–3 showed no signs of improvement; in all but one
    of these schools, no more than forty-five students who started in
    the ninth grade remained there long enough to enter the twelfth
    grade.

CHAPTER 5: ALICE WASHINGTON: THE DETAILS OF LIFE

107 ALICE WASHINGTON WAS FORTY-TWO YEARS OLD WHEN I GOT TO
     KNOW HER: Alice told me she was thirty-nine when she became
     homeless. I met her three years later.

120 EMBARRASSING STORY ON HARVARD CLUB: *New York Times*,
     April 23, 1994.

121 "IT WASN'T MUCH OF A WEEK TO BE A HORSE": *New York Times*,
     July 18, 1993.

125 "NEEDLE EXCHANGES": As this book goes to press, the needle
     exchange is still there on the sidewalk outside of St. Ann's.

     NEARLY 4,000 PEOPLE IN MOTT HAVEN WERE KNOWN TO BE INTRA-
     VENOUS USERS: New York City Department of Health, cited in
     unpublished memorandum (August 27, 1993), by the Hunter Col-
     lege Center on AIDS, Drugs, and Community Health; New York
     State Division of Substance Abuse Services, cited in "Reaching
     Low-Income Women at Risk of AIDS," by Nicholas Freudenberg
     and other staff members of the Hunter College center, in *Health
     Education Research*, Vol. 9, No. 1 (1994); author's interviews with
     staff members of the center. Some estimates of intravenous users
     in Mott Haven exceeded 7,000.

139 REMEMBERING ALICE WASHINGTON: In earlier writings, I have de-
     scribed how Alice and I got to know each other in the Martinique
     Hotel and how our friendship deepened in the years that followed
     after she had moved to the South Bronx. As with other people
     who had reason not to want to be exposed to public scrutiny—
     the punitive workings of the welfare system, for example, were
     a persistent factor of concern—I disguised her heavily. Now that
     she has passed away, I have told her story with less inhibition.
     I have followed the same pattern in other sections of this book
     that touch upon the lives of those who had the same concerns,
     or other reasons to avoid exposure, at the time when I initially
     described them. All these adults and their children, nonetheless,
     remain disguised to some degree, as I have said, to defend their
     privacy or, in the case of those who are deceased, that of their
     family-members.

CHAPTER 6: SURVIVORS

144   THE EMERGENCE OF WHAT THEOLOGIANS TERM "A SENSE OF CALL-
      ING": Many others who are not theologians, such as the psychia-
      trist and author Dr. Robert Coles, use this term in speaking of the
      search for moral values and the pursuit of useful purpose on the
      part of young adults as they move into maturity.

CHAPTER 7: THE BOY WHO ATE A GIANT BAG
OF COOKIES WHILE HE WALKED ME ALL
AROUND THE NEIGHBORHOOD, AND HIS
VERY INTERESTING MOM

149ff. MEDICAL WASTE INCINERATOR IN MOTT HAVEN: *New York Newsday,*
        October 16, 1991 and September 8, 1993; *New York Times,* No-
        vember 2, 1991, September 8, 1992, September 5, 1995, May 11,
        1997, June 27, 1997, and May 6, 1999; *Riverdale Press,* May 13,
        1993; *New York Daily News,* May 14, 1996, September 18, 1998,
        and May 6, 1999; *City Limits,* June/July 1996 and July/August
        1999.

149   AT LEAST 6,000 CHILDREN RESIDED WITHIN CLOSE PROXIMITY OF
      THE WASTE INCINERATOR: As many as 4,000 children lived in the
      Diego-Beekman Houses. At least 2,000 more lived in other pri-
      vately owned buildings, as well as in large public housing towers
      in the area.

150   "WASTEFUL PROTEST IN THE BRONX": The editorial condemning
      neighborhood activists and parents who opposed construction of
      the medical incinerator appeared in the *New York Times,* Novem-
      ber 11, 1991.

      ASTHMA HOSPITILIZATIONS IN MOTT HAVEN AREA IN 1995 WERE
      FOURTEEN TIMES HIGHER THAN ON EAST SIDE OF MANHATTAN: *City
      Limits,* April 1998. Also see notes for chapter 1, p. 11.

151   BROWNING-FERRIS CORPORATION'S VIOLATIONS OF ENVIRONMEN-
      TAL AND AIR-POLLUTION LAW: A partial summary of the legal vio-
      lations committed by the owners of the medical incinerator, and
      penalties provisionally imposed upon them, is provided in a con-
      sent order drafted by the New York State Department of Envi-
      ronmental Conservation on July 22, 1998. The document, which
      was distributed to people in the nearby neighborhoods, recorded
      100 violations of environmental law and proposed, among other
      penalties, that the owner of the incinerator, Browning-Ferris
      Industries, Inc., contribute money for asthmatic children to go
      to asthma camp. The *New York Daily News* (February 24, 1998)
      noted that the operators of the waste facility had, in fact, violated
      air-pollution laws more than 500 times. Browning-Ferris finally
      paid $250,000 in settlement of the dispute (*New York Daily News,*
      May 6, 1999). Also see *New York Daily News,* February 4, 1996,
      June 4, 1996, and March 11, 1999.

158   LEONARDO'S MOTHER BELIEVES THAT HIS RELIEF FROM ASTHMA
      IS CONNECTED WITH THE SHUTDOWN OF THE BURNER: The waste
      incinerator was shut down when he was eleven, in 1997 (*New
      York Daily News*, April 1, 1997). Over the course of the next three
      years, asthma hospitalizations in Mott Haven declined by 56 per-
      cent. (See "Asthma Facts," a report by the New York City Depart-
      ment of Health and Mental Hygiene, May 2003.)

CHAPTER 8: PINEAPPLE COMES OF AGE

175   THE DIEGO-BEEKMAN COMPLEX: See notes for chapter 4, p. 84ff.
186   LARA'S CLASS ESCAPED THE RUN OF SHORT-TERM TEACHERS
      PINEAPPLE HAD HAD: In spite of this advantage, Lara had to pay
      a price for one of the irrational and arbitrary practices that were
      put in place at P.S. 65. New examinations that had no connection
      with the content of the courses that her class was taking were im-
      posed upon the school when she was in fifth grade. Like several
      others in her class who were receiving good grades up until that
      time, she was suddenly informed that she wouldn't be promoted
      because her test scores were too low. She was obliged to stay at
      P.S. 65 for an extra year. Fortunately, she did not permit this to
      undermine her appetite for learning and went on to do extremely
      well in secondary years.

CHAPTER 9: PINEAPPLE IN ALL HER GLORY
(AND STILL BOSSING ME AROUND)

193   A LAWYER IN PROVIDENCE WAS HELPING PINEAPPLE'S FATHER TO
      FILE AN APPEAL: This appeal, according to the U.S. Citizenship
      and Immigration Services, is technically a "motion to reopen or a
      motion to reconsider with the same office that made the unfavor-
      able decision." The applicant for reconsideration is not permitted
      to go to a higher level of appeal.
208–09   MOST OF THE PEOPLE IN RHODE ISLAND WERE TOO ENLIGHTENED
      TO DENY PINEAPPLE AND HER SISTERS THEIR AUTONOMY OR DE-
      MEAN THEIR FATHER: Among the people who have been most
      supportive and most sensitive are a woman named Kim Ander-
      son, who remains a stalwart friend and ally to Pineapple and her
      sisters, and several members of the church that brought Pineap-
      ple to Rhode Island in the first place.

CHAPTER 10: A LIFE OF THE MIND
(JEREMY, PART ONE)

224   JEREMY'S CLASSMATE RAPED AND STRANGLED: *New York Daily
      News*, April 11 and 16, 1997; *New York Times*, April 11, 1997.

CHILDREN AND TEENAGERS WHO HAD DIED OF VIOLENCE NEAR ST. ANN'S IN THE PRECEDING YEARS: See *Amazing Grace,* cited above.

227 JEREMY'S QUOTATION FROM "THE TELL-TALE HEART": He got it pretty close. Poe's exact words: "It is impossible to say how first the idea entered my brain; but, once conceived, it haunted me day and night." "The Tell-tale Heart," first published in 1843, is included in *Complete Stories and Poems of Edgar Allan Poe* (New York: Doubleday, 1984).

CHAPTER 11: NO EASY VICTORIES
(JEREMY, PART TWO)

258 BOOK THAT PROMPTED JEREMY'S QUESTION: *Ruby Bridges,* by Robert Coles (New York: Scholastic, 1995).

CHAPTER 12: THE KILLING FIELDS

264 ANGELO'S THIRD MIDDLE SCHOOL: The school was known as ACES, an acronym around which the full name of the school ("Academy for Community Education and Services") had been awkwardly constructed. A report in February 2003 from Insideschools.com confirms that most of the teachers there were new and that class size averaged thirty. Orlando Ramos, the principal of ACES when I visited in November 2002, has since left the New York City schools.

270 ANGELO SWIPES A STRANGER THROUGH THE TURNSTILE: It's possible, according to Martha Overall, that Angelo's Metro card was the kind that's called an "unlimited pass," good for either seven days or thirty days, but only for the purchaser. She noted, however, that this is often overlooked by transit officers unless they have some other reason to suspect a person of wrongdoing.

272 PROFIT-MAKING FIRMS THAT OFFERED A DEGREE OR SOME OTHER DOCUMENT: Information on the Technical Career Institute's degrees, courses, tuition, and admission is available in the TCI Catalog for 2010–11, which indicates the cost of $5,960 per semester for a two-year program to obtain an associate degree or certificate. The catalog's final item under the heading "Admissions"—a well-obscured paragraph preceded by immunization specifications for enrollment—states the school's graduation rate, "in accordance with the federal Student Right-to-Know reporting and disclosure requirements as well as the New York State Regents Accreditation Standards." In August of 2009, "163 of the 859 students (19.0 percent)" who had enrolled in the fall of 2006 "had graduated or completed their program of study within 150 percent of the normal time to completion."

273   WARNINGS TO POTENTIAL APPLICANTS: The complaints cited were
      posted to the consumer website RipoffReport.com on March 26
      and October 26, 2009, September 29 and November 11, 2010.
276–77   THE PRISON RUNS A NUMBER OF EDUCATION PROGRAMS: A spokes-
      person for the New York City Department of Corrections verified
      to me (August 8, 2011) that the prison continues to offer Adult
      Basic Education and preparation for the GED. For younger in-
      mates, Rikers runs its education programs through the East River
      Academy, part of District 79—"Alternative Schools and Pro-
      grams"—of New York City's public schools.

CHAPTER 13: NUMBER OUR DAYS

287   BENJAMIN'S SISTER WAS PERMITTED TO ATTEND THEIR MOTHER'S
      WAKE BUT NOT HER FUNERAL: Whether or not an inmate in New
      York is allowed to visit the deathbed or attend the wake or fu-
      neral of a close family member is decided at the discretion of the
      superintendant of the prison where the inmate is held. See New
      York State Department of Correctional Services, "Handbook for
      the Families and Friends of New York State DOCS Inmates," De-
      cember 2007.
289   QUESTIONS ABOUT MARTHA'S PREDECESSOR AT ST. ANN'S: The
      man who'd been the "interim priest" later wrote to me and shared
      with me his strong belief that the reason he had been suspended
      was political. He spoke in terms of "oppressor" and "oppressed"
      and referred to the writings of a man we both admired, the Bra-
      zilian educator Paulo Freire, who, he knew, had been my friend
      and mentor. I appreciated his attempt to explain things to me
      from his point of view. It was a thoughtful letter. I felt that he was
      reaching out to me for my support. At the same time, I knew that
      Paulo Freire, whom I'd met in Mexico in 1968 and with whom
      I had a deep and personal attachment in the ensuing years,
      would never have allowed himself, or have encouraged his fol-
      lowers, to demonize a woman on the basis of her race or gender.
      Freire's personal behavior was consistent with his principles and
      politics, which were characterized above all else by a capacious
      generosity.

EPILOGUE

305   NEW HOUSES IN MOTT HAVEN SELL FOR UPWARDS OF $200,000:
      Some of these houses were already selling for $185,000 in 1997
      (New York Times, November 2, 1997). In spite of two recessions,
      $200,000 might be too conservative an estimate after fourteen
      years. (One real estate website indicates that a number of these
      houses in Mott Haven were valued at $350,000 or more in De-
      cember 2011.)

306 "IT HAS THAT FEELING OF SOMETHING ABOUT TO HAPPEN TO IT": "Potential Awaits Its Moment," *New York Times*, September 2, 2011. Mott Haven and surrounding neighborhoods have long been the subjects of optimistic press reports. See, for example, "Slouching Toward Utopia in the South Bronx," *New York Times*, December 5, 1993; "A South Bronx Very Different from the Cliché," *New York Times*, February 14, 1999; and "Goodbye South Bronx Blight, Hello Trendy SoBro," *New York Times*, June 24, 2005.

307 THE SOUTH BRONX REMAINS THE POOREST CONGRESSIONAL DISTRICT IN THE NATION: The 16th Congressional District incorporates the entire South Bronx and a few additional sections of the Bronx. The district's boundaries are given on the website of U.S. Representative José Serrano, under the heading, "Our District" (December 2011). As of the latest census, this district is still the poorest in the nation, with a poverty rate of 38 percent (*New York Daily News*, September 29, 2010).

THE MEDIAN HOUSEHOLD INCOME IN THE SOUTH BRONX IS LESS THAN $24,000: The figure, as determined by the U.S. Bureau of the Census in 2010, is $23,773 for the 16th Congressional District.

IN MOTT HAVEN, MEDIAN HOUSEHOLD INCOME IS LESS THAN $17,000: The City of New York's "Community District Needs" report for the Bronx, Fiscal Year 2011, cited in note for chapter 2, p. 15, places the present figure in Mott Haven at $16,800.

THE FEDERALLY ESTABLISHED POVERTY LEVEL FOR A HOUSEHOLD OF FIVE PEOPLE: Poverty levels from the *Federal Register*, current as of January 20, 2011, are provided on the website of the U.S. Department of Health and Human Services under the heading "Poverty Guidelines, Research, and Measurement."

14 PERCENT UNEMPLOYMENT IN THE BRONX: As this book went to press, the Bureau of Labor Statistics, which updates statistics monthly on its website, gave the unemployment rate for Bronx County as 14.1 percent (February 2012). New York City as a whole had a rate of 9.6 percent for the same month.

MORE THAN 300 PEOPLE SHOW UP FOR JOBS AT SNEAKER STORE: *New York Post*, September 11, 2011.

308 UNEMPLOYMENT FIGURE UNDERSTATES THE JOBLESS RATES IN POORER AREAS: The Bureau of Labor Statistics, cited above, does not break down its numbers below the city or county level, making corresponding figures unavailable at district and neighborhood levels—which is one reason, among many, why consistent unemployment numbers for the South Bronx are not easy to pin down. As long ago as 1997, the *New York Times* estimated unemployment at 45 percent (November 2, 1997). More recently, the *New York Daily News* calculated the unemployment rate within three South Bronx housing projects at 51 percent (November 25, 2011). The U.S. Bureau of the Census, meanwhile, in its 2010 American Community Survey, calculates the figure for the South Bronx to be 19.2 percent.

"DISCOURAGED WORKERS" NOT INCLUDED IN UNEMPLOYMENT FIG-
URES: According to the Bureau of Labor Statistics, people who
"want and are available for work, and who have looked for a job
sometime in the prior 12 months," are not counted among the
unemployed if they have not "searched for work in the four weeks
preceding the survey.... Discouraged workers were not cur-
rently looking for work specifically because they believed no jobs
were available for them or there were none for which they would
qualify." For this and other information as to who is counted, or
not counted, as part of the labor force, I have relied on the website of the Bureau of Labor Statistics, as updated on November 17,
2011. (See under heading "Labor Force Characteristics.")

309 STORIES PUBLISHED ON DRUG DEALERS IN THE BRONX AND EAST
HARLEM DRUG LORD: *New York Daily News,* June 18, 2011.

310 SON OF ST. ANN'S EDUCATION DIRECTOR SHOT AND KILLED: The
boy was shot in the Morrisania section of the Bronx. See *New York
Daily News,* September 22, 2011.

JEREMY DESCRIBES NEW MALL IN SOUTH BRONX: The mall, which
is near the 149th Street Bridge, just off an expressway, is called
the Gateway Center.

311 GOVERNMENT OFFICIAL SAYS "CONDITIONS ... WERE HORRENDOUS"
IN DIEGO-BEEKMAN COMPLEX: *Village Voice,* December 14, 1999.
Some of the other details on the termination of Continental Wingate's ownership were reported in the *New York Times,* March 31,
1999.

TRANSFER OF OWNERSHIP TO A NONPROFIT CORPORATION REPRE-
SENTING INTERESTS OF THE TENANTS AND SUBSEQUENT CHANGES
IN THE DIEGO-BEEKMANS: I've relied primarily on Reverend
Martha Overall's chronology of these events, her balanced as-
sessment of improvements in the buildings, and my own on-site
observations.

312 THE FIFTH-GRADE TEACHER AT P.S. 30 WHOSE CLASS I USED TO
VISIT: Jasmine Harrinarine Gonzalez is the new principal of
P.S. 65.

P.S. 30 IS RATED VERY HIGH FOR ITS ACADEMIC PROGRESS OVER RE-
CENT YEARS: The school has been rated A (the highest rating) on
its Progress Reports by the New York City Department of Education for the 2008–9, 2009–10, and 2010–11 school years. P.S. 65
received B, C, and B for the same years.

313 STATISTICS FOR OTHER ELEMENTARY SCHOOLS SERVING THE SAME
NEIGHBORHOOD OR NEIGHBORHOODS NEARBY: *New York Times,*
September 2, 2011.

313–14 MIDDLE SCHOOLS IN SOUTH BRONX: New York City Department of Education Progress Reports, 2009–10, for M.S. 203,
J.H.S. 162, M.S. 343, and P.S./I.S. 244.

314 72 PERCENT NONCOMPLETION RATE FOR BLACK MALES IN NEW
YORK CITY: "The 2010 Fifty State Report on Public Education
and Black Males," released by the Schott Foundation for Public Education, Cambridge, Massachusetts, and New York City.

Michael Holzman, chief researcher for the Schott Foundation study, notes that New York City students who cannot qualify for graduation by the standards of the state, which are established by the New York Board of Regents, may, as an alternative, be given "local" diplomas, which are, he says, "in effect, certificates of attendance." Some of the unsuccessful black male students included in the figures given in the Schott Foundation study, Holzman observes, have graduated in this limited respect "but not in the sense of having been prepared (or even qualified) for college" and, he adds, "not qualified, or prepared, for much of anything." (Memo to me from Michael Holzman, November 23, 2011.) The question of what kind of document a student receives at the end of senior year is somewhat academic in the case at hand, since the vast majority of black male students in the New York City schools drop out of school before they enter the twelfth grade—typically, in my experience, at least a year or two years earlier.

315 AT BOTH ELEMENTARY SCHOOLS SERVING ST. ANN'S NEIGHBORHOOD, ZERO PERCENT OF STUDENTS WERE CAUCASIAN: New York State School Report Card, 2009–10, for P.S. 65 and P.S. 30.

INDEX

About the Author

JONATHAN KOZOL is the National Book Award–winning author of *Savage Inequalities, Death at an Early Age, The Shame of the Nation,* and *Amazing Grace.* He has been working with children in inner-city schools for nearly fifty years.

New from Jonathan Kozol

The Theft of Memory

Losing My Father, One Day at a Time

Jonathan Kozol

CROWN PUBLISHERS
NEW YORK

Available wherever books are sold

Also by Jonathan Kozol

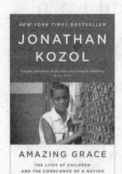

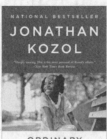

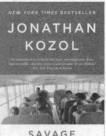

AMAZING GRACE

*The Lives of Children
and the Conscience
of a Nation*

**ORDINARY
RESURRECTIONS**

*Children in the Years
of Hope*

**SAVAGE
INEQUALITIES**

*Children in America's
Schools*

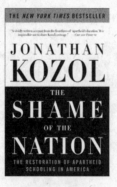

**RACHEL AND HER
CHILDREN**

*Homeless Families
in America*

**THE SHAME OF
THE NATION**

*The Restoration of
Apartheid Schooling
in America*

**LETTERS TO A
YOUNG TEACHER**

B\D\W\Y
BROADWAY BOOKS / NEW YORK
Available wherever books are sold